"In this book, Somaiyeh Falahat engages in a deep analysis of space in Fez, Tunis and Isfahan. Using the Persian concept of 'Hezar-to', she shows us how the relationship between spaces and in-between spaces constitutes a unique nature that reveals and conceals reflecting continuity and separation simultaneously. The work provides a significant contribution to the study of abstract space in the 'Islamic City'."

Nezar AlSayyad, *University of California, Berkeley, USA*

"This book is an invitation to take a fresh look at the historic Islamic cities, change our perspective and think about them in a new way. It explores the cities of Fez, Isfahan and Tunis from a phenomenological perspective to capture and describe the experiential and sensual aspects of the urban space, and to become sensitive to their interiority, ambiguity and liminality."

Ali Madanipour, *Newcastle University, UK*

"The importance of this book lies in its author's carefully substantiated argument that the sensually perceived, spatial characteristics of premodern Islamic urbanism have been neglected in scholarship; an oversight she attributes to an excessive reliance on cartographic methods for the comprehension of urban space and an inadequate conceptualisation of this space. Avoiding the first error by proceeding phenomenologically, and the second by unpicking and simultaneously developing, from an emic perspective, the etic concept of the labyrinth, Somaiyeh Falahat opens up new ways of knowing historic Islamic cities."

Simon O'Meara, *University of London, UK*

T0397095

Cities and Metaphors

Introducing a new concept of urban space, *Cities and Metaphors* encourages a theoretical realignment of how the city is experienced, thought and discussed.

In the context of 'Islamic city' studies, relying on reasoning and rational thinking has reduced descriptive, vivid features of the urban space into a generic scientific framework. Phenomenological characteristics have consequently been ignored rather than integrated into theoretical components. The book argues that this results from a lack of appropriate conceptual vocabulary in our global body of scholarly literature. It challenges existing theories, introduces and applies the concept of Hezar-tu ('a thousand insides') to rethink the spaces in historic cores of Fez, Isfahan and Tunis. This tool constructs a staging post towards a different articulation of urban space based on spatial, physical, virtual, symbolic and social edges and thresholds; nodes of sociospatial relationships; zones of containment; state of intermediacy; and, thus, a logic of ambiguity rather than determinacy. Presenting alternative narrations of paths through sequential discovery of spaces, this book brings the sensual features of urban space into the focus.

The book finally shows that concepts derived from local contexts enable us to tailor our methods and theoretical structures to the idiosyncrasies of each city while retaining the global commonalities of all. Hence, in broader terms, it contributes to a growing awareness that urban studies should be more inclusive by bringing the diverse global contexts of cities into the body of our urban knowledge.

Somaiyeh Falahat is a Feodor-Lynen Research Fellow in the Department of Geography and a Research Associate at Trinity Hall College, University of Cambridge, UK.

Routledge Research in Planning and Urban Design

Routledge Research in Planning and Urban Design is a series of academic monographs for scholars working in these disciplines and the overlaps among them. Building on Routledge's history of academic rigour and cutting-edge research, the series contributes to the rapidly expanding literature in all areas of planning and urban design.

Unplugging the City
The Urban Phenomenon and Its Sociotechnical Controversies
Fábio Duarte and Rodrigo Firmino

Planning for Greying Cities
Age-friendly City Planning and Design Research and Practice
Tzu-yuan Stessa Chao

Heritage-led Urban Regeneration in China
Jing Xie, Tim Heath

Tokyo Roji
The Diversity and Versatility of Alleys in a City in Transition
Heide Imai

Cognition and the Built Environment
Ole Möystad

Public Space Unbound
Urban Emancipation and the Post-Political Condition
Sabine Knierbein and Tihomir Viderman

Cities and Metaphors
Beyond Imaginaries of Islamic Urban Space
Somaiyeh Falahat

www.routledge.com/Routledge-Research-in-Planning-and-Urban-Design/book-series/RRPUD

Cities and Metaphors

Beyond Imaginaries of Islamic Urban Space

Somaiyeh Falahat

Routledge
Taylor & Francis Group
LONDON AND NEW YORK

First published 2018
by Routledge
4 Park Square, Milton Park, Abingdon, Oxon OX14 4RN

and by Routledge
605 Third Avenue, New York, NY 10017

First issued in paperback 2022

Routledge is an imprint of the Taylor & Francis Group, an informa business

Publisher's Note The publisher has gone to great lengths to ensure the quality of this reprint but points out that some imperfections in the original copies may be apparent.

British Library Cataloguing-in-Publication Data
A catalogue record for this book is available from the British Library

Library of Congress Cataloging-in-Publication Data
Names: Falahat, Somaiyeh, author.
Title: Cities and metaphors : beyond imaginaries of Islamic urban space / Somaiyeh Falahat.
Description: Abingdon, Oxon ; New York, NY : Routledge, 2018. | Series: Routledge research in planning and urban design | Includes bibliographical references and index.
Identifi ers: LCCN 2017054397 | ISBN 9780415728225 (hardback) | ISBN 9781315851754 (ebook)
Subjects: LCSH: Islamic cities and towns. | Public spaces—Islamic countries. | Architecture—Islamic countries. | Urbanization—Islamic countries. | City planning—Islamic countries.
Classifi cation: LCC HT147.5 .F35 2018 | DDC 307.76—dc23
LC record available at https://lccn.loc.gov/2017054397

ISBN: 978-1-03-247624-7 (pbk)
ISBN: 978-0-415-72822-5 (hbk)
ISBN: 978-1-315-85175-4 (ebk)

DOI: 10.4324/9781315851754

Typeset in Sabon
by Apex CoVantage, LLC

Contents

Acknowledgements viii
Note from the author x
List of illustrations xi

Introduction: diversifying global urban vocabulary 1

1 The idea of the 'Islamic city' 16

2 City as labyrinth 58

3 Hezar-tu as an urban concept 81

4 City as Hezar-tu: Fez, Isfahan and Tunis 93

Epilogue 166

Glossary 169
Bibliography 171
Index 184

Acknowledgements

I am indebted to many who have inspired me throughout this work. I am immensely grateful to Nezar AlSayyad, Ali Madanipour, Eduard Heinrich Führ and M. Reza Shirazi for the numerous talks we had about the idea of the book, and its methodology in particular, and cities and urban life in general. I sincerely thank Simon O'Meara, Matthew Gandy, Riklef Rambow, Katharina Fleischmann, Achim Hahn, Inken Baller, Philipp Misselwitz, Amira Bennison, Ash Amin and Eckard Ehlers for their valuable insights during the course of work. For fieldwork assistance, on-site support and providing or preparation of documents, I am indebted to Chiraz Chatara, Sofien Dhif, Omar Gumrahe, Zakariae Moujazi, Yousef Fihri, Eya Mahrough and Sanae Aljem. A major part of the translation in the section of historic evolution of Tunis was provided by Sofien Dhif. I thank Anton Escher for his generosity in making available the detailed maps of Fez al-Bālī. The advice of Hasan Radione, Assia Lamza, Nora Lafi, David Amster, Maryam Ghasemi and Ahmad Montazer gave me an enormously helpful introduction to each of the case study cities and neighbourhoods. I am grateful to them for this, and to Kamal Raftani for patiently responding my questions about Fez. My special thanks also go to Alex Hollingsworth, previously at Routledge, who believed in the book, and Sade Lee, Aoife McGrath and Kerry Boettcher who supported me to its completion. I am also sincerely grateful to Ahoora Baranian, Mohsen Sadeghi, Marie-Louise Karttunen, Cody Valdes and Wael Itani for their valuable help at different stages of the work. My especial thanks also go to the Gerda Henkel Foundation, Berlin Institute of Technology (TU Berlin) and German Academic Exchange Service (DAAD) for their financial support which made the fieldwork possible. I am thankful to the Iran Cultural Heritage, Handcrafts and Tourism Organization, the branches in Isfahan and Tehran; Association de Sauvegarde de la Médina de Tunis (ASM); L'Agence pour le Développement et la Réhabilitation de la ville de Fès (ADER-Fez); Naghsh-i Jahan Pars Consultation and Isfahan Organic Consultation for providing permission to use their archives and databanks.

I met many incredibly amazing people during fieldwork in the three cities, especially among residents of the neighbourhoods of Sīdī Muḥamad al-Ḥāj,

Sabac Lūyāt, Bin Zīān, Ṣāfī, Dīwān, Jūybārih and Pusht-i Masjid. They not only inspired me in my research but broadened my view of the world. They were so kind as to offer me their hospitality, share with me their belongings, give me their books as gifts, invite me to their wedding ceremonies, let me take their dough to the neighbourhood oven and engage me in their daily life in many other ways. I learnt much more than architectural and urban theory from them, for which I am indebted to each and every one. My admission that I am in love with their cities is apparent throughout this book.

I dedicate this book to my parents, for their precious love and kindness.

Note from the author

For the transliteration of Arabic and Persian terms, I follow the transliteration system of the International Journal of Middle East Studies. The Arabic words are transliterated mostly based on their high Arabic equivalents. As an exception to the transliteration system, I use term *Hezar-tu* to replace *hizār-tū*. In my previous publications I have used two transliterations for this term, *Hezar-too* and *Hezar-tu*, interchangeably. All translations from foreign languages to English are mine, except when otherwise noted. All photos have been taken by myself.

Illustrations

1.1	Dārulsalṭanih-yi Isfahan map, 1924; with facsimile edition of Saḥāb Geographic and Drafting Institute, Saḥāb Geographic and Drafting Institute Archive, Tehran	31
4.1	The distribution of mosques or schools and some main routes along the water network system	101
4.2	Urban fabric on the walking routes, Fez al-Bālī (2015). Sīdī Muḥammad al-Ḥāj, Sīāj and Shāwī *dirbs*; Saba^c Lūyāt *dirb*	108
4.3	The courtyard, al-Dabāghīn *zāwīya*, Sīdī Muhammad al-Ḥāj *dirb*, Fez al-Bālī (2015)	110
4.4	The courtyard, Zūwītan *zāwīya*, Sīdī Muhammad al-Ḥāj *dirb*, Fez al-Bālī (2015)	111
4.5	Steps at the entrance of al-Dar^cī *zāwīya* – view from interior, Sīdī Muhammad al-Ḥāj *dirb*, Fez al-Bālī (2015)	112
4.6	The gateway and sign that mark the beginning of the Shāwī zone and Sīāj *dirb*	115
4.7	Shāwī *dirb*, a residential alley, Fez al-Bālī (2015)	116
4.8	Urban fabric on the walking route in Isfahan (2013)	122
4.9	The bazaar, Isfahan (2013)	123
4.10	Isfahan (2013)	125
4.11	Ornamentation, Shiykh Lutfullāh mosque, Isfahan (2013)	127
4.12	Tārīkīhā alley, Pusht-i Masjid neighbourhood, Isfahan (2013)	129
4.13	Urban fabric on the walking route: Sīdī bin Arūs, Qasba, Siyyida ^cAjūla and Dīwān *dirbs*, medina of Tunis (2016)	134
4.14	In front of the Ḥamūda Pāshā mosque, Sīdī bin Arūs alley, medina of Tunis (2016)	136
4.15	Dīwān *dirb*, medina of Tunis (2016)	137
4.16	The mosque and the *zāwīya* in the ^cAbdil Ghādir complex, Dīwān passage, medina of Tunis (2016)	142
4.17	Friday prayer in the ^cAbdil Ghādir complex, Dīwān passage, medina of Tunis (2016)	143
4.18	A residential *dirb* at Dīwān passage, medina of Tunis (2016)	144
4.19	Landmarks like minarets function as visual and symbolic components of the passages. Sīdī Muḥammad al-Ḥāj *dirb*, Fez al-Bālī (2015); Pusht-i Masjid *kūchih*, Isfahan (2013)	151

Introduction

Diversifying global urban vocabulary

Concepts are vital to the constitution of our comprehension of cities as they introduce thought-motifs to our analytical understandings. Politically and epistemologically embedded, they are tools and instruments of thinking cities and articulating our perceptions of urban space. Each concept can introduce us to new structures of thinking and understanding, opening new realms while concealing other facets; therefore we need the appropriate vocabulary to make legible different aspects of urban life and space. Concepts, on the other hand, are elements of our shared space of thought on cities – the liminal area where the thinking of diverse cultures comes together and connects to create globally shared knowledge. In contemporary urban scholarship, we have a certain set of universal notions through which cities are conceptualised and understood. Yet, by enriching our universal vocabularies with multiple concepts from different geographical-cultural settings, we provide tools not only for contextualising cities marginalised in the existing body of knowledge, but also for multiplying our readings of cities in general. Such enrichment will help diversify our urban conceptual thought and develop an inclusive mode of knowledge-production while embedding new theoretical conversations in analysis of urban space.

In the context of 'Islamic city' studies reasoning in the shape of theorising, mapping and diagrammatising overstates the role of separation, segregation and the public-private duality when it casts paths merely as the urban exterior or linking lines.[1] Relying on reasoning and rationalising has reduced the descriptive, vivid features of the urban space into a common scientific framework. Consequently, such space has often been thus understood through its urban structure and functional divisions, rather than via the experience of it per se, meaning that its phenomenological characteristics have been ignored rather than integrated into our theory-making. One reason for this omission, I argue in this book, has been the lack of conceptual vocabulary in our global body of scholarly literature. For fresh readings of the Islamic city, we need alternative frameworks of understanding which bring the sensual features of Islamic urban space into the focus of the study and provide an appropriate conceptual tool for manifold readings of it: a framework that evades interpreting the city through the lens of existing spatial concepts, metaphors and beliefs that limit alternative apprehensions of settings that come under the rubric of 'Islamic city'.

In this book I introduce the spatial concept, or metaphor, of *Hezar-tu* [hizār-tū] and examine its potential for realigning understanding of urban space and its arrangements in the context of the historic cores of cities in the Middle East and North Africa.[2] Hezar-tu, which I borrow from Persian literature studies, literally means 'a thousand insides', denoting an abstraction, or an ever-elusive core, which is hidden or resides inside insides, requiring the negotiation of multiple thresholds to reach its understanding. I use the term as an alternative tool for rethinking the spatial relations (*Raumkonzept*) in my case study cities. This tool, I argue, inverts the principles of conceptualising space, constructing a staging post towards a different articulation of space-ordering based on in-between spaces rather than nodes, a logic of ambiguity rather than determinacy, the insideness rather than outsideness. I arrived at the notion of Hezar-tu by reworking the concept of labyrinth and rethinking its application in the context and discourses of studies of Middle Eastern and North African cities. Although the two terms are used as synonyms denoting a kind of spatial ambiguity, I argue they introduce two contrasting spatial structures: 'labyrinth' emphasises the element of path and the action of moving, while 'Hezar-tu' highlights spaces and thresholds. Hezar-tu is about in-betweenness, deferring and revealing but also hiding, while a labyrinth is about passing and meandering. Hezar-tu is about interstitiality, liminality and the spatial conditions of edges.

This work, in broader terms, contributes to a growing awareness that urban studies should be more inclusive, challenging Western-centric frameworks by bringing the diverse global contexts of cities into the debates related to urban theory that shape the body of our urban knowledge.[3] This awareness promotes the goal of articulating new geographies of urban theory by dislocating the European-American centre of its production and by recalibrating the geographies of 'authoritative knowledge.'[4] A number of other scholars have also drawn attention to the need for broader theoretical agendas, Edensor and Jayne emphasising that 'making sense of urban life does not have to depend on frameworks laid down by the "Western" academy.'[5] Citing Connell, they confirm that our existing urban theories have originated in the Western geographical-cultural context which marginalises or subsumes non-Western ideas. The result is that the non-Western context is consistently codified and contextualised from a Western standpoint. Edensor and Jayne add that such ideas are typically ignored entirely, as if non-Western space cannot be theorised or that it awaits a Western interpretation.[6] Urban theory has thus been unsuccessful in systematically engaging with broader epistemological and ontological debates because of the persistence of theories and concepts that originate in European and American academies and resonate through scholarly environments around the world.[7] As Tonkiss has also noted:

> the big narratives of contemporary urban theory . . . rarely capture the diverse realities of urban form and process. These large categories have the effect of simplifying the cities that do come under their lens, while consigning the great majority of actual cities to analytic invisibility or marginality.[8]

These views highlight the necessity for proposing points of departure for reimagining cities that are situated outside the West, and for a postcolonial revisioning of how cities are understood. Robinson further states that to reconfigure the field of urban studies, scholars need to rethink fundamental concepts of Western scholarship and examine some of the basic assumptions and key concepts of the field.[9] Urban studies thus should assess the horizon of meaning within which it is currently based, while scholars need to acknowledge the cultural situatedness of their scholarship.[10]

A number of methods and approaches have been proposed to include 'other' cities in the articulation of contemporary urban theories. For example, Robinson decouples understandings of the modern from its association with the West and relocates accounts of urban modernity from a few big European and North American cities to the ordinary cities over the globe.[11] In *Urban Theory beyond the West*, chapter authors contextualise a number of key urban debates – such as modernity, globalisation, neo-liberalism, mobilities, ordering/disordering – in cities around the globe.[12] Edensor and Jayne, for example, discuss how each urban theme has gone through specific processes in each geographical context, exploring the idea that 'urban spatiality is the product of distinctively situated social relations, practices and institutions whilst recognizing broader global processes.'[13] This insight helps diversify our understanding of a number of universalised urban concepts and expand them to apply to globally varied contexts. In a similar vein, Roy suggests a paradoxical combination of specificity and generalisability.[14] She believes theories have to be produced '*in* place (and it matters *where* they are produced), but that they can then be appropriated, borrowed, and remapped.'[15] This generates theory that is simultaneously 'located and dislocated.'[16] Therefore, in order to achieve a 'relational' theory of space, as proposed by Robinson, rather than merely 'adding' the experience of the Global South to already existing frameworks,[17] it is necessary to produce theory in the actual context of the Global South – thereby moving away from existing terms and seeking new structures of understanding based on regionally produced concepts. This course of action is followed, for example, in the edited volume, *Other Cities, Other Worlds*, which discusses and situates the themes of globalisation and modernity in the contexts of cities other than those in the West.[18]

Building on this discourse and setting my discussion within the scope of spatial relations investigation, I argue that a way towards more inclusive theory-building is to expand the range of contemporary concepts and theorisation by examining alternative frameworks for understanding, as well as spatial notions and conceptual vocabularies that have originated and been developed in diverse social, political and geographical contexts across the globe. Employing local concepts in analysis enables the perception and interpretation of urban diversity, drawing out particularities and highlighting the subtle and the hidden.

In line with the views discussed here, a key goal of this work is to experiment with the idea of Hezar-tu in reading the space of cities that are categorised variously as 'Islamic,' 'Arab' and 'Middle Eastern' in urban studies since the early twentieth century.[19] More concretely, I reconceptualise spatial ordering in the historic cores, or premodern fabric, of Fez, Isfahan and Tunis using the concept of Hezar-tu to explore the different layers and dimensions of their sociospatial structure. The urban space of the Islamic city has often been conceptualised in terms of diverse nuances in the dualities of exterior/interior and private/public, incorporating structural characters such as division, exteriority and clarity wherein, for example, walls are seen as the main boundary-makers. An alternative reading of the city can accentuate the continuity of connections between interior/exterior and public/private, introduce interiority as a key structure in urban space, acknowledge ambiguity as an inherent characteristic of cities and emphasise intersections of sociospatial relations as principles of place-making. This multifaceted approach provides a more relevant and dynamic theory of urban space in Islamic cities studies than has been employed to date and, as it is posited in this study, the concept of Hezar-tu contributes to embodiment of these dimensions.

I link this experiment to another argument I make in the context of Islamic cities studies, that is: although phenomenality is one of the main drivers of ideas, and the basis of cognition and perception, yet scholarly conceptualisations of Islamic cities are mainly devoid of the phenomenological aspects of urban space. I argue there are two reasons for this: first, sensual features of the cities have been overlooked or ignored by being rationalised or downplayed within reasoning processes – despite perceptions of space having been key sources for the production of place-images and place-myths of the cities. For example, attributes like labyrinthine, maze-like or mysterious are widely used in describing or representing the space of Islamic cities. Although criticised by postcolonial authors, these remain the dominant sensual perceptions, stimulated by images and narratives produced in diverse sources ranging from novels, itineraries, travel stories, tourist brochures and social media to scholarly representations.[20] These place-images are generated by perceptions of how urban space is ordered and by feelings about the cities that emerge while walking through them.[21] The expression of these feelings in the sources embrace sensations of getting lost in the city, incomprehensible urban logic and a lack of clarity of purpose and usage which are seen in the scholarship as associated to a number of physical characteristics such as the form of the alleys, the typology of buildings, and architectural elements such as obscure walls.[22] The scientific conceptualisation of space in the context of Islamic cities studies, however, took shape principally based on investigations of the structure of cities that focused on urban functions, social structures or administrational-political frameworks as the main departure points for understanding their logics and patterns. The second reason for the elision of phenomenality is that we have lacked proper terminologies to express the outcomes of cognition and perceptions. I discuss this in more detail in the next chapter. Another potentiality that the term Hezar-tu offers is to provide us with a conceptual vocabulary to think the space of the city including its phenomenological aspects and sensual perceptions.

I do not aim to elaborate on forces that shape space, or deal with the question of why a particular kind of space has been produced. I do even not try to give or suppose a function for the form and geometry of cities – to justify the tortuousness of street networks, for instance. Similarly, I certainly do not claim that cities were built and the space produced with the intention of attaining Hezar-tu-ness or that the thought-motif of Hezar-tu contributed to the formation of space. Rather, my principal aim is to present an alternative framework of understanding the case study cities. I argue that Hezar-tu is an expression that offers an alternative foundation on which to rethink how space has been ordered in cities in a particular spatial milieu. My study is not a historical investigation, although most of the fieldwork takes place in the historic cores of the cities and inherited-from-the-past materiality. I do not aim for a morphological or anthropological study of cities in this book. Yet, I reference all these fields to achieve the goal of the study, which is to present an alternative concept for a rereading of spatial relations.

I hope this approach will offer a new way of observing urban space, on the one hand, while reiterating the importance of integrating local particularities into our theory-making, on the other. The work goes beyond the existing literature in three ways: it incorporates phenomenality; it assimilates local characteristics into the theoretical vocabulary; and it introduces a different focus for understanding the structure of space.

The concept of 'Islamic city'

In addition to exploring the application of the Hezar-tu, the book contributes to discourse on the notion of the Islamic city, whose meaning and points of reference are still disputed. The term first appeared in the early twentieth century as the product of the modern encounter with cities whose structure and space took shape in the premodern age. In the late nineteenth century, the first scientific conceptions of Islamic urban phenomena began to be developed in the texts of European historians or geographer-historians who sought to comprehend the cities they resided in, or visited, the Middle East and North Africa. An understanding began to take shape in which the cities were conceived in oppositional terms to those in Europe, or the West more broadly. In the descriptions produced during the early decades of the twentieth century a number of characteristics were associated with a typical city in the region – such as the centrality of a mosque and bazaar, and a tortuous street network – which were then expressed by the category Islamic city. The description was used in these earlier studies as a concept which, on the one hand, referred to a set of urban-structural features understood to be typical of all cities in North Arica and the Middle East, and, on the other, resonated with 'recurring images of the Other.'[23] Thus it embodies the accumulation of both ideologies (concerning ideal and non-ideal cities), and perspectives on the material or functional characters of Middle Eastern and North African cities.[24]

In a number of other usages, the attribution of Islamic has a literal connotation and Islamic city thus expresses its exact literal meaning. This perspective foregrounds the idea that as the city has been shaped by Islamic laws, it is Islamic in absolute terms. What shapes the city's structure, in this approach, are the legal, cultural and juridical forces derived directly from statements written in the religious texts such as the Quran or the words of the prophets. For example, Hakim uses the term *Arabic-Islamic Cities* in his book on building and planning principles in the region, arguing that the urban structure of Tunis during the period of the al-Ḥafṣīyūn (thirteenth to sixteenth centuries) was formed by following the statements of the religious school of Maliki: a set of principles and guidelines which were based on either the Quran verses or Hadith texts. These principles, according to him, had direct influence on conduct and decision-making within the urban milieu, at both architectural and urban scales, as religious scholars and judges followed them to guide and control the activity of urbanism.[25]

In a different, more general way, the notion of the Islamic city also represents a topology or mode of city-making that began in about the eighth century along with the rise of Islam, transforming over the centuries yet maintaining some key spatial characteristics, and continuing until the emergence of urban modernisation processes. This kind of city-making is observable across a large region stretching from Iran to Morocco and is represented by some key urban functions such as the existence of mosques, bazaars and almost autonomous residential neighbourhoods. Being a schematic representation, this application of the term refers to formal resemblances, on the one hand, and common, distinguishing characteristics in urban structures, sociocultural systems and administrational frameworks, on the other. Bianca states that the respective regional styles of Islamic architecture show 'inner affinities which are clearly based on related customs, patterns of use and corresponding structuring principles,' rather than formal resemblances.[26] In this view the term is used interchangeably with 'the Arab city,' 'the Middle Eastern city,' 'the Oriental city' or 'the city in the Islamic world.'

Classifying a number of cities under one spatial milieu, as I also do in this work, presumes, in the first place, the existence of diverse types of space-making pertaining to different groups of cities occupying certain geographical and temporal positions.[27] I build on Lefebvre's observation that there have always been distinctive modes of production of space with 'specific relations of production of space' in cities globally.[28] Each of these modes of production may subsume variant forms but all subvariants follow the same general space-making concept.[29] For example, the city of the ancient world, the Greek city, with its genesis, form, specific daily rhythms and particular centres and polycentrism (agora, temple, etc.), exemplifies one mode of production; likewise, the praxis of European medieval society or an Asiatic mode of production may be inferred from specific urban space 'or the relationship[s] it embodies.'[30] The overarching concept reflects, and contributes to, the generation of shared sensual and logical spatial characters among the cities within a category. The characters/spatial relationships were created in the course of processes whereby the space was thought about, built, practiced or imagined in the realms of the material, the social and the virtual (e.g. symbolism), so they belong to all these spheres. This interpretation intersects with what Shields calls 'cultures of space.'[31]

In light of these considerations, discussion proceeds on the assumption that it is possible to think of a group of cities as belonging to a single category of the concept-of-space, of culture of space or spatial milieu,[32] which is virtual, on the one hand, since although physically embodied, the shared commonality of character among cities lies mainly in the realm of an intangible set of spatial principles and relations; it is real, on the other, since it exists as part of the reality of the cities and shapes them in concrete ways. The concept-of-space, which defies precise definition, is the source of the commonality of perceptions and conceptions of space across a category of cities which allows the loose classification of large numbers of cities into a single spatial category. Assuming that the production of space is the outcome of continuous interactions between the three realms of perception, conception and practice,[33] the general concept of space is at home in many levels of space-making, referring to, or influencing, spatialisation in diverse realms ranging from the material to the virtual.

The other assumption of this work is that a major part of the spatialisation of the Islamic city goes back to the string of descriptive terms used in imaginaries, narrations and conceptions of the cities of the Islamic world. Through such representations, whether of single locations or of characteristics attributed to the pattern, the city attains a specific kind of spatial formation. In other words, the elements of the imaging – the concepts and theories and 'the discourses, symbols, metaphors and fantasies'[34] through which we ascribe meaning to the city – are equally important in constructing its space and in generating processes leading to *re*-production of space within its boundaries. Furthermore, the terms applied in descriptions of cities also contribute to determining how spatial formation is imagined, (re)constructed and (re)spatialised in scientific discourses. Said engages with the production of knowledge and meaning in interpreting and perceiving the space in the Orient by stating this body of knowledge promotes a 'mode of discourse with supporting institutions, vocabulary, scholarship, imagery, doctrines.'[35] He adds that a tradition of 'thought, imagery, and vocabulary' has given the Orient its presence.[36]

Based on these assumptions, I employ the term Islamic city to refer to a kind of spatialisation which consists of two equally significant types: the actual morphological characters shared by historic cores of most of cities in the Middle East and North Africa (actual reality); and the body of concepts used in connection with these cities in scientific discourses (virtual reality). The former refers to both tangible heritage like the material body at the historic cores of cities, and less tangible cultural practices and expressions. This is the usual domain of archaeological and historical studies whose avowed goal is to explore the concrete evidence that has passed from the past to the present, endeavouring to understand it in a form as close as possible to its actuality. This approach has been the basis of most of studies contributing to the discourse of the Islamic city. Yet the notion of the Islamic city also incorporates the diverse spatialisations that are formed by words, symbols, thought-motifs, disciplinary frameworks and cultural constructions. Inevitably, the virtual reality, which has evolved over the decades since the first conceptualisations and modern representations of the Islamic city appeared, has been superimposed onto tangible heritage and is continuously being (re)constructed in the present; it has shaped our understandings and imaginaries of the city, it is manifested in representations and conceptualisations and, arguably, it instantiates distance from the actual reality of the city.

In this usage, therefore, the spatiality of the Islamic city is shaped not only within the process of producing spaces but also by the set of meanings, metaphors and concepts through which it has been interpreted, understood and represented in contemporary scholarship. Together, these result in the generation of a vague but roughly united framework for the term, an inchoate representation of an entity with all that relates to it: discourses, representations, cultural spatialisations and the built physical environment. Thus I do not use the term Islamic city in its literal sense, namely, to evoke the idea that the city has received its characteristics and quintessence only from Islam. Nor do I employ it as a fixed term, referring to static geographical or temporal boundaries. Rather the notion here represents a number of spatial characteristics embedded in a network of codes of understanding.

The two types of spatialisations discussed, actual and virtual, are intensively interlinked: words, concepts, metaphors and patterns influence the way in which we conceive of space and define the context of spatial relationships. Thus, the scientific conceptions enfold inherited spatial formations (heritage) with a set of produced-in-the-present means and relationships including codes, images, concepts, patterns and symbols. On the other hand, the reference point of the virtual (where meanings are made) is the actuality of the city: we give meaning to the space and characterise it based on what can be seen, explored and measured as/in the space. In this way each description or analysis of the city creates a particular spatiality based on what exists in inherited actuality and in produced virtuality. This causes different temporalities to become part of the notion of Islamic city and removes the monopoly of the past.

In this work I mainly address the second type of spatialisation, virtual reality, which I believe has not received enough attention in studies of Islamic cities. Islamic city studies are largely dominated by the historical perspective and remain dependent on the research scope of archaeologists, architectural or urban historians and historian-geographers, yet the historiography of Islamic city studies shows that cultural constructions have played an important part in directing approaches and explorations.[37] There is little work that rethinks the commonly applied, normative theoretical frameworks, reconsiders widely employed spatial concepts and terminologies, or deconstructs thought-motifs. Nonetheless, there have been turning points where authors have foregrounded the theme of knowledge-production and discussed how different approaches and epistemological or ontological viewpoints can affect our understanding of cities.[38] Based on this premise, they profoundly criticised the approach of the Orientalists due to the ways in which the latter imagined and represented Islamic cities. We need constant re-examination of the terms, concepts and thought-motifs through which we understand and think the urban space.

In addition, in what represents a pastiche of past and present, the new urban and architectural (re)developments in the cities have used the past as a key source for constructing or maintaining identity and distinctiveness in a globalised world. In recent decades the belief that modern urban elements and patterns are not the sole domain of 'others' (i.e. Westerners) has convinced most architects, urban planners, policy makers and scholars of the need to discover or create localized forms of architecture and city construction, related to or found in traditional and premodern patterns that offer regional distinctiveness and particularity.[39] Narrating the past plays a crucial role in constructing identity and in bridging the modern and the traditional. Therefore, the way the Islamic city as a spatial entity is defined has a part in shaping the identity of contemporary Islamic cities, not only by virtue of the inherited material but also by the ways we approach it, by the words and other symbols we use to describe it, by the framework of understanding and the way it aligns with cities in a global context.

The structure of the book

The book contains four chapters. In the first I review the different ways in which the Islamic city has been conceptualised as a mode of city-making. The ideas discussed are samples of a wide range thought that shapes the body of knowledge in Islamic cities studies, representing the key theoretical approaches developed in a range of disciplinary backgrounds. The goal is to review how urban space and the city have been understood so far in international scholarship in two categories: *theories* and *perceptions*. I discuss which elements, factors and forces have been highlighted as the determinants of urban space or the means of its distinctive formation, and how spatial relationships are defined at different scalar or thematic levels.

In many cases theorising efforts have been devoted to defining a pattern or organisation (of space, social structure, administrational system) for the city as a functioning whole.

This chapter reveals how urban space has been conceptualised in relation to the notion of the Islamic city and how the phenomenality of space has been constantly overlooked by being rationalised in scientific discourse. One of the reasons for this neglect in studies that elaborate on the phenomenality of space in Islamic cities is that, beyond seeing it as mere 'disorder,' there have not been adequate vocabularies to express experiences of it accurately, or to import spatial experiences into the body of theory and scholarship. I explain that among the concepts used to understand the cities of the Middle East and North Africa the quality of labyrinthinity has been the most repeated and most disputed. The labyrinth as a particular spatial metaphor invokes multidimensionality and can denote diverse aspects of space, including its phenomenality. It conveys a pastiche of practices connected with using space, feelings in space and culturally constructed spatial associations. Thus I argue in this chapter that it has been, to date, the most phenomenological concept that has been used to reify a code of space in the spatial milieu of Islamic cities – although, as I will elaborate, it is a deformed perception and representation.

In the second chapter the meanings, patterns and concepts that have been associated with the notion of the labyrinth will be discussed from a historical perspective. Using the term as a framework for observing and describing cities prioritises 'the path' as the spatial unit of understanding, and movement as a spatial practice that positions the 'spaces of place' in the background. Flow is an inherent part of urban life in the modern city and seeing a city as a labyrinth imposes the modern(ist) way of thinking onto a non-modernist phenomenon and ignores the most important urban spatial practices of 'nuclei' and 'halting'. This chapter concludes that the term labyrinth actually plays down those phenomenological characteristics that originally played a part in generating the view of (Islamic) cities as labyrinthine. Therefore, although application of this notion can gather together diverse metaphorical, physical and practical spatialities, it reduces the experience of space. New concepts are, therefore, needed to direct the focus onto the spaces of place as the most articulated, with the highest intensity of everyday life activities. Reworking the labyrinth, as the closest explanatory terminology in the context of Islamic cities, leads us to the metaphor of Hezar-tu and thus opens the tradition of the usage of labyrinth to other ways of knowing the city.

The third chapter introduces the concept of Hezar-tu as a spatial metaphor, a theoretical framework, suited to new explorations of urban space, particularly those that are present in Islamic cities. I elaborate on the terminology of Hezar-tu, studying its literal meaning and the meaning of its constituent words, that is, *hezar* (*hizār*) and *tu* (*tū*). The literal meanings span a range of significance with references to tendencies like insideness, foldedness, in-betweenness, sequential discovery and performance as a curtain. The usage of the notion in literature studies will also be elaborated, elucidating the spatial connotations of the term and their relationships to other fundamental concepts, such as *barzakh*, developed in the context of Islamic spiritual studies. The ideas imparted by *barzakh* are connected to partitions, barriers, midlands and intermediate zones between two states or things. It is both a limit and an *entre-deux*: something that stands between two things, both separating and joining. Hezar-tu, in this context, is connected to explorations of the spatial conditions of edges, borders and boundaries in a city. The spatial quality that Hezar-tu represents the character of spatial organisation and inspires phenomenological readings of cities that include the feelings of enclosing, enfolding, involuting, protecting and covering that are experienced in different scales in urban life. The chapter ends by summarising the five elements foregrounded by the concept of Hezar-tu: (a) in-betweenness, in-between spaces and transitional boundaries, where in-between elements or spaces function as boundaries, as they defer access to the inner realm; (b) spatial depth, with the added nuance of sequential experiencing of layers of meanings or spaces; (c) the feature of revealing but hiding, that is, deferring by multiple in-betweens which function as loci for the presence of opposites: at once impenetrable and offered to the gaze; (d) the containment which is created by a (porous) boundary; (e) a logic of ambiguity which is essential and ontological in the concept of Hezar-tu.

In the fourth chapter, I re-describe (urban) space in the historic cores of Fez, Isfahan and Tunis as a Hezar-tu, as a fluid assemblage of in-between spaces, each with its own character, that follow each other (towards a central core). I have selected Fez because it provides an extreme example of a profusion of *tūs*, Tunis as a contrast to Fez, and Isfahan as an example from outside the Arab world. In analysing the cities, I first review the evolution of their historic cores, and then narrate the urban space while walking a number of routes through them, selected on the basis that they have, to a large extent, survived modernising impacts on their urban form.

Field research had two main steps. First, using historical sources, on-site observations and interviews with residents I collected diverse types of information on the elements, details, structures and daily rhythms of each of the case study routes. Knowledge of the different urban architectural elements and sociocultural aspects of the spaces around the routes gained during this stage of research is fragmented. Secondly, against the background of the information achieved in the first step, I walked through the route, narrating it. The goal was to piece together the knowledge gained in the first stage, and also to combine it with the (subjective) sensual experience of walking through the space. Roping together all its diverse physical or non-physical characteristics, the walk presents 'a narration of the path.' The main focus of observation is in-between spaces; that is, the project provides a reading of the Hezar-tu-ness of each city. Reviewing the current theories and methods in urban studies reveals the crucial role of walking in understanding cities and their spaces, yet this way of knowing can be insufficient, easily falling into the trap of presenting a distinctive subject position wherein the emphasis is only on the primacy of personal, sensory experiences. Using a combination of different means of study provides a richer framework of understanding.

The exploration is based on the assumption that studying the historic cores of cities involves a constant oscillation between different temporalities, something which also necessitates the use of diverse knowledge sources. My main such source in studying the physical space of the urban fabrics was the existent architectural fabric, while further knowledge was gained from documents illuminating the cities' historical evolutions. To understand the sociocultural context, this work moves back and forth between historical and modern sources, using (secondary) historical sources to gain information on the past functions of spaces, everyday life rules and norms. Other sources include on-site observations and interviews with residents that explore the daily usages of spaces.

In the last section of chapter 4, I argue against a myth present in literature discussing the urban space of the Islamic city: that walls are the mere or main boundary-makers in the city and the urban form is articulated in such a way as to strongly preserve the private sphere against the public realm. I would argue against this myth, suggesting that the ordering of relations takes place mainly through in-between spaces, rather than by walls, which create diverse sorts of edges such as virtual, symbolic and social. In addition, despite the large amount of scholarship on the importance of privacy and its strong preservation from the public realm in Islamic cities, I would argue that belief in the extent of this is not well founded. There is, in fact, a different private-public spatial juxtaposition in the city to the model that suggests that the inside of the house is preserved as a private sphere against the rest of the urban environment.

Notes

1 I will use the term 'Islamic city' as a familiar, if unsatisfactory, shorthand with awareness of its weaknesses which are detailed in the existing scholarship. Definition of the usage of the term in this book follows in the later discussion.

2 This book primarily examines the idea of *Hezar-tu* in a limited geographical, temporal and discursive context ('Islamic city' studies and more specifically the historic cores of three case study cities of Fez, Isfahan and Tunis). Yet I believe this term has broader geographical and temporal scope.

3 See, for instance, Tim Edensor and Mark Jayne, 'Introduction, Urban Theory beyond the West', in *Urban Theory beyond the West*, ed. Tim Edensor and Mark Jayne (Abingdon: Routledge, 2012); David Bell and Mark Jayne, 'Small Cities? Towards a Research Agenda', *International Journal of Urban and Regional Research* 33, no. 3 (2009): 683–99; Andreas Huyssen, ed., *Other Cities, Other Worlds: Urban Imaginaries in a Globalizing Age* (Durham: Duke University Press, 2008); Ruth Panelli, 'Social Geographies: Encounters with Indigenous and More-Than-White/Angelo Geographies', *Progress in Human Geography*

32, no. 6 (2008): 801–11; Raewyn Connell, *Southern Theory* (Cambridge: Polity Press, 2007); Jennifer Robinson, *Ordinary Cities, between Modernity and Development* (Abingdon: Routledge, 2006); Jennifer Robinson, 'Postcolonialising Geography: Tactics and Pitfalls', *Singapore Journal of Tropical Geography* 24, no. 3 (2003): 273–89; Catherine Nash, 'Post-Colonial Geographies', in *Envisioning Human Geographies*, ed. Paul Cloke, Mark Goodwin, and Phil Crang (London: Arnold, 2004); Robinson, 'Postcolonialising Geography: Tactics and Pitfalls'; Dipesh Chakrabarty, *Provincialising Europe: Postcolonial Thought and Historical Difference* (Princeton: Princeton University Press, 2000).

4 Ananya Roy, 'The 21st-Century Metropolis: New Geographies of Theory', *Regional Studies* 43, no. 6 (2009): 820, original emphasis.

5 Edensor and Jayne, 'Introduction, Urban Theory beyond the West', 1.

6 Connell, *Southern Theory*; cited in Edensor and Jayne, 'Introduction, Urban Theory beyond the West', original emphasis.

7 Edensor and Jayne, 'Introduction, Urban Theory beyond the West'.

8 Fran Tonkiss, *Cities by Design, the Social Life of Urban Form* (Cambridge: Polity Press, 2013), 10.

9 Robinson, *Ordinary Cities, between Modernity and Development.*

10 Ibid.; Chakrabarty, *Provincialising Europe: Postcolonial Thought and Historical Difference.* It should be noted, however, that the critique of the dominance of European or North American cities in building contemporary urban theory is not an argument about the inapplicability of current ideas to the cities of the Global South. As Roy observes, 'It is not worthwhile to police the borders across which ideas, policies, and practices flow and mutate. The concern is with the limited sites at which theoretical production is currently theorized and with the failure of imagination and epistemology that is thus engendered.' Roy, 'The 21st-Century Metropolis: New Geographies of Theory', 820.

11 Robinson, *Ordinary Cities, between Modernity and Development.*

12 Tim Edensor and Mark Jayne, eds., *Urban Theory beyond the West* (Abingdon: Routledge, 2012).

13 Edensor and Jayne, 'Introduction, Urban Theory beyond the West', 27.

14 Roy, 'The 21st-Century Metropolis: New Geographies of Theory'.

15 Ibid., 820, original emphasis.

16 Ibid.

17 Ibid., 821.

18 Huyssen, *Other Cities, Other Worlds: Urban Imaginaries in a Globalizing Age.*

19 Each of the terms has evoked its own disputes in the discourse, but no better designation has yet been suggested. The term Islamic city raises the question of whether the prefix Islamic is accurate for the cities of the region, given that they have inherited their distinctive characteristics from pre-Islamic ages see Eugen Wirth, *Die Orientalische Stadt Im Islamischen Vorderasien Und Nordafrika: Städtische Bausubstanz Und Räumlische Ordnung, Wirtschaftsleben Und Soziale Organisation*, vol. 1, 2 (Mainz: Philipp von Zabern, 2000); 'Die Orientalische Stadt, Ein Überblick Aufgrund Jüngerer Forschung Zur Materiellen Kultur', *Saeculum* 26, no. 1 (1975): 45–94. Other scholars claim, however, that the commonalities of cities in the region are due to the direct or indirect impact of Islam. See Simon O'Meara, *Space and Muslim Urban Life: At the Limits of the Labyrinth of Fez* (London: Routledge, 2007); Nezar Alsayyad, *Cities and Caliphs, on the Genesis of Arab Muslim Urbanism* (New York: Greenwood Press, 1991); Janet L. Abu-Lughod, 'The Islamic City – Historic Myth, Islamic Essence, and Contemporary Relevance', *International Journal of Middle Eastern Studies* 19, no. 2 (1987): 155–76. It is believed that '[t]here is an unmistakably Islamic character that can only be attributed to a prevailing spiritual identity,

as materialized through a consistent daily practice and the corresponding built environment' (indirect impact) Stefano Bianca, *Urban Form in the Arab World, Past and Present* (New York: Thames & Hudson, 2000), 9. Islam, in this view, while not the only cause of the urban form, was an important contributing element: 'the social, political and legal characteristics of Islam . . . shaped . . . the processes whereby Islamic cities were formed, transformed, and transformed again,' generating the distinctiveness of Islamic cities Abu-Lughod, 'The Islamic City – Historic Myth, Islamic Essence, and Contemporary Relevance', 162. For example, Islamic institutions provide influential frameworks for urban life by regulating the relations between the individual and the community Albert H. Hourani, 'Introduction: The Islamic City in the Light of Recent Research', in *The Islamic City*, ed. Albert H. Hourani and Samuel M. Stern (Oxford: Bruno Cassier, University of Pennsylvania Press, 1970), 9–24.

20 See, for example, the novel Sophie El Goulli, *Les Mystères de Tunis* (Tunis: Dar Annawras, 1993).

21 For example, Christian Norberg-Schultz, *The Concept of Dwelling* (New York: Rizzoli, 1985), 69. depicts the morphological fabric of the city as a 'labyrinthine settlement' into which the regular and orthogonal patterns of mosques bring a general order. The urban space of everyday life, according to him, generally appears as a 'multifarious labyrinth' Christian Norberg-Schulz, 'The Architecture of Unity', in *Architectural Education in the Islamic World*, ed. Ahmet Evin (Singapore: Concept Media/Aga Khan Award for Architecture, 1986), 9. There were also similar statements in the early twentieth century descriptions. Roger Le Tourneau, *Les Villes Musulmanes de L'Afrique Du Nord* (Virginia: La Maison des Livres, 1957), 20, for instance, claimed the aerial photography of any Muslim city brings to mind 'Daedalus' labyrinth.'

22 See, for example, Jean Sauvaget, *Alèp: Essai Sur Le Développement D'une Grande Ville Syrienne, Des Origins Au Milieu Du XIXe Siècle* (Paris: P. Geuthner, 1941); Jean Sauvaget, 'Le Plan de Laodicée-Sur-Mer', *Bulletin D'études Orientales* 4 (1934): 81–114; Robert Brunschvig, 'Urbanisme Médiéval et Driot Musulman', in *Revue Des Etudes Islamiques* (Paris: Librairie orientaliste Paul Geuthner, 1947), 127–55; Le Tourneau, *Les Villes Musulmanes de L'Afrique Du Nord*; John Gulick, 'Private Life and Public Face: Cultural Continuites in the Domestic Architecture of Isfahan', *Iranian Studies* 7 (1974): 629–38.

23 Edward W. Said, *Orientalism* (New York: Vintage Books, 1979), 1.

24 In later studies, the view of duality between European and Islamic cities (self/other) was strongly criticised and a body of studies has developed involving more diversity in disciplinary backgrounds, more variety in points of view, and engaging detailed fieldwork research on specific case study cities.

25 Besim Hakim, *Arabic-Islamic Cities: Building and Planning Principles* (New York: Routledge and Kegan Paul, 1986).

26 Bianca, *Urban Form in the Arab World, Past and Present*, 9.

27 Assuming common shared spatial characters among the premodern cities in the region has generated another disputed point in the discourse (cf. footnote 19): whether the generalisation evoked by the term Islamic city, or other equivalent notions such as Middle Eastern city, is scientifically and analytically valid given the wide temporal spectrum of their development – from the seventh century until the industrial era. On the one hand, there is a strong awareness that the urban peculiarities that arose from geographical differences, historical circumstances and national or local administrational structure were so marked that categorisation only produces reductions and simplifications. This approach may see theorising based on spatial characters common in cities of the region as generalisation that underestimates individual cities' particularities. On the other hand,

it is believed a number of specificities differentiated cities of the region from other cities across the globe; consequently, though each place differed in detail, they had certain formal or organisational qualities in common. For example, Wirth writes that the fundamental difference to the Western city is obvious. See Wirth, 'Die Orientalische Stadt, Ein Überblick Aufgrund Jüngerer Forschungen Zur Materiellen Kultur'. In line with that, Lapidus notes: 'It is perilous to make generalisations for such an immense region and period in which the cities discussed differed from one another and changed internally in numerous important ways. Nonetheless, certain features of geography and social structure seem to have been held in common, and differences in detail do not vitiate all efforts at generalisation. Though historians are disposed to stress the immediate, the concrete, and the unique in historical experiences, models or "ideal types" which define the whole as well as assess the significance of differences in detail are equally important.' Ira Marvin Lapidus, 'Muslim Cities and Islamic Societies', in *Middle Eastern Cities*, ed. Ira Marvin Lapidus (Oakland, CA: University of California Press, 1969), 48, original emphasis.

28 Henri Lefebvre, *The Production of Space*, trans. Nicholson-Smith (Oxford: Basil Blackwell, 1991), 31.

29 Lefebvre, *The Production of Space*.

30 Ibid., 31.

31 Rob Shields, *Spatial Questions, Cultural Topologies and Social Spatialisations* (Los Angeles: Sage, 2013).

32 Qualitative spatial characters are the key constituent elements of the spatial relations. Among these features we can mention the specific constellation of relationships in and between space, for the type of spatial patterns and space-ordering vary according to society; see Bill Hillier and Julienne Hanson, *The Social Logic of Space* (Cambridge: Cambridge University Press, 1984); Ali Madanipour, *Public and Private Spaces of the City* (London, New York: Routledge, 2003).

33 Lefebvre, *The Production of Space*.

34 James Donald, 'Metropolis: The City as Text', in *Social and Cultural Forms of Modernity*, ed. Robert Bocock and Kenneth Thompson (Cambridge: The Open University, 1992), 427.

35 Said, *Orientalism*, 2.

36 Ibid., 5.

37 See, for example, Nezar Alsayyad, *Cities and Caliphs, on the Genesis of Arab Muslim Urbanism* (New York: Greenwood Press, 1991); Said, *Orientalism*.

38 See, for example, Said, *Orientalism*.

39 See, for example, Bianca, *Urban Form in the Arab World, Past and Present*.

1 The idea of the 'Islamic city'

Two approaches to understanding space have been developed in the body of discourse and knowledge on cities in the Middle East and North Africa. Most scholarly conceptualisations of the city and space are based on cognitive interpretations in which the city is understood through rational relations, producing a model which is very close to what de Certeau calls 'the concept city.'[1] The other approach lies in the realm of immediate perception and sensual experience represented by the accounts of both scholars and visitors. Although the two sometimes coexist in a single description, a certain degree of distance between them has been retained: while the former has been the basis for most analytical discussions, the latter has remained confined to descriptive formulations. Reviewing the development of these two approaches reveals the dominance of cognitive conceptions in the discourse, highlighting that conceptualisations of the cities have not taken into account their sensual characteristics. It also reveals which urban features have been overseen or misrepresented in the process.

In the following pages I review conceptions from a range of valuable studies, chosen because they exemplify both the diversity and the key approaches that have had salience in international scholarship on Islamic cities. Some of the views represent the most commonly referenced ideas and some hint at themes to which I will refer when discussing the ideas central to the thesis of this book. I begin with theories of the city, and then address descriptions of the immediate perceptions of both scholars and travellers. Each approach has developed a set of vocabulary, terms and prototypes, many of which have become keywords and key concepts in the body of knowledge connected to the notion of Islamic city. While these examples are fragments, they do come together to produce an enduring picture of the Islamic city; they represent and shape the dominant narrative that in turn shapes the study of Islamic cities, which this book revisits. The results show that the phenomenality of space has not been used as the foundation for theorising cities, but rather as a rationalisation, and among the concepts applied when representing the Islamic city, labyrinth is a keyword that spans rationality and phenomenality.

Theories and maps

The Islamic city and its space have been cognitively interpreted and conceptualised from diverse angles and disciplinary backgrounds including urban, architectural and social history, geography, social geography, archaeology and symbolic philosophy, each presenting a particular spatial representation of the city. The level of focus varies from individual case study cities in specific timeframes, to regional inductive conceptions, to more holistic theorisations. Similarly, the focus of study has varied widely from physical elements and patterns, through architectural monuments and urban form, to social structures and functional systems.

While the descriptions and analyses discussed below might at a first sight seem to be fragmented or mutually exclusive, most of them share some key points and fill out the mosaic to form a whole picture. All have contributed to building a body of knowledge which shares the belief that the Islamic city represents a distinctive type of city-making which has a specific form, pattern, sociocultural structure, administrational system and urban logic, and needs to be studied as a unique system of urban relations and elements. Resulting conceptualisations have mainly been textually presented, yet have also been accompanied by modern cartographic maps and diagrams. While terms and concepts are the elements of discursive constructions, lines and figures are the means of expression in diagrammatic representations. By conceiving and representing the studied city through a select set of factors, each author spatialises it on the basis of a defined set of elements and spatial relationships and 'represents the city as a certain kind of place'[2] embodied within a particular constellation of codes, signs and metaphors.

Different understandings of space that have been constructed in the historiography of Islamic city display two major trends: the first pays greater attention to physical layout; the second has a more anthropological perspective.[3] In the texts produced during the early decades of the twentieth century, as in the dominant modernist trend of the time, understandings depart from rational-analytical comparisons between the patterns of streets in Islamic cities and the regularity of normative, modern street patterns. Yet the results of the comparisons were often expressed using phenomenological descriptions involving sensual spatial concepts. In these texts the space of the city was constructed in the course of unregulated negotiation between rational and phenomenological interpretations.

In these first studies space was largely conceptualised through constant references to the pattern of the street network and the private sphere's character of introversion, keeping in mind regularity as the criterion of an ideal city. It was believed that Islamic cities comprised a series of inconsistently juxtaposed cells, welded to each other by narrow, irregular streets, a combination which was regarded as the negation of urban order. Buildings, in this composition, were thought not to be integrated into a preconceived pattern but, rather, as individually defining the course taken by the roads and passages, resulting in a large number of cul-de-sacs and pathways. It was also presumed that there were hardly any open spaces or squares to relieve the narrowness of the streets and byways of the cities, while houses were oriented away from the street.[4] The resulting space was largely perceived as tortuous, labyrinthine and complicated, with manifold secret nooks and shadowy recesses. De Planhol writes, for instance: 'the people conceal their private life' behind the 'forbidding walls' of their houses in 'the maze of alleys and back streets.'[5] Similarly, Brunschvig states that a Muslim city has tortuous, complicated and sometimes labyrinth-like paths lined with closed houses; the city favours culs-de-sac, shadowy folds and secret corners.[6]

In the second half of the twentieth century an important transformation took place in studies of Islamic cities in which their social and anthropological aspects were highlighted. Since then much more diverse readings and perspectives have appeared, based on which Islamic cities been explored by scholars from different disciplines whose range of points of view reveals similarly different aspects.[7] In the decades since then, urban space has mainly been understood within a series of structural-functional relationships which scholars have observed in the cities' structures and systems. Investigations have focused on the social, economic or administrational-political structures of the city during the course of which diverse reasons were presented to justify early twentieth century understandings. Reviewing the texts shows that the most common statements with regards the characteristics of space accorded Islamic cities usually contain elements of an interpretation that can be summarised as follows: the cities may look formless but they have quite definite and logically patterned organisations. That is, the syndrome of twisting lanes does not imply disorganisation, as there is a definite urban organisation in that there is a clear skeleton for the city with the bazaar as the main artery and other routes branching off it. The main urban functions are lined along the main arteries. The residential districts fill the rest of the city and they have their own urban utilities such as neighbourhood mosques, markets and baths. The introversion (courtyard typology) of houses and the encroachments of buildings onto public thoroughfares, the twisting narrow streets and numerous blind alleys, culs-de-sac and blank walls were understood as connoting withdrawal from public life.[8]

In other similar statements diverse arguments have been put forth to demonstrate the regularity of the pattern of spatial organisation in the city. For example, the street network is described as consisting of a number of principal commercial roads with a network of regular and relatively wide roads connected via other streets to the outskirts of the town. Raymond argues this pattern invokes a relative regularity which 'contradicts the stereotype of an anarchic "Islamic" street-plan.' He continues by noting that it is in the residential districts that we enter the 'famous network of irregular streets and alleys without exits which some scholars have seen as a specificity of the whole city . . . such impasses made up no more than forty to fifty per cent of the total street network, concentrated in the residential zone.'[9] So the argument goes that as the irregularity of the streets is not a general characteristic of the whole city, the city cannot, therefore, be characterised as labyrinthine or irregular. Other statements by Raymond following a similar reasoning assert that the irregularity of the streets and the abundance of blind alleys were a particular local phenomenon and answered to the needs of people who inhabited the residential neighbourhoods, such as their need for privacy.[10] This set of theoretical conceptions can be scrutinised in seven major approaches:

(a) *Schematic conceptions:* Schematic representations of the Islamic city spatialise it based on three fragmented points of focus as key underlying forces shaping the city: its functional pattern, the network of passage and urban administrational-legal systems. The way that the city is seen in this understanding, derived from the related texts, can be summarised as follows: the city is an agglomeration of a number of urban functions such as mosque and suq, and a number of residential quarters. Due to their importance in a Muslim's life, the mosque and suq created a functional centrality in the city. The principal government building, namely, the palace of the ruler, is located near the central mosque. The suqs follow a particular functional-spatial hierarchy according to which the less clean and silent jobs are positioned at the furthest distance from the mosque, while the cleanest and most intellectual are more closely positioned. The central mosque as the spiritual, political and religious centre is placed on the main thoroughfare (function and geometry). In the city the residential and commercial districts are spatially and physically separated, comprising the two main typologies of the urban fabric. The residential area is divided into a number of neighbourhoods settled by distinctive groups of people who have built separate communities based on their ethnic, tribal or profession-related commonalities. The morphology of the neighbourhoods is a distinctive characteristic of the city. It has a network of tortuous passages with a large number of blind alleys, which is created due to the lack of a determining (i.e. top-down) administrational system in the city. By orienting houses away from the public thoroughfares, this form has encouraged the enormous moral distance between the private (family) and public (city) life of individuals.

Authors argued that the roots of reifying this model in the body of knowledge on the Islamic cities lie in the studies of the late ninetieth and early twentieth centuries and resulted from the Orientalists' patriarchal perceptions of the cities in the region.[11] It was at that time that (European) scholars, mainly historians or geographer-historians, began to study Islamic cities, particularly those North Africa and Syria, initiating a body of knowledge that elaborated on a schematic urban understanding.[12] For example

Le Tourneau describes the urban structure of Fez as a typical Islamic city. He writes:

> [There were] three principal gates of the city . . . through which passed the main external traffic of Fez . . . these streets were blocked by gates and closed at night . . . Each quarter could . . . try to isolate itself from the rest of the city; access was shut off each evening after nightfall. Consequently, it was difficult to circulate during the night . . . Outside the main arteries, the number of blind alleys was great. In fact, Moslem [Muslim] cities of North Africa were not laid out according to street plans; the location of the streets was determined by the arrangement of the buildings. As a result, these were numerous dead-end passages winding between houses in order to provide access to those located in the centre of a residential block.[13]

It was through this type of comprehension that the first scientific depictions of spatial relationships in the Islamic city emerged. That is, the city was analysed for the first time as a spatial-physical object with the aim of understanding how the elements work together and why they take the form they do.[14] Here, the city is understood and represented based on an identified rationale of the relationships, patterns, functions and forms in the city as a whole: an assemblage of a number of distinctive urban functions (such as mosque and bazaar), administrational-religious structures and pattern of streets. The descriptions of the urban form are limited to the geometry and pattern of the path network while the key terms and concepts applied include mosque, labyrinth, suq, quarter and irregularity.

(b) *The mosque as the navigator of urban space:* In a number of accounts, the Islamic city is conceptualised based on the networks and relationships generated by religious buildings and their functions in the city. These networks are discussed in terms of their arranging or being arranged by the community, the government and religion; sources for the studies have been mainly archaeological and textual evidence. Grabar, for example, examines the role of religious buildings, with particular emphasis on the mosque, in determining spatial arrangements in the city as he considers religious buildings to have had long-term continuous existence in, and an extensive influence upon, the functional and spatial structures of cities; they are, therefore, significant elements in defining the city's pattern.[15] Subsequently he conceptualises the model of the traditional Islamic city based on the historical development of the symbolic and structural character of the religious buildings. He studies how these kinds of buildings emerged as spatial and functional poles in the city and how their urban role and position evolved over the centuries. Different types of religious buildings, their spatial typology and historical evolution, and the way they take part in making particular spaces in the city (for instance, in the creation of monumental avenues such as Shāri[c] Biyn al-Qaṣrīn in Cairo) are also among key discussed points.

In this school of thought, religious buildings are suggested as reflectors as well as navigators of the principal relationships and structures of urban systems. The spread of mosques over the city, the hierarchy of their legal status, their religious and spiritual values and the role they play in local social identifications illustrate how they functioned as focal points in the city, serving as centres around which various city sections were organised. For example, as Grabar states, in the eighth through tenth centuries there were only a few mosques providing focal spiritual points in the city, which created strong religious centres in the functional pattern as well as imposing particular spatial orders.[16] But later, due to the extension of patronage, the number of spiritual buildings largely increased and, rather than imposing new orders on the pattern of the city, they adapted themselves to the existing designs: 'They no longer transformed the city by becoming its obvious centres but fitted themselves wherever space was available.'[17] The adjacency of mosques and palaces or their divisions into separate urban units also resonated with the relationships between the religious centre of the city and the government, both reflecting and inscribing changes in the nature of the community of faith (society). Although Grabar confirms that developing his idea based on only one aspect of urban life may have methodological problems, he believes it offers an advantage over other studies that only provide either theoretical generalisations or specific data on local conditions.[18]

(c) *Socio-administrational structure as spatial regulator:* The city has also been interpreted through its socio-administrational fabric, the pattern of distribution of socio-political communities over the city and their cross-spatial (cross-regional) relations and scopes of action. For example, Lapidus sees the Islamic city as a juxtaposition of a number of quarters with settled communities that came together due to a degree of social solidarity among their residents.[19] Having differing social and political capacities meant that the quarters acted as geographical as well as administrative units in subdividing the city into various territorial parts. Among the few institutions that cut across the boundaries of these units and acted at the city scale or even beyond, to include rural areas, were the fraternal associations, bazaars and law schools of religious elites. These institutions, also performing in adjudicative and administrative roles, created communities which linked people across and beyond cities. 'Within cities a single school might come to dominate a particular place, and for all intents and purposes create a kind of communal unity.'[20] The structure leads Lapidus to conclude that the towns did not have 'a highly developed sense of the importance of public spaces and ways.'[21] In a slightly different approach, Hourani explains the administrational and social structure by describing the influence of key urban institutions such as the religious leaders (ulema), emphasising that the physical shape of the Islamic city is not only a reflection of its social structure but affected by numerous other physical and non-physical factors.[22] Based on this premise, he roughly constructs a typical Islamic city as one that largely consists of a citadel, a royal quarter, a central urban complex including the principal religious buildings and the bazaar, suburbs, and residential quarters which had relative separateness and autonomy.[23]

(d) *The public-private sociospatial pattern as the distinctive character:* Public-private sociospatial relations have been among the main sources of comprehension of the Islamic city. Many authors have referred to the existence of a scrupulously preserved private sphere that contrasts with the public realm of the city, conceiving of it as the main instigator of the structure of the city and the most salient characteristic of the urban spatial pattern.[24] In architectural terms, the typology of courtyard houses has largely been interpreted as based on the requirement of (gender-based) privacy. Le Tourneau, for instance, notes that houses in Fez 'were all built around a patio, more or less large, where there was no risk of the women's being seen from the outside;' the

> entrance is almost always into a corridor so bent and narrow that it is impossible to see from the threshold what is happening in the courtyard: the women thus have time to conceal their presence as soon as a stranger enters the door. The corridor leads to a courtyard, the patio, generally square in form.'[25]

In stronger terms the home is also understood as 'primarily a wall, with a gate that can be closed.'[26]

Wirth elaborates extensively on the public and private spheres in Islamic cities.[27] He conceptualises the city as based on its spatial arrangements (*räumliche Gliederung* or *räumliche Organization*) and describes distribution patterns and structures as they feature at different levels. In terms of functional divisions, he believes, there is a clear distribution pattern across the city which consists of three areas: the residential area (neighbourhoods); the trading area (the bazaar as the commercial centre); and the governing area. With regards to the structure of public-private division, he suggests that the city is also divided into three zones possessing different legal and social qualities: the public realm (such as mosques and main passages), the individual intimate realm of private houses, and the collective-private realm of cul-de-sacs (the intermediary realm).[28] The morphological character of the city, according to Wirth, clearly reflects the latter structure with its three main urban architectural elements: the courtyard typology of buildings which are penetrated from the outside; the cul-de-sac and passage network of the neighbourhoods with pre-determined levels of accessibility, circulation plans, aesthetics and legal and administrational responsibilities; and the structure of city's division into disconnected quarters.[29]

The architectural principle of the houses is one in which living spaces are grouped around a courtyard, and the outer side of the house, opening onto a cul-de-sac or a passage, is composed of windowless walls deterring observation.[30] This phenomenon confirms, as Wirth puts it, the tendency for withdrawal, enclosure and privacy.[31] The culs-de-sac and the structure of the neighbourhoods support the protection of the private sphere and spatially extend the domestic area of private life. According to Wirth, the passages and culs-de-sac did not develop by chance and are two significant components and principles integral to the notion of the 'Oriental' city.[32] In this type of analysis – which represents a typical understanding of Islamic city space – mosques, bazaars, public squares, public baths and all main passages, as important connection lines in the traffic network, constituted the public sphere. The reason behind this assumption was that these spaces were open to the public and controlled by the authorities. The opposite side of the coin is assumed to be the individuated, intimate sphere of private houses, where not only access and control but even viewing by outsiders was strongly prohibited. This pattern is also reflected in the statements of law and religious schools according to which the principal passages are under public ownership and accessible to all members of society, while the cul-de-sacs are subject to the shared private ownership of the residents with a defined extent of accessibility.[33] According to this assumption, there is a clear division between public and private spheres and most of the city belongs in the private realm. Van Nieuwenhuijze writes, 'The traditional Middle Eastern town has a ratio between private and public land use that is decidedly disfavourable to the latter.'[34] The spatial and social organisation of the residential quarter – culs-de-sac and private courtyards – is seen as the embodiment of the general tendency towards a retreat from the public sphere into preserving the intimacy and privacy of family life: a tendency towards privatising and enclosing houses and culs-de-sac.[35]

Wirth adds that the public space in this sphere is limited to the 'negative space' of the passages which are defined by the walls of houses or other buildings: 'the pathways and squares are negative spaces, that means space that is spatially *excluded* from the private sphere rather than being spatially *enclosed* by public, common urban open spaces.'[36] This is related to the compatible tendency towards 'insideness' (*Innerhalb-sein*). One of Wirth's theses throughout his long-term research on Islamic cities is that if we define the social and 'spatial organisation' of cities in relation to the private-versus-public dichotomy, then the Islamic city is one of privacy and the 'occidental' city one of public(ness). He summarises the exclusive elements of the 'Oriental city' as the cul-de-sac structure of the residential neighbourhoods; the privacy and inward-orientation of houses due to their courtyard typologies; numerous residential quarters that do not communicate with each other; privacy as the dominant distinguishing attribute in urban life; and the bazaar as the vital core of the city.[37]

With a similar focus, Bianca conceptualises space-ordering (*Raumordnung*) and the concept of space (*Raumkonzept*) by paying particular attention to the underlying social, cultural and metaphysical forces in visual and morphological structures.[38] He understands the city in two main ways: in terms of its functional structure and its pathway network. The system of the 'dominant functional model' is explained in association with urban form and private-public relations.[39] According to him, the functional model presents a multifunctional core structure wherein the central mosque, enmeshed in a series of interconnected suqs, has the main role. The network of suqs, on the other hand, is interspersed with other key urban institutions such as schools, baths, and caravansaries. The large courtyard of the Friday Mosque, which facilitates multiple uses, is the primary public space of the component and probably the whole city. The spatial narrowness and compactness of the suqs are balanced by the public courtyards of surrounding building units such as caravanserais.[40]

Beside the functional model, according to Bianca, the city has another particularity: the layout of the pathway network whose main spines connect the core structure to the gates, framing the primary movement flows.[41] At various intervals the entrance points of residential neighbourhoods, which are autonomous social units, are marked on the spines by small gates. 'The residential districts . . . provide the private quarters . . . and are structured along similar principles . . . but with greater emphasis on the articulation of intermediate passages.'[42] The entrances

> were followed by an elaborate system of narrow alleyways, internal passages and gateways before the thresholds of individual houses could be reached and the transition into the domestic communication system on the other side of the entrance door could occur. These devices helped filter the flow of people, managing step by step the shift from public to private space.[43]

The system of progressive sequences of gates, passages, dead-ends and thresholds follows, and reciprocally builds, the spatial logic in which the private life of houses in residential quarters is assumed to be 'shielded off from the main streams of public life.'[44]

(e) *Segregation as the key mediator of spatial organisation:* Abu-Lughod locates the distinctiveness of the Islamic city in the social, gender-based and functional segregations that, she believes, rule the sociospatial structure of the city.[45] A striking characteristic of the cities of the Islamic world, in her view, is their 'subdivision into smaller quarters whose approximate boundaries remain relatively constant over time and whose names continue to be employed as important referential terms.'[46] The spatial logic of the city, which was always intended to subdivide it into a certain number of units, meant that boundaries and nomenclature

> have persisted for a long time. So the city has been characterised by two main elements: boundaries and a number of segregated cores. While segregation can be constructed materially, visually or culturally, the cities of the region were strongly influenced by Islam and Islamic reasons for boundary-making which go beyond mere Islamic property law or other similar customary laws developed within a given society.[47]

The logic of the subdivision can be observed in the 'common creator[s] of boundaries.'[48] Three types of boundary, creating three kinds of segregations at different scales, developed based on social distinctions, gender-based separations and socio-functional divisions. Islam made rough juridical distinctions between people on the basis of their relation to the community of believers (*umma*): Christians, Jews, Copts and so on.[49] These social distinctions were reflected in the spatial structure of cities, mainly through concentrations in pre-determined residential neighbourhoods. Only in a few specific circumstances – such as during social tension and military or economic threat, and at specific points in time such as in Moroccan cities in the nineteenth century – were juridical distinctions solidified into oppressive physical spatial segregations. Commonly, 'voluntary concentrations' based on economic functions or political advantages were widespread and could 'gather the density required to support common special services and institutions. These common services and institutions, in turn, created markers for quarters which indicated to outsiders who was supposed to live there and indicated to insiders that they belonged there.'[50]

The segregation of the sexes, as Abu-Lughod observes, generated another particular solution to the question of spatial organisation. Islam imposed a set of architectural and spatial requirements by underlining gender segregation: 'What Islam required was some way of dividing functions and places on the basis of gender and then of creating a visual screen between them.'[51] Consequently, it encouraged a particular, concomitant type of spatial structuring and division: 'the creation of male and female turf is perhaps the most important element of the structure of the city contributed by Islam.'[52] She goes on to note that

> the rules of turf were not only to establish physically distinctive regions; more important, they were to establish visually distinctive or insulated regions. The object was not only to prevent physical contact but to protect visual privacy. Line-of-sight distance, rather than physical distance, was the object of urban design. Thus, Islamic law regulated the placement of windows, the heights of adjacent buildings and the mutual responsibilities of neighbors toward one another so as to guard visual privacy. Architecture assisted this process. Not only the devices of *mashribiyya* (lattice wood) screening but the layout of houses and even of quarters created the strangely asymmetrical reality that women could see men but men could not see women, except those in certain relationships with them.[53]

According to Abu-Lughod the blind alleys or dead-end paths were also devices for achieving the aimed-for protection of the neighbourhood pattern.[54]

Another level of space division, according to Abu-Lughod, is that between residential and commercial sectors which created systems of relatively autonomous neighbourhood units across the city. She relates this system to Islam which neglected to 'concern itself with matters of day-to-day maintenance.'[55] Abu-Lughod believes the segregation left the neighbourhoods a certain measure of autonomy in terms of, for example, municipal services: 'a legal system which, rather than imposing general regulations over land uses of various types in various places, left to the litigation of neighbors the detailed adjudication of mutual rights over space and use.'[56] The units functioned as protection, defending their residents against any kind of invasion, particularly when the central authority was not strong enough to overcome chaos or external (and internal) threats. When the central power was in control of the city and the hierarchical structure worked smoothly the neighbourhoods were in constant communication with each other, sometimes serving as administrative units in this latter incarnation. Thus the Islamic city had a number of cells of residence which constituted the building blocks of urban society.[57]

(f) *The (concept of the) wall as the key spatial element:* In O'Meara's view, separation, reversal and segregation are the urban spatial principles which most extensively define the city's space.[58] The physical manifestation of these principles is the wall, which is the principal structural element and shaper of the architectural space and typical urban morphology of Islamic cities: walls make 'inside, separate and inviolable from outside'[59] at the architectural level, and without walls 'there would be no paths and alleys, no labyrinth'[60] on an urban scale. Passages are not only bordered by walls, as O'Meara notes, but they are also formed by them, along with territorial expression in the neighbourhoods:

> [The walls of Medina] steer our changes of place; enclose, delimit, and protect our activities, objects, and tools; receive us and make us pass from one location to another. They separate and structure the architectural space, and by way of this they allow us to dwell. They can, therefore, signify the nature of this dwelling.[61]

The walls, however, are understood as 'more than just background bricks and mortar, but once signified a protective notion of shame and commonly symbolized a politically, juridically, and religiously desired form of gendered urban society; a society which walls helped coerce into existence.'[62] Therefore, in broader conceptual terms, the wall in this view embodies a cultural principle which pivots on the idea of shame and, subsequently, related sociospatial notions of limit, separation, division and reversal. Walls are protective and delineate cultural valuables. Investigating diverse dimensions and interpretations of this element – social, religious, legal, juridical – in the city, O'Meara concludes that the cultural concept of shame informed the space and caused the ubiquity and longevity of the particular morphology which was consistent, with minor modifications, throughout much of North Africa and the Middle East from 1400 to 1800 AD.[63]

(g) *Symbolic conception of urban space as representative of the cosmos:* Ardalan and Bakhtiar read the city – its elements and space-time – symbolically, and with references to spiritual dimensions.[64] Basing their argument on an overarching paradigm that all traditional architecture follows a cosmic order and that man is analogous to the cosmos, they elaborate on shapes, surfaces, geometries, patterns, colours and space/place meaning in Iranian-Islamic cities, concluding that it is a key concept in the tradition of Islamic Iran that space generates the form and not the shape (here meaning the solid): 'in the conception of "place" . . . a central space is created by enveloping it in walls.'[65] This is manifested in the courtyard architecture, the centripetal organisation of space and space usage.

Large-scale cities, according to Ardalan and Bakhtiar, have two key elements: the city walls which define 'the cities' positive shapes in space and their correspondence to cosmic laws,' and the centre 'as a single point in space that moves in time and creates the line, or the linear element of the bazaar.'[66] Central to this system is the belief that 'man exists most wholesomely within a physical environment that is analogous to him. The city, in its disposition, is thus thought to emulate the human anatomy which, by inverse analogy, relates to the cosmos.'[67] In this interpretation, which conceptualises the city as a whole and as a positive space or three-dimensional mass, the palace precincts symbolise the spiritual head of the body, the main mosque (*jāmī*) the city's symbolic heart, and bazaar which connects these two vital elements the backbone of the city; the passages of the neighbourhoods leading into the 'city's body' represent the ribs. Within this structure and overall framework the main organs of the city develop: hammams, madrassas, caravanserais, granaries, bakeries, water cisterns, and numerous stores of the merchants and craftsmen. The governing concept – that of being analogous to the human body, and thus the cosmos – is one that can grow indefinitely and produce a multiplicity of geometric elements. Within the mass or material shape of the total city, 'positive space carves out a hierarchy of negative, geometric volumes through which man moves.'[68]

Based on this approach, an interior space that preserves distance and privacy is the intent, while objects such as minarets exist as landmarks witnessing the significance of internal spaces. In the spatial arrangement what is pivotal is the rhythmic continuity of space itself and the synthesis of space and time, which are brought together by a harmonic order:

> a continuous space, defined by symmetrically repeated geometric forms, cumulatively sensed through movement. Movement coalesces space and

> time into a unity that is infinitely extendible in space, yet finitely complete as any given point in time.[69]

The moving architecture, as Ardalan and Bakhtiar note, is created in the city through geometric forms and patterns, and by symmetrically repeating them.[70] The way the spatial units are placed together, their juxtaposition in symmetrical repetition, maintains the spatial flow. For example, the loggia (*iyvān*) connects the courtyard of the mosque to the interior domed area of sanctuary, thereby balancing the two different spaces.[71]

So a boundary is drawn that separates and yet does not break the continuity of rhythms and patterns. The rhythmic flow is the manifestation of the particular role of time in the city; thus movement and flow are the key concepts that define and form the space of the city. Ardalan and Bakhtiar conceptualise Safavid Isfahan as based on the concept of movement, defining three levels at the city scale: primary, secondary and tertiary movements.[72] The first is illustrated by Isfahan's long covered bazaar which stretched from the Miydān-i Kuhnih Square in the north to the Zāyandihrūd river in the south. The secondary system is represented by the neighbourhood pathways which are analogous to the veins of a leaf sustaining the tissue of residential quarters. The third system of movement relates to the network of water canals which provides the city with water, a prerequisite for urban life. The outstanding architectural buildings, such as the Khājū Bridge and Naqsh-i Jahān Square, are built at the intersections of the movement systems.

On the architectural level, movement takes place in the 'rhythmic continuity of space, shape, and surface' when architectural units such as loggias provide transitions that connect different spaces, or when the two geometries of square and circle harmoniously and continuously transform into each other in, for example, a domed chamber that exhibits a cupola rising from double pairs of columns with a square base.[73] Another example of spatial continuity in the Masjid-i Shāh[74] is the formation composed of three courtyards, four major porches and seven interior spaces, in which 'a series of interlocking space modulations are then woven into one continuous spatial experience. The main court flows through the porches into the domes chambers which open in turn to the side courts.'[75]

This symbolic interpretation of the city or space is based on the belief that the principles which govern Islamic art, especially architecture, can be found in the gnostic aspect of the religion (Islam) – the Way (*ṭarīqa*) – the esoteric dimension which contrasts with the exoteric dimension of Islam that concerns the Divine Law (sharia). The main assumption of the Way is that there is a hidden meaning in all things. That means everything has an outer as well as an inner meaning. So the external forms bear inner realities which are their hidden essence. Islamic art comes into being as a result of the wedding of formal sciences and the crafts, both of which were strongly influenced by gnostic Islam, while the Divine Law regulated daily life in the city.[76] This view differs from the postulations of authors like Hakim and Akbar who postulate the exoteric dimension of Islam that concerns the Divine Law as a source for understanding the city and urban space.[77]

Maps

Aerial representations and maps have been among the main sources of conceptions in Islamic cities studies. Discursive elaboration and modern understanding of Islamic cities have been accompanied by a wide range of cartographic mappings since the nineteenth century, the era in which surveys, maps, directories and guidebooks proliferated across the globe. The abundance of modern maps appeared as governments began to require more detailed information and knowledge about cities in order to plan, regulate and tax them. Consequently, maps became instruments of power as well as sources of education and were influential in shaping further actions, such as preparing redevelopment plans.[78] In colonial cities of the Middle East and North Africa, mapping was undertaken by colonial authorities in the form of large-scale, detailed, city-wide surveys that related to administration's need to obtain enough knowledge and information on the cities to govern them. Pier Colin's map (1860) of Tunis and the Bureau Topographique du Maroc Occidental (1913) of Fez are two examples of this kind of work. In other, non-colonial cities, modern cartographic maps were drawn either by local experts – for example, Dārulsalṭanih map of Isfahan in 1923 – or by local engineers in cooperation with their European peers, like the Tehran map drawn by August Kriziz, an Austrian teacher at Dār-ul-Funūn school, in close collaboration with his Iranian colleagues in 1857. These maps also had the goal of gaining the information needed to govern and design the cities.

The method of representing cities through maps provided a new and different perspective from that which had previously existed in local manuscripts or travellers' panoramic, picturesque depictions, wherein the cityscape was the original source of representation and constituted its codes. The change from pictorial representations to cartographic images highlighted physical characters of streets and foregrounded their narrow tortuousness. In these modern representations of the Islamic city, the visual dominance of the linear network of streets constituted the streets as the principal representatives of the city, presenting a rationale of movement between places. By highlighting pathways, cartographic maps demonstrated and contributed to the emerging importance of outdoor space and its new roles in city life, thus testifying to a more general shift in the arrangement of spaces from a tendency toward interiority in traditional configurations into an emphasis on exteriority in modern settings. The maps marked exteriors which were understood as confined merely to outdoor spaces, thereby excluding indoor (public) exteriors, or courtyards,[79] due to the belief that the interior (the indoor) was 'too private' to be presented on a map. Subsequently, the urban spaces constructed by the maps were categorised into two groups: private space associated with the indoor and public space which is seen in connection to the outdoor. As the passageways that constituted the major percentage of the outdoor and public buildings, such as mosques and madrassas, are absent from the logic of the maps, the perception is evoked that the public space of the city is mainly present in the pathways that offer movement between places.

On the other hand, the visual dominance and pattern of roads in the maps connotes a set of spatial engagements of the subject in urban space. The long narrow pathways appear as mere linkages between individual built spaces, depicting the city as a place for the kind of movement that involves no sensual engagement with the space. This conception reduces the element of the path to a neutral, physically linking line whose only representative feature is its geometry, while its phenomenological or social qualities are disregarded. As Chambers observes, city plans present 'an outline, a shape, some sort of location, but not the contexts, cultures, histories, languages, experiences, desires and hopes that course through the urban body.'[80]

Features of the representation of space in maps influence the understanding and interpreting of cities for, once drawn, the maps become a part of reality and also shape it:

> Once a space has been represented in map-form the representation becomes a potent reification – a construct, which is both treated as reality at the same time as it shapes it . . . Once imagined, the representation assumes a reality that is unassailable. It is impossible to disentangle analytically or discursively the site as it is from the way in which it is being represented and its future imagined. And these 'realities' are inseparable from how the site is remembered. In other words, the representation is simultaneously the real and the real is the imaginary, and the negotiation of both is political.[81]

To discuss an example, the Dārulsalṭanih-yi Isfahan map is the first cartographic map of Isfahan (figure 1.1). It was drawn by Sūlṭān Siyyid Riżā Khān, a member of the *naẓmīyih*[82] of Isfahan, between 1920 and 1923. The map has three main characteristics which are observable at first sight:

(a) A network of lines visually dominates the overall image of the map. As a result, the geometrical elements of the routes become the key visual features that the map presents of Isfahan to the viewer.
(b) A large number of words are spread across the map: mainly the names of alleys or neighbourhoods, they create a vague patchwork of urban units. Referencing different occupations, ethnicities, religions or cities of origin, the names connote diverse social units or groups in the city whose spatial embodiments on the map are alleys or vaguely delineated neighbourhoods. For example, one alley is named Brokers which refers to a craft union (*ṣīnf*) in the city and, therefore, the spatial presence of

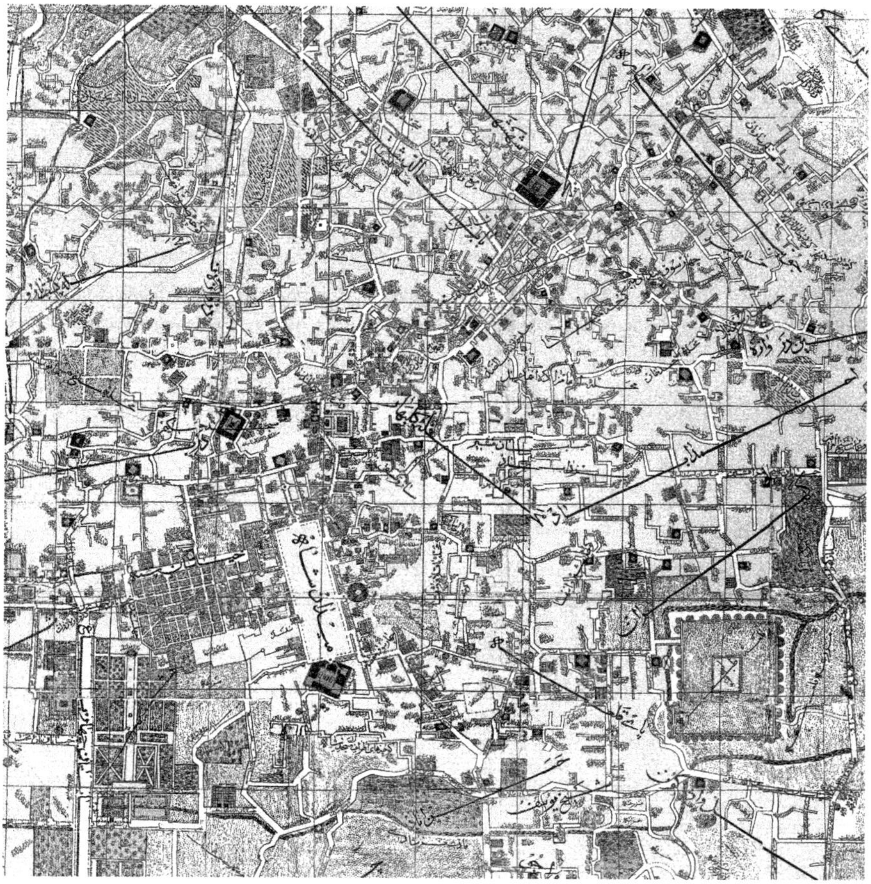

Figure 1.1 Dārulsalṭanih-yi Isfahan map, 1924; with facsimile edition of Saḥāb Geographic and Drafting Institute, Saḥāb Geographic and Drafting Institute Archive, Tehran

that craft union in the urban fabric, indicating that those belonging to it occupy the area either for work or for residence. The name used on the map, in other words, separates each area from its surroundings by connecting it to a specific group of people that belong to the craft union. Many alleys are named after individual persons, probably the best-known residents of each alley or neighbourhood; other pathways or neighbourhoods reference local places of worship. Marked, for example, is the neighbourhood of the Imāmzādih Īsmāʿīl shrine. The separations through naming are blurred, as the boundaries of the separated areas are not clearly marked on the map. Nonetheless, they vaguely present a system of division in the city with fuzzy delineations.

(c) The routes are classified based on their topological typologies. Depending on their shape, and surrounding elements or functions the pathways are categorised as *kūchih, khīābān, bunbast*, and *kūchihbāgh*. The routes that were long and to a certain extent straight are named *khīābān* – the word that in today's Persian language translates as street; culs-de-sac are named *bunbast*, literally meaning a place closed at one end. The alleys flanked by gardens are called *kūchihbāq* (or alley-garden), while the remainder are grouped under the name *kūchih*.[83]

The Dārulsalṭanih-yi Isfahan map oscillates between a modern logic of urban representation and Isfahan's premodern sociospatial characters. On the one hand, we have a clearly determined system of understanding the city by mapping its roads and classifying them based on their functional and physical typologies and geometries. The representational dominance of this classification – and the urban routes themselves – foregrounds exteriors and introduces pathways as key urban spaces, as required by a modern understanding of cities, and also rationalises movement across urban space, another typical element of a modernist approach. The words and names used, on the other hand, invoke and preserve some premodern cultural principles and features in the map. The names are historically embedded in everyday urban life and in people's orally transmitted memories, and these depictions are among their first documentations. Western travellers' bewilderment when visiting these cities was partly caused by the lack of street names or numbers, and vice versa: in Persian travellers' descriptions of European cities, it is evident that they wondered why the streets had names and the buildings had numbers.[84]

Yet the style of delineation that the written layer of the map promotes still resists the modern approach of precise rationalising of the division system in cities; although the names and words denote the existence of distinct areas and units in Isfahan, they do not mark the units with exact, concrete boundaries. The superimposition of the modern way of representation combined with preservation of premodern elements can also be seen in the urban functions that are marked on the map. The telegraph, for example, is marked as newly emergent modern infrastructure, alongside spaces like caravanserais whose existence dates back centuries.

The footnotes of maps provide pointers to the 'priorities and values that guided the representation and the social, cultural and historical context within which it was drawn.'[85] In the footnotes of the Dārulsalṭanih-yi Isfahan map, we read:

> In general the availability of a local map is necessary for each location, particularly for the use of the *naẓmīyih* of the city. The director of the *naẓmīyih*, Ahmad Alīkhān Zand, demonstrated effort in preparing a map of the city in 1298 [1919]. Due to the mentioned reasons, I, Sūlṭān Siyyid Riżā Khān. . ., despite the unavailability of sufficient equipment,

> began to work in . . . 1299 [1920] and finished a detailed map in the scale of 1/4000, in . . . 1302 [1923]. The map shows all the neighbourhoods, routes, religious places, hammams, gardens and other places that were, in my belief, important . . . What at first sight presents previous engineering conditions are: the beautiful style of the buildings in Isfahan; streets and pathways stretch from north to south and from east to west in parallel to each other and in beautiful condition . . . and good climatic conditions. After the different invasions of the country and the construction of castles, towers, gates and other buildings, the initial image of the city has disappeared and it has fallen into an unacceptable state. Fortunately, at the time that I was preparing the map a period of prosperity began in Iran. And, thanks to the efforts of Sardār Sipāh . . . [and] Mr Amīr Iqtidār Hukmrān and his contributions (for example in paving and widening the pathways and developing streets), Isfahan starts to flourish and there are hopes that it may return to its original condition. . . .
>
> [signed by Sūlṭān Siyyid Riżā Khān][86]

> The top-down map of each city is one of the important tools of every institution, particularly the *naẓmīyih* and *baladīyih*.[87] Unfortunately, no map was available for this big historic city [Isfahan]. The Frenchman, Chardin, presented some maps in his books from his travels to Isfahan in the era of Safavid kings. But they are limited to governmental buildings. Fortunately, in the current time of prosperity, and due to the efforts and attentions of Mr Sulṭān Mīrzā Siyyid Riżā Khān Dār Jalaleh, who is among the high officers of the *naẓmīyih* of Isfahan, he has managed this huge work in a short time . . . Anybody who is familiar with the science of cartography can confirm the extension of efforts he [Riżā Khān] has put in to drawing this map. . ..
>
> [signed by . . . Muhāsib-ul-Aval dated . . . 1302 [1923]].[88]

The main goal of the Dārulsalṭanih-yi Isfahan map, according to its footnote, was to provide the necessary tools for (early-modern or semi-modern) urban administrational institutions such as the *naẓmīyih* and the *baladīyih*. There are many other similar maps produced from the cities in the region during the late nineteenth and twentieth centuries which have provided the bases of studies and interpretations of urban space and cities. In a map from 1913 drawn by the Bureau Topographique du Maroc Occidental, the city of Fez, similarly, is represented mainly through networks of streets and names of alleys and neighbourhoods. In this map, however, the boundaries of Fez neighbourhoods are clearly determined and listed in the legend, which also mentions a number of principal elements – ranging from an alley to a sanctuary (*zāwīya*), a mosque or a house – in each neighbourhood. The way the city is shown as an assemblage of sociospatially divided units with clear-cut boundaries reduces the complexity of interconnections between different units and ongoing urban dynamics.[89]

Mapping always involves some kind of 'exploration, selection, definition, generalisation and translation of data.'[90] It rationalises space and time based on particular sets of values and criteria which determine what is worth signification, and thus remembering, and what can be neglected: maps are selective representations of spaces, realities and spatial relationships and thus they prioritise some worldviews over others.[91] In this way, the drawing of a map is not a purely objective or technical procedure; rather it reproduces the sociocultural context – the hierarchies of social values and power structures, and the languages – within which it takes place.[92] As Dennis states, a map is 'as selective, as ideologically grounded, as subject to individual interpretations, as more obviously subjective sources such as novels and paintings.'[93] So maps filter the spatial relations and the real, lived space through a set of ideologies, politics, norms and sociocultural understandings. The filtration creates a distinction between the represented and the reality and determines a certain type of rationality which directs how space is understood and presented. As a result, each map constructs a particular definition of urban space in a city, and redefines which spaces constitute 'the city' and of what the urban space consists.

Cartographic maps direct attention towards the routes, linkages and acts of movement.[94] They represent the city as an accumulation of networks of pathways with a number of public buildings shown as solid volumes around them. So 'the city' was assumed to be taking place in outdoor space as the only space that enables the movement and connection around and across it. In this way, urban space equates with exterior space, where the exterior refers to the area outside the outer walls of buildings. This current cartographic understanding not only puts emphasis on outside spaces but also gives primacy to clarity and exact scientific determination. In these maps, clear-cut delineations of built cells by walls define the boundaries of pathways, that is, the public space, and also constitute the limits of spatial cells in the city. Yet there are cases, for instance in the historic fabric of Fez, where the contours of buildings do not accord with occupation and usage boundaries and thus do not represent the real, actual spatial units of the city.[95] The real boundaries are a complex overlay of ownership borders which vary on different levels of adjacent buildings because the areas owned by each resident might differ vertically from building to building. The complexity and ambiguity are accelerated by the fact that these boundaries are negotiable between neighbours and can change over time.

The way a map presupposes a meaning for the concept of boundary also has a part in the way it imagines the space. Whether the spatial units are defined in a map based on the courtyards whose immediate boundaries are the architectural spaces around them, or based on the physical walls which can lack a concrete association with the reality of urban life, will result in two different (re)constructions of the space. For example, if we shift our focus from outdoor passages to courtyards, acknowledging the dynamic character of ownership boundaries in a city, the maps will no longer only foreground a linear fixed network of pathways as 'the city.' Consequently, the courtyards will be rightly considered the key spaces of the city and urban life, forming the nodal spatial foci that gather not only architectural sub-spaces around them but also a complex network of sociocultural and political relationships; sociocultural issues include, for instance, the extent of privacy or publicness, while political forces refer to control, ownership, access and events. The diverse overlap of these elements gives each courtyard a unique character. Thus, in this new way of mapping, the representation of the space will change to an agglomeration of regular squares meticulously carved out of a larger solid block. Then the pathways take on a secondary importance and analysis of urban space shifts to 'irregular' routes whose functions are mainly seen as linking spaces to diverse types of indoor exteriors with different functions, social meanings, degrees of privacy, spatial behaviours and so on. This potential diversity in setting the norms and elements of mapping – that is, the basic framework of understanding – acknowledges and appreciates the fact that cities have diverse ontological characters.

Diagrams have also been key elements in imaging the Islamic city whereby theoretical descriptions of cities conclude in diagrammatic representations. In these cases, the diagrams present structures or logical systems for a typical Islamic city: a set of connections between different elements in the city that illustrate functional or social zonings and relations between different functions in the city. Principal among these, and repeated in numerous diagrams of Islamic cities, are the main mosque, the market, baths, caravanserais, residential quarters, sub-centres of quarters, main thoroughfares, walls, castles, city gates and suburbs. Sometimes characteristics of urban form are also included – for example Wirth symbolises the residential areas with an assemblage of culs-de-sac.[96] By applying specific techniques of abstraction this mode of representation extracts from the dynamics of urban life a schematic presentation of certain elements of that life in the form of points, lines or sections. The human experience is thereby translated to a kind of abstraction.[97]

Perceptions

There is a common feeling, derived from sensual experience of urban space in an Islamic city, that each one has something special: a character or an existence, perhaps, which differentiates it from others. Yet the nature of this something has been described or interpreted differently: Abu-Lughod calls it a code that unites the elements of an Islamic city at different levels in terms of sociospatial characters and, she suggests, as it is common in all Islamic cities, it also unites them in general; Bianca, on the other hand, sees it as an inherent order and a vocabulary while, in contrast, De Planhol claims it is a lack of order.[98] This 'something' has remained obscure and is not yet clearly conceptualised in the existing scholarship. Descriptions of experiencing space pivot on a number of key elements in the cities where the pathway network, again, takes first place. The urban space and form have been widely interpreted in terms of perceptions of networks of passages – named as a particularity of the Islamic cities.[99]

Abu-Lughod suggests the existence of a commonly perceived code of space in Islamic cities. She states that 'one always "knows" when one is in the presence of an Islamic civilization.'[100] She goes on to ask:

> Is it merely the superficial decoration, the insistently repetitive arches, the geometry of tiny spaces aggregating to vast designs that signal the Code? Is it the basic architectonic concept of square-horizontal and rounded vertical space that announces the unity underlying external diversity in shape? Is it the overall emphasis upon enclosing, enfolding, involuting, protecting and covering that one finds alike in single structures, in quarters, indeed in entire cities? There appears to be certain basic 'deep structures' to the language of Islamic expression in space.[101]

This code appears to be a vague feeling, evoked by visual characteristics and geometrical patterns as well as architectural elements, that results in an image of the given city. Connections observed between the details and large-scale patterns (the whole city), all give rise to the character of enfolding.

Discussing a similar perception of unity, Bianca emphasises that there is an 'inherent concept of order' which produces an Islamic city's 'singular physical character,' a sense of inner unity and homogeneity which is also observable from a bird's-eye view,[102] observing that the continuous cellular structure blurs the division between individual architectural components.[103] When moving through the space of the city, the walker experiences a 'distinct feeling of spatial continuity transcending the limits of individual buildings and connecting the various realms of public life.'[104] Yet, at the same time, the walker

> receives clear physical guidance with respect to the differentiation between different sectors. A subtle visual reference system relates to accepted (and expected) codes of social behaviour within the given urban compartments. Each individual realm carefully retains its specific spatial character, while interacting with neighbouring units through distinct architectural devices, such as intermediate gateways, internal passages, thresholds and communicating doors. Hence the impression of meandering through a seemingly endless series of interconnected chambers within a highly articulated and yet homogenous urban universe.[105]

According to Bianca every single part of the urban structure, ranging from the smallest particle to the entire urban fabric, carries the attributes of wholeness and unity produced by this vocabulary or code. The spatial logic (of the Islamic city) is based on constant differentiation of interior niches from exterior spaces, where both notions are relative values within a large spatial spectrum ranging from the small private room to the complete urban structure. Consequently, there is a division of space into included and excluded in which the whole structural order of the city promotes 'a paradoxical physical experience which is characteristic of most traditional Arab cities: one always has the feeling of being at the centre of things, in whatever sub-unit of the composite urban structure it may be.'[106]

In a different account, O'Meara calls Fez an 'inscrutable' city; it appears to be 'defined and determined by its walls,' 'a city of distancing, non-reflecting transpositions' whose space is the space of separation and reversal, which keep the occupant or visitor 'mindful of an inner life.'[107] In O'Meara's account, premodern Fez is a walled enclosure, yet it is not entirely enclosed. It is, rather,

> *entr'ouvert*, ajar: simultaneously open and closed. Visually, for example, it consisted of a liminal realm of perforated surfaces in multiple planes; not the plunging voids of Euclidean space characteristics of modern cities. Shuttering and weaving the visual field, framing and reframing space, layering it into bays and arcades . . . The city's neighbourhoods provide a second illustration: a passage taken through them reveals to the gaze an intercalation of openings in an otherwise closed, almost telescopic mesh of walls.[108]

The effect of such an ambiguous visual realm is that for either a complete outsider or a familiar inhabitant there is a constant feeling of remaining within and without at the same time, with arrival always deferred. For a complete outsider, the whole city, except its main thoroughfares, is entirely closed: 'to this visitor the medina must have seemed forbidding and obscure. Although physically within the city, he, or less likely she, yet remained without all but the most public spaces; a double position that would likely have been disorienting.'[109] For an acquainted resident to whom the doors of the houses are in principle traversable

> a play between open and closed operated to seemingly deliberate effect. For although they might have traversed increasing degrees of interiority from the city gate to the main thoroughfare, to the side street, to the dead-end alley, to at last entering the house, they yet remained within and without. Opening onto the heavens, the courtyard's well of sky returned them to the *entr'ouvert*.[110]

The most common perceptual understanding of urban space of Islamic cities is presented in Wirth's explanation of the sensual experience of walking through one.[111] He describes the difficulty of finding one's way in the continuously branching labyrinthine alleys of the bazaar, but then, from its seemingly chaotic entanglements and crushes, one enters the residential area. This is much quieter, empty of people, surrounded by blank, windowless walls and closed doors, where one repeatedly gets into cul-de-sacs which necessitate reversing and finding a new way out. The public passages – except in some cases such as in Cairo and Istanbul – have no representative or aesthetic function. The idea behind them was not to implement some predefined conceptual ideas through, for example, ruler-straight building rows. Rather the goal was to create the possibility for flowing movement in the city. He adds the cityscape of the Islamic city is dominated by city walls, minarets, gateways (their façade) of mosques, religious schools and the narrowness of alleys in residential areas.[112] Paintings and travel stories also express similar perceptions of the urban space of Islamic cities. Çelik observes that in the Orientalists' paintings Algerian urban houses were represented in a dual way: 'If the exterior representations of the indigenous urban house conveyed the prevailing characteristics of the old town, interior views elaborated on more imaginary scenes . . . [which] reinforce the introverted nature of the Algerian house.'[113] The exterior views focused on the terraces and the narrow, winding streets lined with irregular buildings, while the interiors were represented by fantasy scenes dominated by ornaments.[114]

The pathway network also dominates the image of urban space in the travel stories of early-modern visitors to Islamic cities. De Bode, visiting Isfahan, writes:

> at last [I] reached the gates of Isfahan . . . I had to traverse the whole breadth of the town from north to south; first by cut-throat lanes between high-raised walls which enclose the gardens of the suburbs; then by covered bazaars . . . till I reached the Chahar-Bagh of Shah Abbas, that celebrated alley, bordered by eastern plane-trees.[115]

Similarly, Arnold, visiting Shiraz, writes:

> A stranger to Persian ways and means, seeing us fording watercourses, winding round ruined walls, passing between miserable sheds scarcely eight feet apart, would hardly suppose that by the most frequented route, we were entering the chief city of the Persian Empire . . . The ragged roof of boughs and straw, which was intended to cover the way, but the result of which was to chequer the path with patches of sunlight, was supported by saplings just as they were brought from plantations by the river side, and the road was as it had pleased the population to make it.[116]

He adds:

> Through a small maze of mud walls [we] approached the house . . . In Persian eyes the construction would indeed be faulty if anything of the interior could be seen through this one opening of communication with the outer world. There is always a turn in dark, covered entry.[117]

These diverse perceptions have resulted in cultural constructions of place-images, like 'mysterious', 'labyrinthine' and 'ambiguous', which are associated with Islamic cities. Çelik, for instance, notes that the casbah of Algiers 'evoked mystery. It represented the attraction of unknown dangers'; and the 'mystery' has been an element of the triad on which the myth of the casbah of Algiers is based.[118] These kinds of namings have a part in city identification and give a shape to cities.[119] Through these languages we get images of places to which we have never been that will affect our performance in the city. We practice the city based on its labels: 'Each of these images . . . represents the city as a certain kind of place. By representing specific cities as certain kinds of places, we are in a way determining our potential actions in those places.'[120]

Rationalised phenomenality

The experience of walking through cities has evoked key perceptions of urban space which have been among the main sources of inspiration in characterising Islamic examples. Yet, pushed into the background, the phenomenality of space and its immediate experiencing has not been used as the foundation for theorising cities. Rationality has dominated the studies and theorisations, while phenomenality has often played a background role: rarely the direct, pivotal point of conceptualisations, it has, however, been the reference point of their inspiration. The neglect of sensual spatial characters has taken three forms: firstly, when translated into academic analyses, the phenomenality of space is interpreted as 'uncommon irregularity'; secondly, in analysing urban space practical reasons and accounts have been sought for a perceived 'disorder' in the city; thirdly, in studies that elaborate on the very phenomenality of the space, beyond seeing it as a mere 'disorder,' there have not been adequate vocabularies to express the described experiences accurately and to import spatial experiences into the body of theory and scholarship.

The first and second forms presume the same spatial criteria, although they are developed by two groups of authors with opposing points of view. Based on these criteria, a city is supposed to be a modern one of reason which is expected to be organised on the foundations of some spatial order, best expressed in geometrical regularity. And the space should be comprehensible, accessible and clear. Therefore, experiencing the space of the Islamic city, which is neither accessible nor easily comprehensible, led the authors to interpret the spatial pattern of the city as 'irregular.' Meanwhile, the character of 'irregularity' is supposed to reduce and question the urbanity or perfection of a city, making of it an incomplete example. The first form emerged from early scientific encounters with Islamic cities by authors who developed many of their ideas based on immediate experience of the space.[121] Yet the tortuousness of the paths, the feeling of getting lost and trapped in the private sphere only led them to interpret the cities as 'disintegrated' and 'not like a real city,' but rather, for example, chaotic agglomerations of isolated blocks. The spatial organisation has thus been seen as a negative quality since it did not accord with the modern analytical structure and framework for understanding dominant in the contemporary scholarship on Islamic cities.[122]

The second group of scholars believe there are rationales and reasons behind the irregularity and chaos in an Islamic city. This view provides accounts of why it has the form it has, thereby justifying the urban structure; this is a search for underlying orders, causes, rationales and forces behind the structure and formation of the cities and their material urban fabric. Discovering different layers of interrelationships among elements, objects and structures in Islamic cities has been a key goal in order to answer why and which historical, religious, juridical, legal or physical dynamics shaped the urban form. The established foundation or anchor for justifying the urban (dis)order in these accounts 'is a key social institution, which acts as a medium of developing, justifying and spreading a particular account.'[123]

To account for what is directly experienced in the city, in these studies, the authors refer, for example, to social systems,[124] ethnic structures, legal urban institutions,[125] urban organisation,[126] early Arab practice,[127] property rights,[128] religion,[129] traffic control,[130] limiting circulation,[131] cultural codes/lack of municipal administration,[132] providing defence,[133] a best answer to the challenge of desert living,[134] responsibility and property rights,[135] religious law and building codes[136] and privacy.[137] The Islamic city is, for instance, seen as an urban society which has divided essential powers and functions among its different component groups, and where the interactions between these subsidiary groups have produced the urban form. Or it is seen as a distinctive whole with an opposition between a vast private zone and a public centre which has shaped the city's vigorous centrality.

Various similar explanations have been put forth to emphasise that the Islamic city is rational. As another example of a typical approach, Wheatley notes that life in an Islamic city is concentrated in the internal courtyard of houses, not on the street; this priority reveals that the street layout is 'rational and systematic.'[138] Similarly, Kostof states, 'the labyrinthine medina' is 'quite rational' and the city has a highly unique spatial order.[139] Jianni also believes the Islamic city forms a 'complex urban fabric of houses built around courtyards within a labyrinthine network of narrow roads,' yet it has a highly unique spatial order.[140] He declares the private world of the residential district is 'a complex labyrinthine structure' because it is 'purposely meant to be difficult of access to outsiders.'[141] In all these approaches there is a tendency towards rationalising the sensual perceptions of the city and presenting reasons to prove that the city is 'rational,' 'has a logic,' 'follows a clear logical pattern' and has 'a certain level of regularity.' Or, alternatively, some scholars emphasise that the irregularity only appears in a limited number of cities of the region because cities such as Baghdad in the era of al-Mansur, Herat and Safavid Isfahan were planned and thus had regular street networks. They conclude from this fact that a chaotic and completely irregular cul-de-sac pattern was not a characteristic feature of Islamic cities.[142]

Raymond's statements on spatial structure appropriately represent the examples of the functional view in the above mentioned studies.[143] He notes that the major features of urban structure in large Arab cities of the region from Morocco to Iraq, and from Syria to Yemen, in the period between the sixteenth and nineteenth centuries, appear 'fairly constant and exhibit a rationale such that we are justified in speaking of a coherent *urban system*.'[144] These characteristics are discussed as products of the existence of a separation between areas of economic activity and areas of residence which encourages the existence of two strongly contrasted zones: the public zone of the city centre and the private zone of residential areas. He further observes that the urban centre or public zone was organised around the main suqs and the principal mosque and responsibility for broad avenues, large markets or important mosques fell to the political authorities; the private zone, on the other hand, was devoted to private dwellings comprising the urban quarters which are among distinctive the features of the Arab city. These quarters were relatively enfolded; one street connected a quarter to the outside and branched into streets that were usually irregular and ended, finally, in cul-de-sacs.[145] Outlining the reasons and rationales for these structural characters, he suggests:

> The irregularity of the streets and the abundance of cul-de-sacs which has so intrigued Orientalists was thus a local phenomenon within the city, one answering to the various needs of the population living in the city's quarters, and not a general characteristic. We have noted how in the centre and towards the gates traffic was catered for by direct, regular thoroughfares. Within their quarters, the inhabitants could be content with irregular streets and cul-de-sacs which in point of fact, were conductive to their security. The only communications they needed were with the city centre where their active life was passed and where they fulfilled their chief religious obligations (Friday prayer); they had no need of direct contact with the outside. Each quarter consisted of a kind of population pocket, open only towards the centre. In actual fact, the cul-de-sacs represented statistically a little less than half of the road network, their development being restricted to within the quarters: 52 per cent of road system in Fez and 41 per cent in Aleppo. In Algiers there was a very marked contrast between the lower city, corresponding to the centre (24.5 per cent cul-de-sacs), and the upper city, where the indigenous population lived (59.9 per cent). The cul-de-sac was thus a functional feature, localized within a specific sector of the city.[146]

Highlighting the public-private composition or functional hierarchy of street networks has been an important element of the reasoning behind urban space-ordering in the cities, also discussed by other authors. Hakim states that street systems are primarily of two types: the through-traffic, open-ended street which was considered part of public space and had to be wide enough for two packed camels, at least, to pass; and the cul-de-sac which, according to Islamic law, is considered the private property of the people having access from it to their front doors.[147] According to Çelik, the network of streets in Algiers revealed a system of filtered access, and the neighbourhood pathways, which were narrow, irregular and often dead-ends, effectively accommodated the introverted residential spaces that centred on the privacy of the home and the family. The configuration of the streets, she notes, also enabled the use of gates to close off a neighbourhood in the evenings for safety reasons. Therefore, it revealed 'a carefully articulated logic.'[148]

Spatial separations or sociospatial segregations throughout the city, the protection of domestic space and the existence of extreme distinctions between private and public spheres in the city have provided a consistent anchor in conceptualisations of the urban space of the Islamic city. It is widely argued that preserving private space by sealing it off from a perceived external threat was one of the integral features that gave the cities the forms embodied in the courtyard pattern, tortuous lanes and an overall tendency towards inwardness. As discussed, according to O'Meara the wall as a key spatial organiser in the material structure is the embodiment of segregation as a key idea in space-making.[149] Abu-Lughod sees Islamic cities as divided into areas of ethno-religious homogeneity where the spatial boundaries are culturally constructed and then transform into physical segregation.[150] Le Tourneau states that a house in Fez is a closed space turned entirely toward the patio;[151] similarly, Çelik, when explaining the role of the courtyard in Algiers, notes: 'gender-based separate "turfes" prevented physical contact and relegated the lives of the women to their homes. Privacy thus became a leading factor and resulted in the emergence of an interiorized domestic architecture' (interiorised court).[152] She concludes:

> [T]he cumulative analyses of ethnographers and architects [of Algiers during French rule] produced a list of characteristics that defined the 'Algerian house.' With its courtyard as the key space, the Algerian house was interiorized. It enclosed itself to the street and the external world by its blank, planar facades with minimal openings.[153]

It is believed that the reason behind this typology was the respect for privacy which 'dictated the design of facades as well: windows and doors were carefully located to prevent views into the houses across the street.'[154]

This process of reasoning and the accounts it produced are means of presenting convincing explanations for beliefs, values and actions: the capacity to make convincing judgements.[155] In reasoning we deal with complexity by breaking it down to manageable pieces. In subdividing a phenomenon into pieces we assign them with symbolic values which generate social and psychological meanings for these pieces. Then, we reassemble them to establish new understandings in a new model of interpretation. That is, we reconstruct the complexity in 'an intelligible way, hence controlling its complexity to a level . . . graspable by the human mind, so that it can be expressed in words.'[156] The use of reason is an interpretive process which consists of analytical and synthetic stages – as Descartes notes.[157] These stages of analysing and synthesising both generate scales of abstraction and are, therefore, socially constructed: 'the way we subdivide a phenomenon . . . depends on our perspective and our purpose. Different people may generate different ontologies,' and people may disagree on how to reconstruct the segmented pieces.[158] Thus, our knowledge – which is ultimately formed through this process of segmentation and reconstitution – is socially and culturally constructed.

Another key feature of reason is its contrast with feeling. Feelings, as Madanipour notes, make us aware of our inner states in response to the outside world; reason, on the other hand, is our tool to respond to social norms and conventions, many of which are set to tame emotional impulses. We use reason to judge between true or false. The contrast between feeling and reason also seems to refer to the distinction between scientific knowledge and reflective action, or between knowing and acting. In understanding urban space and the city from the outside, from the scientific third-person viewpoint, we analyse and break down the space in order to comprehend it. In doing so, we impose an order on an infinite substance which we cannot grasp with our senses. Understanding urban space from the eyes of the individual observer means moving from a bird's eye view to the human perspective: from a structured and subdivided pattern, to a phenomenological view in which the space is bodily experienced by every individual in the process of movement.[159]

It is vital to study and understand cities as maps or panoramas which reveal the underlying forces and dynamics that created the form, social structures and other reasons behind the urban life that have dominated Islamic cities studies to date. Yet it is also important to go beyond that and read the city through characteristics that are perceivable through immediate experience of its space. In recent urban theory (of everyday life), there is 'a sense of the need to grasp a phenomenality that cannot be known through theory or cognition alone.'[160] Amin and Thrift endorse an approach that strives for a 'phenomenality of practices.'[161] They believe that urban practices constantly exceed the disciplinary envelopes in which they embedded. So they turn to 'another urbanism . . . which reads cities from their recurrent phenomenological patterns.'[162] It is necessary to know the city 'beyond powers of cognition, venturing into the realms of poetic invocation and sensory intimation.'[163] For Lefebvre, too, there is an existential and phenomenological condition in the production of space in the course of everyday life processes.[164]

The third form and reason for the neglect of sensual spatial characteristics is the lack of terminologies or spatial concepts. The descriptions reviewed so far provide deep insights into the phenomenological aspects of the space in urban cities, yet they have not been consolidated in the main body of our knowledge of these cities. While analytical conceptions have revolved around a definite number of architectural elements or sociospatial patterns determined to be the main representative components of the city – such as the wall, boundary, passageway, courtyard, preserved privacy and so on – perceptions have been mainly expressed in descriptive statements applying terms such as tortuous, ambiguous and labyrinthine.

Verbalising the perceptions has culminated in a variety of recurrent terminologies, images and concepts which shape a major body of work on the Islamic city. The employed spatial metaphors, or concepts, for expressing the phenomenological perceptions that are used throughout the scholarship have largely contributed to the creation of the place-images and understanding of space in the cities and thus become a vital part of constructing notions of them. As Shields states, 'this geography of difference is socially constructed over the long term and constitutes a spatialisation of places and regions as "places-for-this" and/or "places-for-that."'[165] Symbols and metaphors liken the things to forms with which we are already familiar in our literary culture.[166]

The set of descriptive concepts used in reference to Islamic urban space includes, for example, enclosed, enfolded, involuted, protected, covered; *ent'rouvet*, being at the same time within and without;[167] incomprehensible, homogenous, continuous, endless, interconnected, united, causing the feeling of being at the centre, with blurred divisions, labyrinthine, ambiguous, mysterious, vague, inextricable and introvert. Or this can be perceived and expressed on another level as dominated by crooked alleys,[168] with a hodgepodge pattern of street communication,[169] shapeless, fluid, twisting, amorphous and physically formless,[170] maze,[171] chaotic,[172] with winding passages,[173] narrow twisting alleys,[174] without plan (*planlos*)[175] and labyrinth.[176] Most of these concepts, like 'tortuous' and 'winding', do not go beyond two-dimensional qualities of space, reducing it to a linking line between two points in the city. Other terms such as irregular and non-geometric refer to the absence of a quality instead of the existence of it.

Yet another group of terms – such as enfolded, *entr'ouvet*, being at the same time within and without, and being-inside (*Innerhalb-sein*) – helps fill in the mosaics of a general patchwork that hints at the phenomenality of space. The main reason for this lies in the potential these terms have to introduce spatial qualities that go beyond mere form or function, on the one hand, and encompass specific qualities of urban space, on the other.[177] For example, 'enfolded' does not merely describe a two-dimensional geometry; rather, it refers to the coalescence of a set of qualities including, for instance, the courtyard typology (material configuration of space), space that hides and does not expose itself to observers (perception of space) and the notion of nonporous borders (aesthetics of space). Thus, 'enfolded' also foregrounds a common understanding of space particular to the Islamic cities. Persistent hints of phenomenological perceptions of space in conceptualising the particularities of urban space in Islamic cities reconfirm the distinct importance of the aspect of phenomenality in this regional spatial context. Therefore it needs closer scrutiny; it also needs to be concretised analytically and theoretically in the body of knowledge on Islamic cities.

Labyrinth, the linking metaphor

Among concepts applied when representing the Islamic city, 'labyrinth' is a key term that both explains the experience of space in Islamic cities and spans rationality and phenomenality. There are three reasons for this particularity: the persistent presence of the term in interpreting and representing the cities since at least the mid-eighteenth century; the multifaceted meaning of labyrinth as a spatial concept; and the embeddedness of the notion in a particular geographical-historical context. It has been a persistent concept in the discourse on Islamic cities in both scientific conceptions and popular representations, whether the city is understood as a 'map' or experienced in a 'tour'.[178] In current scientific discourse, although there is a clear awareness that the term attaches a negative character to the structure of the Islamic city, it is still preferred to other notions. For example, O'Meara writes, 'the labyrinthine web of frequently narrow and half-lit streets, alleys, and cul-de-sacs that unites the urban infrastructure and does so much to define the space' is amongst the parameters of the typical morphology of cities in the Islamic world.[179] He applies the term labyrinth as shorthand to refer to the typical characteristics of Islamic urban space, yet, cautiously, he adds that he uses the term 'solely in the sense of a convoluted network of segmentalized, interconnecting passageways bordered by tall, seemingly impenetrable walls.'[180] Thus, labyrinth is used throughout the book, but with an adopted definition. We can also observe the term in writings of other recent authors like Champbell, Madanipour, Çelik and Alsayyad.[181] Can we conclude that the notion of a labyrinth is thought to be the best way to describe the phenomenality of Islamic urban space – probably due to its potential in expressing qualities related to three-dimensional space – but that there is also a strong awareness that it does not fully coincide with realities?

It is a concept that goes beyond mere function, pattern or form, and involves phenomenality and intimacy in the comprehension of the city.[182] It 'goes beyond appearances'[183] by engaging emotions, practices and memories as different layers of interaction with space. In terms of physical characteristics, the concept denotes incomprehensible, 'irregular' geometries which can be successively explored by walking through them (movement as spatial practice). The attribution is not merely a simple representative of the tortuousness of the paths; rather it carries inherent qualities drawn from the phenomenological aspects of the space: its walls, colours, cloth signs, spatial practices of self and others and feelings related to imagined territorial or culturally defined boundaries. That is, the sensual characters of the urban space also have role in its being perceived as incomprehensible and labyrinth. Yet, ultimately, the experience of perceiving the space of the Islamic city as a labyrinth is based on a vague (sensual) impression of space that is, for example, unreadable and which loses people in its twists and turns. These spectral feelings, drawn from the sense of 'incomprehensibility,' are made legible by being assimilated into the image or symbol of labyrinth – which also incorporates the obscurity what exactly the form or space is. This is a vague sense of the flavour of the city that describes a sensibility or a state of mind.

Rooted in the cultural history of Europe, the labyrinth as a symbol reinforces cultural-geographical associations, involves memory in the process of interaction with the Islamic city, thereby conjoining sensual, imaginary, metaphorical and symbolic spaces. As the term spans diverse facets of experiencing (perceiving), conceiving and representing space, it touches a layer of understanding that differs from the other concepts used so far in the context of Islamic cities studies. In addition, its application in both cognitive conceptions and sensual perceptions confirms the role of labyrinth in bridging rationality and phenomenality in the context. We can observe three types of presence of the term in this discourse:

(a) Studies that follow rational, cognitional approaches in analysing or mapping the Islamic city, equate a labyrinth-like city with a chaotic city. According to the norms and ideals of a modern mind, a city should offer connectivity, permeability, clarity and movement. Any exception to this rule is challenged as an abnormal, inappropriate or dysfunctional case. And when no logical reason is found to explain this dismissal of the presupposed spatial principles, the structure of the city concerned is often interpreted as being labyrinthine or maze-like – whether observing the city from above or within. A 'labyrinth city,' in these cases, is regarded as equal to and denoting an 'irrational city.' Assuming that the city should follow a clear rationality in its structure and movement patterns, authors are 'obsessed with the capture of movement, imbued with the values of precision.'[184] In this way, the city is characterised rather than being explored or reflected upon.

Two groups of studies understand the Islamic city as a 'labyrinth-like' city: the first is mainly influenced by Orientalists or modernists' ideologies, which saw the cities outside Europe or the modern world as inferior. They used terms like labyrinthine, labyrinth-like and maze-like to question the virtues of the cities due to their so-called chaotic structure. For instance, Le Tourneau writes: Nothing is more foreign to a Muslim city of the Maghreb than the straight avenues of a Roman city or a modern city; it is a maze, a labyrinth that makes one think the aerial photograph of any Muslim city.[185] Or de Planhol sees the Islamic city as a maze behind which a 'Muslim' hides herself to stay safe.[186]

The second group detaches the attribution of labyrinth from the Islamic cities' spatial structures by presenting reasons and foregrounding rationalities behind the form of the cities.[187] For both groups the notion of labyrinth denotes an incomprehensible, unjustifiable chaos in the pattern of street networks, whereby 'labyrinthinity' is understood as an improper quality for a city. Using the concept to refer to a two-dimensional geometry – the 'map' type – and rationalise movement patterns, this view presents a two-dimensional understanding of space.[188]

(b) Other investigations take a sensory, cognitional approach based on bodily encounters with urban space. The main source for labelling the Islamic city as a labyrinth, in these cases, are the feelings resulting from experiencing the city by walking its pathways or the successive experiencing of urban spaces. Presenting a level of interaction that differs from rational approaches, this perspective highlights features or feelings such as getting lost in the city, incomprehensibility and unexpectedness, ambiguity or vagueness of space. It evokes the idea that the city and its space are as inextricable as a labyrinth. Perceiving the city as a labyrinth at this level is the result of sensual, practical experiencing of the space, which produces an imaginary space interleaved with the notion of the labyrinth, encouraging the viewer 'to imagine what is not there.'[189] The spatial practice of tracing street networks, along with the phenomenological aspects of elements such as the obscurity of walls, generated the feeling that the space is not readable. The culs-de-sac which are neither connected to other passages nor terminate in any type of open space accelerated this feeling. However, as Stevenson states 'spatial practices create a myriad of narrative maps which, although mythological, imaginary and partial, are central to the process of transforming cartographic space into places of meaning and memory.'[190] In this view, the city is spatialised as a three-dimensional structure based on the network of streets. Different parts of this network are, however, homogenous in terms of social significance.

(c) At another level of construction, the labyrinthinity is a myth culturally produced in association with the Islamic city and its space. Shields states that specific images or representations associated with a place in different ways – such as metaphorically, through history, or directly through photographs of a place – constitute place-images.[191] An image here is not only a representation but 'a virtual image, a cultural *imago*.'[192] Overwriting a place with sets of place-images can lead to the production of place-myths which are, thus, a series of place-images that constitute an overall image or representation of a place or location. The myth here is meant as a qualitative understanding of the 'nature' or 'capacity of space.'[193] Attributions of labyrinth-like or labyrinthine qualities – among others – have nearly become place-myths of the Islamic cities. They are engraved in the collective imagination on these cities expressed both in popular representations and in scholarly debates.

We can take this level of understanding as a starting point from which to delve into new realms of comprehension of space in the context of Islamic cities. In this work, I argue that the attribution of labyrinth implies some spatial characteristics of the spatial milieu of Islamic cities, but it expresses them in a distorted way; the term keeps the character undefined. Criticising and questioning the attribution of labyrinth in this context is not new. Yet the authors who disregard the attribution of labyrinth focus mainly on the functions, rationalities, and usages or religious rules that underlie the form of the city. Their approaches understand the labyrinth not as a spatial metaphor but rather as a sign of irrationality and negative order. Their discussions remain at the descriptive level and no analytical framework has been developed from the discourse. Despite critique, the labyrinthinity of the Islamic city should be considered as a part of the city's reality. All representations of the space contain 'truth claims (not necessarily scientific) about space';[194] they need to be elaborated as a key part of the conceptualisation of urban space. Such attributions comprise levels of understanding and perceiving the space of city, each or which has its own shortcomings but also revelations. What I aim to do is elaborate on the concept of labyrinth, unpacking its different dimensions and using it as the grounds for introducing another spatial concept, Hezar-tu. Moving from labyrinth to Hezar-tu can be a step towards freeing theorisation from its dependence on pre-existing frameworks and rationalisations, and revealing the features which are 'concealed by the form of rationality.'[195]

Notes

1 Michel de Certeau, *The Practice of Everyday Life* (Oakland, CA: University of California Press, 1988).

2 Kevin Hetherington, *Expressions of Identity: Space, Performance, Politices* (London: Sage, 1998), 6.

3 For a detailed review of the history of the emergence of the term Islamic city and 'Orientalist' studies of the cities of the region, see Somaiyeh Falahat, *Reimaging the City, a New Conceptualisation of the Urban Logic of the 'Islamic City'* (Wiesbaden: Springer Vieweg, 2014); Giulia Annalinda Neglia, 'Some Historical Notes on the Islamic City with Particular Reference to the Visual Representation of the Built City', in *The City in the Islamic World*, ed. Renata Holod, Attilio Petruccioli, and André Raymond, vol. 1 (Boston: Brill, 2008); André Raymond, 'The Spatial Organization of the City', in *The City in the Islamic World*, ed. Renata Holod, Attilio Petruccioli, and André Raymond, vol. 1 (Leiden, Boston: Brill, 2008), 47–70; Masashi Haneda, 'An Interpretation of the Concept of the "Islamic City"', in *Islamic Urban Studies, Historical Review and Perspectives*, ed. Masashi Haneda and Toru Miura (London, New York: Routledge and Kegan Paul, 1994), 1–10; Nezar Alsayyad, *Cities and Caliphs, on the Genesis of Arab Muslim Urbanism* (New York: Greenwood Press, 1991). For review of

the evolution of the studies, and diverse mainstream sources for urban studies related to the concept since the early 20th century see Nezar Alsayyad, 'Medina; the "Islamic," "Arab," "Middle Eastern" City: Reflections on an Urban Concept', in *Urban Design in the Arab World, Reconceptualising Boundaries*, ed. Robert Saliba (Farnham: Ashgate, 2015); Falahat, *Reimaging the City, a New Conceptualisation of the Urban Logic of the 'Islamic City'*; Neglia, 'Some Historical Notes on the Islamic City with Particular Reference to the Visual Representation of the Built City'.

4 See, for example, Roger Le Tourneau, *Les Villes Musulmanes de L'Afrique Du Nord* (Virginia: La Maison des Livres, 1957); Gustav E. von Grunebaum, 'Die Islamische Stadt', *Saeculum* 6 (1955): 138–53; Jean Sauvaget, *Alèp: Essai Sur Le Développement D'une Grande Ville Syrienne, Des Origins Au Milieu Du XIXe Siècle* (Paris: P. Geuthner, 1941).

5 Xavier De Planhol, *The World of Islam* (Ithaca, NY: Cornell University Press, 1959), 15, 18.

6 Robert Brunschvig, 'Urbanisme Médiéval et Driot Musulman', in *Revue Des Etudes Islamiques* (Paris: Librairie orientaliste Paul Geuthner, 1947), 127–55.

7 See, for example, Janet L. Abu-Lughod, 'The Islamic City – Historic Myth, Islamic Essence, and Contemporary Relevance', *International Journal of Middle Eastern Studies* 19, no. 2 (1987): 155–76; Jamel A. Akbar, *Crisis in the Built Environment: The Case of the Muslim City* (Singapore: Concept Media, 1988); Nader Ardalan and Laleh Bakhtiar, *The Sense of Unity* (Chicago, London: University of Chicago Press, 1973); Peter Beaumont, Gerald Henri Blake, and John Malcom Wagstaff, *The Middle East: A Geographical Study* (London: John Wiley & Sons, 1976); Eckart Ehlers, 'Capitals and Spatial Organization in Iran: Esfahan, Shiraz, Tehran', in *Téhéran: Capitale Bicentenaire*, ed. Chahryar Adle and Bernard Hourcade, Bibliothèque Iranienne, 37 (Paris, Tehran: Institut Français de Recherche en Iran, 1992), 155–72; Lisa Golombek, 'Urban Patterns in Pre-Safavid Isfahan', *Iranian Studies* 7 (1974): 18–44.

8 See, for example, Richard Ettinghausen, 'Muslim Cities: Old and New', in *From Medina to Metropolis*, ed. L. Carl Brown (Princeton: Darwin Press, 1973), 290–318; Ira Marvin Lapidus, 'Traditional Muslim Cities: Structure and Change', in *From Medina to Metropolis*, ed. L. Carl Brown (Princeton: Darwin Press, 1973), 51–72; Ira Marvin Lapidus, 'Muslim Cities and Islamic Societies', in *Middle Eastern Cities*, ed. Ira Marvin Lapidus (Oakland, CA: University of California Press, 1969), 47–76; Ira Marvin Lapidus, *Muslim Cities in the Later Middle Ages* (Cambridge, MA: Harvard University Press, 1967).

9 André Raymond, 'Urban Life and Middle Eastern Cities, the Traditional Arab City', in *A Companion to the History of the Middle East*, ed. Youssef M. Choueiri (Oxford: Blackwell Publishing Ltd, 2005), 215.

10 Neglia, 'Some Historical Notes on the Islamic City with Particular Reference to the Visual Representation of the Built City'.

11 See, for example, Raymond, 'Urban Life and Middle Eastern Cities, the Traditional Arab City'; Haneda, 'An Interpretation of the Concept of the "Islamic City"'; Alsayyad, *Cities and Caliphs, on the Genesis of Arab Muslim Urbanism*; Abu-Lughod, 'The Islamic City – Historic Myth, Islamic Essence, and Contemporary Relevance'.

12 See, for example, William Marçais, 'L'Islamisme et La Vie Urbaine', *Comptes-Rendus de l'Académie Des Inscriptions et Belles-Lettres* (1928): 86–100; George Marçais, 'L'Urbanisme Musulman', *Reprinted in: Mélanges D'histoire et D'archélogie de L'occident Musulman, Articles et Confrénces de George Marçais* (1939, 1957): 211–31; Brunschvig, 'Urbanisme Médiéval et Driot Musulman'; Le Tourneau, *Les Villes Musulmanes de L'Afrique Du Nord*; Sauvaget, *Alèp: Essai Sur Le Développement D'une Grande Ville Syrienne, Des Origins*

Au Milieu Du XIXe Siècle; Jean Sauvaget, 'Le Plan de Laodicée-Sur-Mer', *Bulletin D'études Orientales* 4 (1934): 81–114; Gustav E. von Grunebaum, *Islam: Essays in the Nature and Growth of a Cultural Tradition* (London: Routledge and Kegan Paul, 1955).

13 Roger Le Tourneau, *Fez in the Age of Marinides* (Norman: University of Oklahoma Press, 1961), 26.

14 Despite the critique, the model is still introduced as a swift preliminary insight to, or summary of, Islamic cities in some teaching courses on urban and architectural history; or on occasions such as when giving the public a general (scientific) impression of the Islamic city.

15 Oleg Grabar, 'The Architecture of the Middle Eastern City from Past to Present: The Case of the Mosque', in *Middle Eastern Cities*, ed. Ira Marvin Lapidus (Oakland, CA: University of California Press, 1969), 26–46.

16 Ibid.

17 Ibid., 39.

18 Grabar, 'The Architecture of the Middle Eastern City from Past to Present: The Case of the Mosque'.

19 Lapidus, 'Muslim Cities and Islamic Societies'.

20 Ibid., 54.

21 Lapidus, *Muslim Cities in the Later Middle Ages*, 72.

22 Albert H. Hourani, 'Introduction: The Islamic City in the Light of Recent Research', in *The Islamic City*, ed. Albert H. Hourani and Samuel M. Stern (Oxford: Bruno Cassier, University of Pennsylvania Press, 1970), 9–24.

23 There are authors who observe the city through the negation of the administrational structure. Stern (1970), for example, discusses the non-existence of municipal or institutional corporation in the juridical-political system of the Islamic city.

24 See, for example, Raymond, 'The Spatial Organization of the City'; Eugen Wirth, 'Zur Konzeption Der Islamischen Stadt: Privatheit Im Islamischen Orient versus Öffentlichkeit in Antike Und Okzident', *Die Welt Des Islams* 31, no. 1 (1991): 50–92; Abu-Lughod, 'The Islamic City – Historic Myth, Islamic Essence, and Contemporary Relevance'.

25 Le Tourneau, *Fez in the Age of Marinides*, 21, 57.

26 Christoffel A.O. van Nieuwenhuijze, *Sociology for the Middle East: A Stocktaking and Interpretation* (Leiden: Brill, 1971), 437; quoted in Eugen Wirth, 'Die Orientalische Stadt, Ein Überblick Aufgrund Jüngerer Forschungen Zur Materiellen Kultur', *Saeculum* 26, no. 1 (1975): 45–94.

27 See Wirth, 'Die Orientalische Stadt, Ein Überblick Aufgrund Jüngerer Forschungen Zur Materiellen Kultur'; Wirth, 'Zur Konzeption Der Islamischen Stadt'; Eugen Wirth, *Die Orientalische Stadt Im Islamischen Vorderasien Und Nordafrika: Städtische Bausubstanz Und Räumlische Ordnung, Wirtschaftsleben Und Soziale Organisation*, vol. 1, 2 (Mainz: Philipp von Zabern, 2000). For his elaborations on the meaning of publicness and privacy and their architectural embodiments see Eugen Wirth, 'The Concept of the Oriental City: Privacy in the Islamic East Versus Public Life in Western Culture', *Environmental Design: Journal of the Islamic Environmental Design Research Centre* 18, no. 1–2 (2001, 2000): 10–21.

28 Wirth, 'Die Orientalische Stadt, Ein Überblick Aufgrund Jüngerer Forschungen Zur Materiellen Kultur'.

29 Wirth, *Die Orientalische Stadt Im Islamischen Vorderasien Und Nordafrika: Städtische Bausubstanz Und Räumlische Ordnung, Wirtschaftsleben Und Soziale Organisation*; Wirth, 'Zur Konzeption Der Islamischen Stadt'; Wirth, 'Die Orientalische Stadt, Ein Überblick Aufgrund Jüngerer Forschungen Zur Materiellen Kultur'.

30 Wirth, 'Die Orientalische Stadt, Ein Überblick Aufgrund Jüngerer Forschungen Zur Materiellen Kultur'. However, he highlights that this typology is not exclusive to residential houses but also appears in commercial spaces like mosques and caravanserai. Wirth notes that the courtyard is a basic concept in the Oriental architecture, which is the obvious canon of the building. The original quote reads: '*Grundidee orientalischer Architektur, auf die man als selbsverständlichen Kanon des Bauens immer wieder zurückgreift.*' Ibid., 76.
31 Wirth, *Die Orientalische Stadt Im Islamischen Vorderasien Und Nordafrika: Städtische Bausubstanz Und Räumlische Ordnung, Wirtschaftsleben Und Soziale Organisation*; Wirth, 'Zur Konzeption Der Islamischen Stadt'.
32 Wirth, *Die Orientalische Stadt Im Islamischen Vorderasien Und Nordafrika: Städtische Bausubstanz Und Räumlische Ordnung, Wirtschaftsleben Und Soziale Organisation.*
33 See Wirth, 'Die Orientalische Stadt, Ein Überblick Aufgrund Jüngerer Forschungen Zur Materiellen Kultur'.
34 van Nieuwenhuijze, *Sociology for the Middle East: A Stocktaking and Interpretation*, 144; quoted in Wirth, 'Die Orientalische Stadt, Ein Überblick Aufgrund Jüngerer Forschungen Zur Materiellen Kultur'.
35 Wirth, 'Die Orientalische Stadt, Ein Überblick Aufgrund Jüngerer Forschungen Zur Materiellen Kultur'. On some occasions, when the accessibility to mosques and other public spaces is highly controlled, these spaces too can be considered to belong to the private sphere, according to Wirth, *Die Orientalische Stadt Im Islamischen Vorderasien Und Nordafrika: Städtische Bausubstanz Und Räumlische Ordnung, Wirtschaftsleben Und Soziale Organisation*; Wirth, 'Zur Konzeption Der Islamischen Stadt'; Wirth, 'Die Orientalische Stadt, Ein Überblick Aufgrund Jüngerer Forschungen Zur Materiellen Kultur'.
36 Wirth, 'Zur Konzeption Der Islamischen Stadt', 68, original emphasis. The original quote reads: '*Die Straßen und Plätze sind gewissermaßen "Negativraum" – das Erlebnis eines räumlichen* Ausgrenzens *aus dem privaten Bereich, nicht eines räumlichen* Eingrenzens *von öffentlich und gemeinsam zu nutzenden städtischen Freiflächen.*'
37 See Wirth, *Die Orientalische Stadt Im Islamischen Vorderasien Und Nordafrika: Städtische Bausubstanz Und Räumlische Ordnung, Wirtschaftsleben Und Soziale Organisation*; Wirth, 'Zur Konzeption Der Islamischen Stadt'.
38 Stefano Bianca, *Urban Form in the Arab World, Past and Present* (New York: Thames & Hudson, 2000); Stefano Bianca, *Architektur Und Lebensform* (Zürich, München: Architektur Artemis, 1979).
39 Bianca, *Urban Form in the Arab World, Past and Present*, 142.
40 Ibid.; Bianca, *Architektur Und Lebensform.*
41 Bianca, *Urban Form in the Arab World, Past and Present.*
42 Ibid., 147–8.
43 Ibid., 149–50.
44 Ibid., 38.
45 Abu-Lughod, 'The Islamic City – Historic Myth, Islamic Essence, and Contemporary Relevance'; see also Janet L. Abu-Lughod, 'Preserving the Living Heritage of Islamic Cities', in *Toward an Architecture in the Spirit of Islam*, ed. Renata Holod (Philadelphia: Aga Khan Award for Architecture, 1978), 61–75.
46 Abu-Lughod, 'The Islamic City – Historic Myth, Islamic Essence, and Contemporary Relevance', 163.
47 Ibid.
48 Ibid., 164.
49 Ibid.
50 Ibid., 165.

51 Ibid., 163.
52 Ibid., 167.
53 Ibid., original emphasis.
54 Ibid.
55 Ibid., 169.
56 Ibid., 172.
57 Ibid.
58 Simon O'Meara, *Space and Muslim Urban Life: At the Limits of the Labyrinth of Fez* (London: Routledge, 2007).
59 Ibid., 67.
60 Ibid., 2.
61 Ali Djerbi, 'Sémiologie de La Médina', in *The Living Medina: The Walled Arab City in Literature, Architecture, and History* (The American Institute for Maghrib Studies [AIMS] Conference, Tangiers, Morocco: Unpublished, 1996), 6; quoted in O'Meara, *Space and Muslim Urban Life: At the Limits of the Labyrinth of Fez.*
62 O'Meara, *Space and Muslim Urban Life: At the Limits of the Labyrinth of Fez*, ix, x.
63 Ibid.
64 Ardalan and Bakhtiar, *The Sense of Unity.*
65 Ibid., 17.
66 Ibid., 89.
67 Ibid.
68 Ibid., 93.
69 Ibid., 95.
70 Ibid.
71 Ibid.
72 Ibid.
73 Ibid., 106.
74 Also known as Masjid-i Imām in current usages.
75 Ardalan and Bakhtiar, *The Sense of Unity*, 124.
76 Ibid.
77 Besim Hakim, *Arabic-Islamic Cities: Building and Planning Principles* (New York: Routledge and Kegan Paul, 1986); Akbar, *Crisis in the Built Environment: The Case of the Muslim City.*
78 Richard Dennis, *Cities in Modernity, Representations and Productions of Metropolitan Space, 1840–1930* (Cambridge: Cambridge University Press, 2008).
79 Consider that in the Islamic city public buildings have the courtyard typology, similar to residential spaces.
80 Iain Chambers, *Migrancy, Culture, Identity* (London: Routledge, 1994), 189.
81 Deborah Stevenson, *Cities and Urban Cultures* (Maidenhead: Open University Press, 2003), 117, 118, original emphasis.
82 Part of the urban administration was managed by the *naẓmīyih* which was the embryo institution that later became the police. The *naẓmīyih* went through major reform and reorganisation with the goal of modernisation in the years between 1878–1890. See Hamid R. Kusha, 'Impediments to Police Modernisation in Iran, 1878–1979', *Policing and Society* 23, no. 2 (2013): 164–82.
83 The term *kūchih* is still in use nowadays in referring to alleys which have the spatial characteristics of a pathway with social boundedness and grouping in terms of sociospatial practices.
84 See Mark Mazower, *Salonica, City of Ghosts, Christians, Muslims and Jews 1430–1950* (London: Haper Collins, 2004); Nile Green, *The Love of Strangers* (Princeton and Oxford: Princeton University Press, 2016); Mīrzā Abūtālibkhān,

Safarnāmih-Yi Mīrzā Abūtālibkhān (1789–1803) (Travel Diaries of Mīrzā Abūtālibkhān), ed. Husiyn Khadīv Jam (Tehran: Sāzmān-i Intishārāt-i va Āmūzish-i Inghilāb-i Islāmī, 1984). As Mazower reminds us, this change in the space of the city represented a sharp break with a past, and witnessed a radical shift in the way the city's inhabitants understood their own surroundings by looking at place-names. Mazower, *Salonica, City of Ghosts, Christians, Muslims and Jews 1430–1950*.

85 John Brian Harley, 'Deconstructing the Map', in *Writing Worlds: Discourse, Text and Metaphor in the Representation of Landscape*, ed. Trevor J. Barnes and James S. Duncan (New York: Routledge, 1992), 240; cited in Stevenson, *Cities and Urban Cultures*, 118.

86 Sulṭān Siyyid Rižā Khān, *'Dārulsalṭanih-yi Isfahan'* (Isfahan: Sahab Cartography Centre, 1923).

87 *Baladīyih* was one of the very first modern urban institutions that aimed at regulating urban space and urban life in Iranian cities. *Baladīyih*, consisting of the Baladīyih Act (1907), the Baladīyih Council, and the Baladīyih Administration, started to develop and set urban regulations in the early 20th century, immediately after the Iranian Constitutional Revolution. The body had a certain degree of independence from the central government in decision-making and implementing regulations.

88 Sulṭān Siyyid Rizā Khān, *'Dārulsalṭanih-yi Isfahan'*.

89 Pandolfo points to what the residents of the Moroccan village she worked in said about maps, which illustrates how Moroccan society associates map-drawing with the colonial forces. Stefania Pandolfo, *Impasse of the Angels* (Chicago: University of Chicago Press, 1997). She writes: 'what was said is that in the [village of] qsar people didn't draw maps. One knew how to get somewhere, house, garden, villages, or tree, or found the way with the help of contextual landmarks. What was said is that the French drew maps during colonial times, and now the Agricultural Office did.' Ibid., 16.

90 Neil Smith and Cindy Katz, 'Grounding Metaphor: Towards a Spatialized Politics', in *Place and the Politics of Identity*, ed. Michael Keith and Steve Pile (London: Routledge, 1993), 70.

91 Stevenson, *Cities and Urban Cultures*.

92 See ibid.; Harley, 'Deconstructing the Map'; John Brian Harley, 'Maps, Knowledge and Power', in *The Iconography of Landscape, Essays on the Symbolic Representation, Design and Use of Past Environments*, ed. Denis Cosgrove and Stephen Daniels (Cambridge: Cambridge University Press, 1988), 277–312.

93 Dennis, *Cities in Modernity, Representations and Productions of Metropolitan Space, 1840–1930*, 53.

94 This is typical of the modern(ised) thought on cities. Movement is important to the modern(ised) mind and streets have been characterised as an important part of the modern urban life. See David Harvey, *Paris, Capital of Modernity* (New York, London: Routledge, 2003).

95 The characters mentioned in this paragraph will be elaborated on in the chapter four.

96 For diverse examples of diagrammatising cities of the region see Eckart Ehlers, 'City Models in Theory and Practice: A Cross-Cultural Perspective', *Urban Morphology* 15, no. 2 (2011): 97–119.

97 See Alan Latham et al., *Key Concepts in Urban Geography* (Los Angeles: Sage, 2010); ibid.

98 Abu-Lughod, 'The Islamic City – Historic Myth, Islamic Essence, and Contemporary Relevance'; Bianca, *Urban Form in the Arab World, Past and Present*; De Planhol, *The World of Islam*.

99 See Zeynep Çelik, *Urban Forms and Colonial Confrontations, Algiers under French Rule* (Oakland, CA: University of California Press, 1997); Abu-Lughod, 'The Islamic City – Historic Myth, Islamic Essence, and Contemporary Relevance'.
100 Abu-Lughod, 'Preserving the Living Heritage of Islamic Cities', 61, original emphasis.
101 Ibid., 62.
102 Bianca, *Urban Form in the Arab World, Past and Present.*
103 Ibid.
104 Ibid., 147.
105 Ibid.
106 Ibid., 158.
107 O'Meara, *Space and Muslim Urban Life: At the Limits of the Labyrinth of Fez*, ix, 57, 69.
108 Ibid., 70, original emphasis.
109 Ibid., 71.
110 Ibid., original emphasis.
111 Wirth, 'Die Orientalische Stadt, Ein Überblick Aufgrund Jüngerer Forschungen Zur Materiellen Kultur'.
112 Ibid.
113 Çelik, *Urban Forms and Colonial Confrontations, Algiers under French Rule*, 106. The Charles Brouty's sketch (1933) of the rooftop of the casbah is mentioned as an example in Çelik, *Urban Forms and Colonial Confrontations, Algiers under French Rule.*
114 In this way, photographs and painting like textual descriptions have also arranged, included and excluded elements in making the space knowable to people. See, also, Kevin Hetherington, 'In Place of Geometry: The Materiality of Place', in *Ideas of Difference*, ed. Kevin Hetherington and Rolland Munro (Oxford: Blackwell, 1997).
115 Baron C.A. de Bode, *Travels in Luristan and Arabistan* (London: J. Madden and Co., 1845), 41.
116 Arthur Arnold, *Through Persia by Caravan*, vol. 2 (New York: Harper & Brothers, 1877), 311.
117 Ibid., II:317, 318.
118 Çelik, *Urban Forms and Colonial Confrontations, Algiers under French Rule*, 25.
119 Ash Amin and Nigel Thrift, *Cities, Reimaging the Urban* (Cambridge: Polity Press, 2002).
120 Richard Marback, Patrick Bruch, and Jill Eicher, *Cities, Cultures, Conservations: Readings for Writers* (Boston: Allyn and Bacon, 1998), 6; quoted in Amin and Thrift, *Cities, Reimaging the Urban*, 23.
121 These early theorisations are outlined later in more detail.
122 Understanding the city as irregular and chaotic, their views are fundamentally criticised and discarded by later authors and in recent scholarship.
123 Ali Madanipour, *Designing the City of Reason, Foundations and Frameworks* (Abingdon: Routledge, 2007), 34.
124 Lapidus, *Muslim Cities in the Later Middle Ages.*
125 Robert Bertram Serjeant, ed., *The Islamic City: Selected Papers from the Colloquium Held at the Middle East Centre, Faculty of Oriental Studies, Cambridge, United Kingdom, from 19 to 23 July 1976* (Paris: UNESCO, 1980).
126 Ettinghausen, 'Muslim Cities: Old and New'.
127 Alsayyad, *Cities and Caliphs, on the Genesis of Arab Muslim Urbanism.*
128 Abu-Lughod, 'The Islamic City – Historic Myth, Islamic Essence, and Contemporary Relevance'.

129 Paul Ward English, *City and Village in Iran: Settlement and Economy in the Kirman Basin* (Madison: University of Wisconsin Press, 1966).
130 L. Carl Brown, 'Introduction', in *From Medina to Metropolis*, ed. L. Carl Brown (Princeton: Darwin Press, 1973), 15–49.
131 Paul Wheatley, 'Levels of Space Awareness in the Traditional Islamic City', *Ekistics*, no. 253 (1976): 354–66.
132 Leonardo Benevolo, *The History of the City* (London: Scholar Press, 1980).
133 Jim Antoniou, *Islamic Cities and Conservation* (Paris: UNESCO, 1981).
134 Christian Norberg-Schultz, *The Concept of Dwelling* (New York: Rizzoli, 1985).
135 Akbar, *Crisis in the Built Environment: The Case of the Muslim City.*
136 Besim S. Hakim, 'Law and the City', in *The City in the Islamic World*, ed. Salma K. Jayyusi et al., vol. 1 (Leiden, Boston: Brill, 2008), 71–92; Hakim, *Arabic-Islamic Cities: Building and Planning Principles*; Spiro Kostof, *The City Shaped, Urban Patterns and Meanings through History* (Boston: Little, Brown, 1991).
137 Raymond, 'The Spatial Organization of the City'.
138 Wheatley, 'Levels of Space Awareness in the Traditional Islamic City', 43.
139 Kostof, *The City Shaped, Urban Patterns and Meanings through History*, 63.
140 Hidenobu Jinnai, 'Microcosm of the Family around the Courtyard', in *The Proceedings of International Conference on Urbanism in Islam (ICUIT)*, ed. Yukawa Takeshi, vol. 2 (Tokyo: Middle Eastern Culture Centre, 1989), 392.
141 Ibid., 394.
142 Jacob Lassner, *The Topography of Baghdad in the Early Middle Ages* (Detroit: Wayne State University Press, 1970); Brown, 'Introduction'; Ettinghausen, 'Muslim Cities: Old and New'.
143 Raymond, 'The Spatial Organization of the City'.
144 Ibid., 58, 59, original emphasis; See aslo André Raymond, *Arab Cities in the Ottoman Period: Cairo, Syria and the Maghreb, Variorumncollected Studies Series* (Aldershot: Ashgate, 2002); André Raymond, *Grandes Villes Arabes À L'époque Ottomane* (Paris: Sindbad, 1985).
145 Raymond, 'The Spatial Organization of the City'.
146 Ibid., 63.
147 Hakim, 'Law and the City', 76.
148 Çelik, *Urban Forms and Colonial Confrontations, Algiers under French Rule*, 14. For a generalisation of this idea, see Masoud Kheirabadi, *Iranian Cities : Formation and Development* (Austin: University of Texas Press, 1991), which discusses the hierarchy of streets in 'Iranian-Islamic' cities.
149 O'Meara, *Space and Muslim Urban Life: At the Limits of the Labyrinth of Fez.*
150 Abu-Lughod, 'The Islamic City – Historic Myth, Islamic Essence, and Contemporary Relevance'. Compare Ardalan and Bakhtiar, *The Sense of Unity*, and Bianca, *Urban Form in the Arab World, Past and Present*, which discuss the fluidity and connection in the architectural and urban spatial structure of the city.
151 Le Tourneau, *Fez in the Age of Marinides.*
152 Çelik, *Urban Forms and Colonial Confrontations, Algiers under French Rule*, 15, original emphasis.
153 Ibid., 103.
154 Ibid., 15.
155 Madanipour, *Designing the City of Reason, Foundations and Frameworks.*
156 Ibid., 3.
157 René Descartes, *Discourse on Method and the Meditations* (London: Penguin, 1968); cited in Madanipour, *Designing the City of Reason, Foundations and Frameworks.*

158 Madanipour, *Designing the City of Reason, Foundations and Frameworks.*
159 See ibid.
160 Amin and Thrift, *Cities, Reimaging the Urban*, 9.
161 Ibid., 4.
162 Ibid., 7.
163 Ibid., 9.
164 Henri Lefebvre, *The Production of Space*, trans. Nicholson-Smith (Oxford: Basil Blackwell, 1991).
165 Rob Shields, *Spatial Questions, Cultural Topologies and Social Spatialisations* (Los Angeles: Sage, 2013), 31, original emphasis.
166 Hayden White, *Tropics of Discourse: Essays in Cultural Criticism* (Baltimore: The Johns Hopkins University Press, 1978).
167 See, for example, O'Meara, *Space and Muslim Urban Life: At the Limits of the Labyrinth of Fez.*
168 See, for example, Ettinghausen, 'Muslim Cities: Old and New'.
169 See, for example, Brown, 'Introduction'.
170 Lapidus, *Muslim Cities in the Later Middle Ages.*
171 See, for example, Larry R. Ford, *The Spaces between Buildings* (Baltimore: Johns Hopkins University Press, 2000); English, *City and Village in Iran: Settlement and Economy in the Kirman Basin.*
172 See, for example, English, *City and Village in Iran: Settlement and Economy in the Kirman Basin.*
173 See, for example, John Innes Clarke and Brian Drummond Clark, *Kermanshah, an Iranian Provincial City* (Durham: University of Durham, 1969).
174 See, for example, Thierry Bianquis, 'Urbanism', in *Medieval Islamic Civilization, An Encyclopaedia*, ed. Josef W. Meri (New York: Routledge, 2006); John Innes Clarke, *The Iranian City of Shiraz* (Durham: University of Durham, 1963).
175 Hans-Eckhard Lindemann, *Stadt Im Quadrat, Geschichte Und Gegenwart Einer Einprägsamen Stadtgestalt*, Bauwelt Fundamente 121 (Birkhäuser, 1999).
176 See, for example, ibid.; Wilfrid Blunt, *Isfahan, Pearl of Persia* (New York: Stein and Day, 1966).
177 Further reasons will be discussed in connection to the space of the city in detail in the chapters that follow.
178 To use de Certeau's terminology, de Certeau, *The Practice of Everyday Life*. See chapter 2 in this book.
179 O'Meara, *Space and Muslim Urban Life: At the Limits of the Labyrinth of Fez*, 1, 2.
180 Ibid., 2.
181 Ian Campbell, 'Tactile Labyrinths and Sacred Interiors: Spatial Practices and Political Choices in Abdelmajid Ben Jalloun's Fí Al-Tufúla and Ahmed Sefrioui's La Boîte À Merveilles', in *World Languages and Cultures Faculty Publications*, vol. Paper 24, 2014, http://scholarworks.gsu.edu/mcl_facpub; Ali Madanipour, *Tehran, the Making of a Metropolis* (Chichester: John Wiley & Sons, 1998); Çelik, *Urban Forms and Colonial Confrontations, Algiers under French Rule*; Alsayyad, *Cities and Caliphs, on the Genesis of Arab Muslim Urbanism.*
182 The spatial characters in connection to the concept of labyrinth will be elaborated in chapter 2.
183 Gregory Seigworth, 'Banality for Cultural Studies', *Cultural Studies* 14, no. 2 (2000): 246.
184 Amin and Thrift, *Cities, Reimaging the Urban*, 121.
185 Le Tourneau, *Les Villes Musulmanes de L'Afrique Du Nord*, 20. The original text reads: 'Rien de plus étranger à une ville musulmane du Maghreb que les

avenues rectilignes d'une ville romaine ou d'une ville moderne; c'est à un dédale, à un labyrinth que fait penser la photographic aérienne d'une ville musulmane quelconque. . ..'

186 De Planhol, *The World of Islam*.

187 See, for example, Lapidus, *Muslim Cities in the Later Middle Ages*; Brown, 'Introduction'; Kostof, *The City Shaped, Urban Patterns and Meanings through History*; Wheatley, 'Levels of Space Awareness in the Traditional Islamic City'.

188 The usage of labyrinth with this interpretation meant that in the later studies the term is attributed to the cities very cautiously.

189 Ibid., 114. To use Amin's and Thrift's terminology.

190 Stevenson, *Cities and Urban Cultures*, 55.

191 Shields, *Spatial Questions, Cultural Topologies and Social Spatialisations*.

192 Ibid., 31, original emphasis.

193 Ibid., original emphasis.

194 Hetherington, 'In Place of Geometry: The Materiality of Place', 189.

195 de Certeau, *The Practice of Everyday Life*, xi.

2 City as labyrinth

The concept of labyrinth as a symbol and metaphor of complexity dates back to the prehistoric era. Representing a condition of entanglement, it originated in the spatial relations associated with the mythic Cretan structure built by Daedalus to hold the half-man, half-monster Minotaur. However, although Daedalus – according to the myth – designed the prison in the form of a labyrinth in order to prevent the prisoner's escape, Theseus managed to find his way out using Ariadne's thread, which raises the issue of the navigability of such a form. There are diverse definitions of 'labyrinth' in contemporary sources that range from Conty's claim that 'any sinuous path, any fortress or fortified enclosure, can eventually represent or evoke a labyrinth,'[1] to Conrad's 'labyrinthine,' which is everything that lacks classic geometry or which is unordered and chaotic.[2] From a different point of view, Kern sees the labyrinth as a well-defined, circuitous path that leads the walker into the centre and back out again; there are no tricks to be solved, no dead-ends or culs-de-sac, no intersecting paths.[3] Dictionaries define a labyrinth as an architectonic device of 'apparently aimless structure, with a complex pattern making it extremely difficult to escape once inside';[4] or as 'a subterranean series of winding and interconnected passages. A maze . . . A labyrinthine is fed with many maze-like turnings, similar to a key pattern, *meander*, or a Greek key.'[5]

The Webster dictionary defines the labyrinth as:

> 1. An intricate combination of paths or passages in which it is difficult to find one's way or to reach the exit. 2. A maze of paths bordered by high hedges, as in a park or garden, for the amusement of those who search for a way out. 3. A complicated or tortuous arrangement, as of streets or buildings. 4. Any confusingly intricate state of things or events; a bewildering complex. 5. a vast maze built in Crete by Daedalus, at the command of King Minos, to house the Minotaur. . . .[6]

The same dictionary introduces the term 'labyrinthine' as something that pertains to or resembles a labyrinth or anything that is 'complicated, tortuous.' The term 'maze', which has been used as synonym or relevant to labyrinth, suggests a 'multicursal design from which confusion arises and is more commonly associated with a children's puzzle or the hedge or garden maze.'[7] The Oxford English Dictionary's definition of 'maze' lists '[a] state of mental confusion,' or 'worldly, vain, or dissolute amusement or diversion,' or even 'a delusive fancy; a trick or deception.' Curl defines a maze as 'a labyrinth cut in turf, formed of plants, or built,'[8] while the Webster Dictionary suggests: '1. A confusing network of intercommunicating paths or passages; labyrinth. 2. Any complex system or arrangement that causes bewilderment, confusion, or perplexity . . . 3. A state of bewilderment or confusion. 4. A winding movement, as in dancing.'[9]

A historical symbol

As a historically embedded concept, the term 'labyrinth' has had diverse applications over the centuries. Before the emergence of ancient Greek culture, it was visualised as a graphical form consisted of a series of seven concentric pathways, connected and surrounding a central goal without any interjectional line.[10] This form, which was either carved on rocks or painted on walls or pottery, spread throughout southern Europe. Matthew describes its pattern as follows:

> Starting from the exterior, the 'path' runs inwards a short distance, turns so as to run parallel with the outer wall until nearly a full circuit has been completed, then doubles back on itself and runs round in the opposite direction, doubles upon itself again, and so on until it finally comes to a stop in a blind end, having traversed all of the space within the outer walls without covering any part twice and without forming any branches or loops.[11]

The proximity of most of the carvings to burial sites gives rise to the assumption that the labyrinths of this era symbolised death, that is, a return to the earth or rebirth. According to this interpretation the winding path of a labyrinth signified the progress of purification through death, by which an individual learned the ultimate mysteries of existence and became ready to re-enter the womb of the earth, thus implying a ritual return to the earth.[12] In tandem with the graphical symbols was a ritual dance called Theseus's labyrinth dance, or crane dance, which Theseus is said to have performed with his youthful companions. A victory dance, it imitated the circling passages in the labyrinth, based on certain rhythmic involutions and devolutions; performing it was a sign of primacy.[13]

In the Roman age, graphical symbols of labyrinths were depicted in wall and pavement mosaics, and continued to play a major role in the culture of the society. Although the general geometrical rules of their pattern changed slightly, they retained the principle of their precedents' pattern: a path with a winding form generated a back-and-forth movement around the middle point until reaching the centre, which might be depicted as a flower or Theseus in battle with the Minotaur.[14] In Roman thought, the decorative labyrinth designs were held to be magically protective and were placed in doorways or near the entrances of houses to ward off evil; it was believed that evil spirits could only fly in a straight line, that is, that they could not find their way through a labyrinth's twists and turns.[15] Rituals connected to the labyrinth also continued to be performed in the Roman era. The Game of Troy, whose complicated movements Vergil associated with the Cretan labyrinth myth, was a common horseback mock battle of the era which was staged in the form of a labyrinth and performed by youths under the age of seventeen to demonstrate their readiness to be accepted into society.[16] Successfully navigating the bewildering movements and misleading corners of the labyrinth demonstrated the qualification of the youths for entrance into the different behavioural world of the adults.

It was during the Roman era that an architectural space was first described as labyrinthine, with Roman historical-geographical writers, such as Pliny the Elder, applying the term to buildings with complex floor plans and confusing or underworld characteristics. They appreciated the ancient labyrinths as works of art, and labyrinthine buildings as architectural splendours, and were absorbed by their complexity and rarity.[17] One of the buildings that was titled a labyrinth by Roman authors was a mortuary temple that had been erected south of a pyramid near Hawara in Egypt; a large structure measuring 305×244 m^2, it was admired as a wonder of the world.[18] The earliest description is by the Greek historian Herodotus (fifth century BC) in his *Histories* where he wrote that it had twelve covered courts connected to each other – thousands of rooms in all – and that the network of passages through the courts, rooms and colonnades were very intricate and bewildering.[19] The characteristics listed by Roman historians and writers – such as Strabo (ca. 64 BC–19 AD) and Pliny the Elder (23–79 BC) – include elements such as the difficulty of navigation and need of a local guide; the large proportions and numerous palaces and courts, and the multiple winding intercommunicating passages which were deceptive at many points.[20] The term 'labyrinth' is used metaphorically here to label a complex, remarkable architectural structure.

In the Christian era the pictorial depictions of labyrinths continued to develop, largely in the form of manuscript drawings where, in a gradual process of Christianising, the previous generic pattern of labyrinth underwent adaptation to Christian ideology. In this new form, the principle of moving from an entrance towards a centre through bewildering pathways was retained. Yet the number of circuits increased to seven and the shape of a cross overlaid the whole pattern; in approaching the middle point and departing from it, one made seventy moves, which paralleled biblical numbers.[21] In addition to manuscripts, visual symbols of Christian labyrinths began to appear as carvings on walls and ultimately evolved into the floor patterns in churches where, in some cases, they were laid across the entire width of the nave as a sort of 'obstacle or buffer.'[22] In preparation for prayer, the pious had first to internalise the labyrinth by tracing its path, and only after that could they continue on their way to the inner sanctum.[23] With a similar understanding of the symbolic content, some worshippers used to trace the labyrinth on their knees to embody the spiritual implications of the pilgrimage to Jerusalem. By undertaking these pilgrimages, the seeker hoped to get closer to God via a practice in which the journey was more meaningful than achieving the goal.[24] In this period the labyrinth was also employed as a symbol of the cosmos, as something symbolising God's obscurity, God's mystery and the extraordinarily intelligent order of creation. It was believed that the tool of human reason, limited in perspective and nature and unable to comprehend this order, was imprisoned by it.[25] On the other hand, while the labyrinth was understood as a symbol of complex visual or verbal genius, the maze was defined as 'anything with no clear, direct way out';[26] it represented the sinful world which created a prison, while the labyrinth was a symbol of the correct way out (the labyrinth was superimposed on the maze): 'the maze transcends apparent disorder to reveal a grand design.'[27]

The meaning, pattern and application of the concept of labyrinth transformed gradually during the Renaissance, resulting in the emergence of a relatively new style with some exclusive features. During this period, the ideological and metaphorical meanings of the notion of labyrinth were weakened.[28] Hedge and flower-bed labyrinths and mazes became important elements in the landscapes of gardens, and hundreds of them were built in Europe between the sixteenth and nineteenth centuries.[29] In this new style, the labyrinth was used as a source of amusement through the illusion of confrontation with the danger of getting lost, and then experiencing the excitement of finding the way out. Trimmed hedges were the preferred form, and the main pattern employed by garden-designers was the puzzle maze in which the partitions were at least the height of the average person, to instil the feeling of being lost.[30] During the Renaissance, the maze, or multi-path labyrinth, was patterned in a variety of designs, the main characteristics of which were the need to choose from various route options and the culs-de-sac. The multi-path pattern was visualized and then implemented in this period for the first time. Previous pictorial representations of the concept of labyrinth were based on one-path designs; the mazes, in contrast, cut the single path into several winding routes.[31] The presence of multiple choices, the potential to take the right or the wrong way and the intentional lingering en route in this new pattern created a sense of lack of clarity and uncertainty about the overall design. These perceptions provided the foundation of the amusement function of the labyrinth in its new form; consequently the most valuable labyrinths were, at this time, 'those that wind most.'[32]

Etymology of labyrinth

Different etymologies have been suggested for the term labyrinth, each emphasising a particular characteristic that labyrinths denote or represent.

For example, as Doob outlines, inextricability is the focus in the two early etymologies.[33] According to one medieval interpretative etymology the labyrinth refers back to the idea that no one can *elabi inde*, namely 'escape from' them, while, according to another, the word is rooted in *laboriosus exitus domus*, meaning 'the house difficult of exit.'[34] Another root that was suggested for the term was *laboriosa ad entrandum* (i.e. 'difficult to enter'[35]), which highlights the understanding that labyrinths are impenetrable. Doob continues that in the most popular etymology the *laborintus* derives from *labor* and *intus*, which can be interpreted in different ways. She notes that the common keyword in medieval etymologies, *labor*, connotes difficulty; however, using it as a verb, the combination of *laborintus* will mean, 'I fall, or perish, or err, or go wrong within,' while, if used as a noun, the *laborintus* signifies 'hardship, or fatigue, or exertion, or application to work lies inside.'[36] The former carries weight as a moral interpretation, whereas the latter represents a difficult process. In these cases, as Doob states, 'etymologically speaking . . . the labyrinth is a process involving internal difficulty (or error, or artistry, or fatiguing effort); and what happens inside is more important than whether it is hard to get in or out.'[37]

Other common synonyms for labyrinth were *domus daedali* and the German word *Irrweg*. The *domus daedali* denotes a three-dimensional physical space, such as a house, with superb architecture which is intrinsic to its nature.[38] The *Irrweg*, meaning the 'path of error,' refers to 'circuitousness, its ability to induce confusion, its nature as process rather than artefact.'[39] This is very much associated with the English word maze, which 'stresses a difficult process, annoyance, confusion.'[40] The word maze itself enters Middle English with *amasod*, meaning 'astonished, and bewildered.'[41] In Middle English Dictionary *ameaset*, *amaiset* are two other words accompanying *amsed* in having the meanings of 'stunned, dazed, bewildered; alarmed, frightened; dismayed/out of one's mind, irrational, foolish.'[42] The noun *mase* appears in 1300 and its meaning, like two other words, maze and *masse*, is defined as 'a source of confusion or deception; vision, fantasy, delusion; deceit; . . . confusion, bewilderment, disorder; . . . in a state of amazement or confusion; . . . confused or useless activity; idle diversion.'[43]

Infinity: the modern implication

In recent years the concept of labyrinth has been considered in association with complex spatial relations developed in works of literature, art and philosophy, such as the short stories of Jorge Luis Borges, the paintings of Giovanni Battista Piranesi or the philosophical concepts of Gilles Deleuze and Félix Guattari.[44] The common feature lies in the way the works produce complexity through the creation of an elaborate conceptual order that is then presented as a folded, twisted phenomenon. Comprehension seems an impossible task to the viewer or reader because numerous interwoven incidents exist in the works, which generate extraordinary relationships: a multilayered combination of signs, symbols, literal or perspectival spaces, elements and metaphors that creates an enigmatic conceptual space with uncommon spatial orders. Indeed, there is a reciprocal relation between the concept of labyrinth and how it appears in these works: sometimes the spatial multiplicity in a text or painting is created by drawing inspiration from a metaphoric understanding of the structure of a labyrinth, whereas in other cases the notion of labyrinth is used to name the 'uncommon' complexity created by the writer or painter.

The series 'Carceri d'invenzione' (the Imaginary Prisons), by Giovanni Battista Piranesi, is one of the most celebrated of artworks whose visual spaces have been interpreted as labyrinthine or labyrinth-like.[45] This series of sixteen copperplate etchings, dating from the 1760s, is an expression of bewilderment and ambiguity.[46] The images represent – and in representing they construct – visual metaphorical spaces which invoke the dynamic of infinity.[47] The odd space in these works is generated by the disorganisation of the spatial and visual relations that the eye normally expects to see in particular arrangements and compositions of architectural elements. The natural directions of movement – the harmony – of the architectural elements are disrupted, the laws of perspective are challenged and different scales infuse into each other repeatedly and sometimes abruptly: sharp, deep diagonals are counterbalanced by flat planes and dense patterns of lines which create interlocking, mysterious compositions.[48] 'This is the source of the unexpected qualitative leap in scale and space,' Eisenstein observes.[49] The out-of-proportion combinations make it difficult to build a unitary space.

In literature, as Hoffmann notes, the labyrinth is the central metaphor for postmodern fiction: 'the crucial figuration for its content, design, narrative strategies, the paradoxicality of its intention and goal is . . . the labyrinth.'[50] Jorge Luis Borges is the best-known author of labyrinthine narratives, which are developed in his short stories and influence the writing of Italo Calvino and Umberto Eco, who also feature the labyrinth as a favoured theme. Borges uses the metaphor to structure narratives, conceptually order the relationships between characters and events, and provide a spatial model and element in the settings of his fiction. A reader will experience the feeling of being lost in the labyrinths of his plots and confused by the unexpected insertion of characters. She will also be puzzled by uncommon architectural compositions such as hexagonal rooms, continuously branching routes, zigzagging paths and asymmetrical houses.[51] The *Garden of Forking Paths* is a fiction of endlessly forking times, spaces and features. The purposefully designed chaos, repetition, branching and deception in the associations of characters and events generate an illusion of infinity in time-space, the labyrinthine, and present it as the main intention of the book: 'I pictured it as infinite . . . I imagined a labyrinth of labyrinths, a maze of mazes, a twisting, turning, ever-widening labyrinth that contained both past and future.'[52]

In Italo Calvino's works, the labyrinth is also a recurrent image. He uses the notion of labyrinth both as a contemporary world condition and a type of structuring narrative. He sees the labyrinth as the archetype of literary image in the contemporary age as, he believes, the contemporary world, being incomprehensible, offers the possibility of multiple, complex representations.[53] So, according to Calvino, it is necessary to face the challenge of the labyrinth – not to overcome it but rather to enjoy the pleasure of wandering and getting lost in it, to enjoy 'the thrill of the endless and very possibly aimless journey over and above any conclusive destination.'[54] He structures his stories likewise; instead of telling a single story a novel consists of diverse fragments of stories, one branching into the next in unexpected and sometimes bizarre turns. His unfinished stories constitute complex connections like those found in a labyrinth: '[t]hey allude, parody, and echo one another and other texts. They form a network of texts that enlace a network of texts that intersect.'[55]

Umberto Eco's detective novels mostly present a branched structure; he claims that people like a detective novel because it is a story of conjecture. In an interview with Rosso, he adds,

> my underlying story . . . branches out into so many other stories, all of them stories of other conjectures, all about the very structure of conjecture itself. One abstract model of conjecturability is the labyrinth. Like any other conjectural space it can be traversed in many ways.[56]

This type of labyrinth is similar to a net in which 'every point can be connected with every other point, and, where the connections are not designed, they are, however, conceivable and designable . . . A net . . . is a tree *plus* corridors connecting its nodes so as to transform the tree into a polygon or into a system of embedded polygons.'[57] The net, or conjectural space, is best expressed by the metaphor of the rhizome – the name Gilles Deleuze and Felix Guattari give to the network structure.[58] Eco states his Guglielmo is structured like a rhizome, whereas the labyrinthine library appearing in *The Name of the Rose*, inspired Borges's *The Library of Babel*, has a maze-like pattern with numerous interconnecting rooms offering multiple path choices giving rise to the senses of obscurity, ambiguity and being lost.[59] It has, however, a single solution path that reaches the goal space. The rhizome has no centre, no exit and no periphery, and is thereby differentiated from both the labyrinth (uni-path) and the maze (multi-path). The rhizome is multidimensionally complicated, and every point is connected to other points in all its dimensions, generating infinity.[60] The rhizome represents the postmodern labyrinth.[61]

In another conceptualisation, Gilles Deleuze, inspired by Liebniz's philosophy, uses the notion of labyrinth to present his philosophical thoughts and concepts, noting that a labyrinth is multiple, has many parts and 'is folded in many ways.'[62] It is 'a piece of fabric . . . which divides into an infinite number of folds or disintegrates into curved movements.'[63] The fold is the constituent unit of the labyrinth, which is not a point but an extremity of the line that continues into infinity.[64] Enumeration, fluidity, continuity into infinity and linearity are key characters discussed in association with the concept of labyrinth in Deleuze's ideas.

We can, therefore, conclude that three different types of labyrinth in terms of perceived structure have emerged throughout history. The first relates to the classic labyrinth, which was a one-path graphical pattern in which there is only one way from the entrance to the centre, thereby ruling out the possibility of getting lost; the complexity is inherent in the tortuousness of the path. The second type refers to the multi-path labyrinth or maze, first depicted graphically and physically built during the Renaissance, in which there are a large number of dead-ends, choices to be made between forked paths and only the right choice leads to the exit. The third type, which Eco defines as a net,[65] is 'an unlimited territory' in which 'every point can be connected with every other point.'[66] The net can be best portrayed by the rhizome.[67]

Labyrinth as a spatial model

The labyrinth is a constellation of spatial elements and relations: there is a path, or a network of paths, which has an entrance, and in some cases a centre or an exit. The path or network gains meaning and identity through a fluidity of movement within it which is experienced by the hypothetical walker. In a one-path or a multi-path pattern, the walker starts at the entry and negotiates a series of bewildering paths to reach the centre or the exit – metaphorically or physically. In a net structure, the walker starts from the entry and negotiates a similarly bewildering network of paths without getting out – conceptually. The path or the network is perceived to be so extraordinarily long and fantastically twisted that the space is not comprehensible, a spatial difficulty that stands for the complexity connoted by the labyrinth. As a spatial model, therefore, the labyrinth refers neither to a concrete structure nor to a precisely defined two-dimensional pattern; rather, it stands for a roughly determined spatial arrangement which is the result of the combination of the three features: incomprehensibility of pattern, confusion in movement and ambiguity in perception. These features represent different realms of our interaction with the space: we cannot logically and/or sensually comprehend the space and we cannot guide our practice of movement in it.

The spatial characteristics and meaning of the labyrinth can be discussed under six principal headings:

(a) *The spatial metaphor:* The idea of the labyrinth is based on a metaphorical assimilation of, and analogy to, an imaginary architectural space that is entangled and ambiguous for the subject who interacts with it and, more precisely, walks through it. This illusionary 'mysterious space' does not necessarily have a clearly predefined pattern or physical structure but is, rather, represented in, or symbolised by, different forms ranging from graphical signs, visual compositions in paintings and literary constructions in stories to conceptual framings in philosophical thought. Thus the concept of labyrinth also transmits a definition of intricacy by being presented as a certain type of spatiality embodied in the realms of the visual, literary, ritual and conceptual.

(b) *Presuppositions:* Using the concept of the labyrinth to express a quality brings ideology into connection with spatiality. In determining the kind of space that is prototypical of complexity and ambiguity, we need to make assumptions about the type of elements that create spatial clarity or obscurity. Based on discussion so far, we can say that non-labyrinth, or 'normal' space, is assumed to have a certain degree of regularity and order so that the subject can understand it without much effort. Direct, regular and/or short routes of access from one point to another, for example, shapes this kind of spatial ordering. A certain degree of lingering is still perceived as normal, except where the lingering is so extreme that produces an 'unusual condition of feeling' in the space. So there is an institutional benchmark, a margin that distinguishes between normal and labyrinthine spaces and applies to all kinds of labyrinths from premodern symbolic graphics to Borges's or Piranesi's masterpieces. The labyrinth challenges quotidian presuppositions of a certain degree of clarity, accessibility, straightness, orientation, reasonable length and limited tortuousness in spatial relations and paths through them; when this clarity is not offered the space is interpreted as a labyrinth with 'corners of secret.'

(c) *Geometry:* This plays an important part in building a labyrinth in terms of both linear patterns (labyrinth, maze) and non-Euclidean geometries (folds). The labyrinth gets its character through its peculiar geometry which guides movement, determines the pattern and, by doing so, produces the spatial characteristics which generate feelings such as entanglement in the hypothetical walker, reader or watcher. Through geometry the complexity is embodied and consolidated in more concrete realms, and it is thus the main regulator of the space and generator of entanglement in the labyrinth.

(d) *The path:* Paths – also referred to as linking lines or folds – constitute the core element of the concept of the labyrinth: a high degree of complexity is the product of difficult paths or ungraspable networks of paths.[68] Mastering the route towards the centre (in the uni-path pattern), finding the right way to the end point (in the multi-path maze), and experiencing the connecting folds are the main constituents of the labyrinth idea. The visual labyrinthinity of paintings or graphical scenes are understood and perceived only when the relations between elements, events and signs are considered – where the relations between the points are the linkages that conceptually constitute the labyrinth.

(e) *Movement:* The model of the labyrinth is a representation of the particular form of moving which takes place along the hypothetical paths of a symbolic labyrinth, or the physical lines of mazes or in conceptual linkages. It is through movement that the sequences of the route, the spaces or events, and the relations between objects are experienced. Intentional lingering, entanglement and ambiguity are defined as such by virtue of defining the quality, pattern and conditions of movement. Thus the spatial practice connoted by the concept of labyrinth is an extraordinarily complex pattern of movement which also brings with it its own temporality.

(f) *Perception:* The metaphorical application of the term labyrinth is the result of perceiving a space as so complex that it is neither comprehensible nor escapable. Immediacy, unexpectedness, waiting, the game of discovery, a lack of knowableness, a multiplicity of choices, unpredictability and loss of one's bearings are among the main features attributed to space perceived as labyrinthine.

A labyrinthine city

In contemporary urban studies the term labyrinth has been particularly used in connection with discourses on modern or postmodern cities. Bernard Tschumi proposes the classical labyrinth as the prototype of what Germano Celant calls 'deprived space' in which 'participants can only find themselves as the subject, aware only of their own fantasies and pulsations, able only to react to the low-density signals of their own bodies.'[69] Shields introduces the labyrinth as a topological archetype.[70] De Certeau's observer, who overlooks the city from above, transforms from a walker into a voyeur and thus 'he can ignore the devices of Daedalus in mobile and endless labyrinths far below' in the city.[71] For Benjamin, Paris was a labyrinth whose entrances were the covered shopping arcades of the nineteenth century. For him, the city is the realization of the labyrinth, the ancient dream of humanity.[72] Spender describing sexualities in German cities during the Weimar period writes:

> a great city is a kind of labyrinth within which at every moment of the day the most hidden wishes of every human being are performed by people who devote their whole existence to this and nothing else . . . the hidden life of forbidden wishes exists in extravagant nakedness behind mazes of walls.[73]

For Elizabeth Wilson the labyrinth is both spatial and metaphorical. She mentions that there is a Minotaur's chamber in a labyrinthine city.[74] For her, personally, the chamber was the reptile house in a zoo from a childhood experience. The attribution of labyrinthine, here, is connected to a kind of fear mixed with an obscure pleasure in the questionable that is assumed to lie in the city's secret courtyards and alleyways. Wilson also uses the Minotaur labyrinth when referring to the ideas that authors of the nineteenth century, such as Tocqueville, or later, Le Bon, developed with regards the features of the urban crowd of that time,[75] which was thought to be inconsistent, out of control and lacking identity. Here the labyrinth is no longer described as a spatial entity; rather, it appears as a metaphor for the ambiguous, ever-changing and uncontrollable side of the reality of urban life in the nineteenth century whose origins were thought to be rooted in common society.[76] It constructs a virtual labyrinth of the city.

Wilson brings up the contradiction between two accounts of a labyrinthine city. She writes:

> The recurring image, of the city as a maze, as having a secret centre, contradicts that other and equally common metaphor for the city as labyrinthine and centreless. Even if the labyrinth does have a centre, one image of discovery of the city, or of exploring the city, is not so much finally reaching this centre, as of an endlessly circular journey, and of the retracing of the same pathways over time.[77]

The labyrinthine city, in Wilson's work, has been seen in connection to elements like pathways and the presence or absence of a centre, practices like endless circular journeys and retracing the same passages, and feelings like obscurity. The linear act of moving around the city, which may or may not have the goal of discovering its centre, lies at the heart of the idea of a labyrinthine city. Although secret chambers and alleyways constitute part of its description, the metaphor's definition references movements and recurrent journeys along pathways, whether to reach a centre or just aimed at undertaking an endless journey across the city's passages – although the latter is more pronounced in terms like 'labyrinthine uncentredness.'[78] Wilson later adds that postmodernism is seen in connection with 'disorientation, meaninglessness and fragmentation', wherein the city becomes a labyrinth or a dream; 'its chaos and senselessness mirror a loss of meaning in the world.'[79] Within her descriptions of a gendered approach to modern and postmodern cities, she points to an imaginary that sees the centre of labyrinth or maze which is 'feared' or 'desired,' as the Sphinx, half-woman, half-animal – while this centre in the Greek legend of the Cretan labyrinth was the Minotaur, half-man, half-bull.[80]

Labyrinth as representation

Cassirer defines three types of space as identifiable in the course of interactions between subjects and space: organic, perceptual and symbolic.[81] Organic space is that which exists materially and physically as 'the world of tactile and sensual interaction with matter, it is the space of experience.'[82] Perceptual space is what our neurological senses tell us as they register the experiencing of space by our body, the first step being our intuitive and direct attempts to understand and feel material space. This process involves our imaginations, fears, emotions, dreams, memories and desires.[83] It constitutes the first level of subjective rearticulation of the space, sometimes manifested as individual imaginaries that become the individual's essential knowledge about the space. The spaces of representation, in this form, remain in the realm of mental imaginations and emerge as the first result of the subject's interaction with space. Space at this stage is thus represented by a number of, often vague, feelings and images, more on the level of the unconscious, the 'dream, a fantasy, a hidden longing, a lost memory or even a peculiar thrill or tingle of fear.'[84] Meanwhile, the users of a city produce their own interpretations of its space, meaning that it is experienced and interpreted in myriad, highly idiosyncratic ways.[85]

Symbolic space is abstract, constructed on the basis of distinctive readings and interpretations of space in which we consciously or unconsciously order the environment around us, assign meanings to its elements and create our own understanding of it.[86] Thus we develop interpretations of spaces out of material space which are contingent upon idiosyncratic factors, including, for example, our background, knowledge, feelings, dreams, archetypical fantasies and so on. Through these perceptions and interactions, imaginary spatial relations emerge in which they and their significance are reset and rearranged in a particular way unique to the subject and the means of representation. Sometimes the symbolic representations are embodied, materially or virtually, in sensually impacted, improvisatory realms such as artistic works, words, images, films, music, archetypes, narrations and travel stories.[87] As Harvey observes, the 'spatio- temporality of a dream, a fantasy, a hidden longing, a lost memory or even a peculiar thrill or tingle of fear as we walk down a street can be given representation through works of art that ultimately always have a mundane presence in absolute space and time.'[88]

All activities that involve representing the landscape are a form of inscription and the concept of 'text' can typify diverse cultural productions such as paintings, maps and narrations. Originating in the postmodern turn, this view considers such representations constitutive of reality rather than mimicking it. They are proposed, in other words, as cultural practices of signification rather than as one-to-one duplications. The meanings that are produced in the representations and texts are dependent on cultural, historical or individual and momentary conditions.[89] Clifford suggests that there is nowhere that offers an overview from which to map and represent the world and human ways of life.[90] Representing takes place in a 'local setting,' as the things we represent are inevitably impacted with our own unique set of interests, views and standards. This means that representations can be critically understood only by exploring the factors bearing upon an author, such as social context, institutional structures, the ontological and political position of the author and, above all, the historical context that impacts all the above factors.[91] Thus, representations are creatures of their authors' making, referencing other texts and cultural constructs which are based on yet further texts; thus 'new worlds are made out of old texts, and old worlds are the basis of new texts.'[92] Representation, therefore, is the product of intertextuality, as are discourses, which are larger structures based on unique practices of signification and including particular assemblages of narratives, concepts and ideologies.[93] Citing Lefebvre, Madanipour writes:

> Our understanding of urban space . . . depends on the frameworks that we adopt at analysis; these frameworks in return depend on our disciplinary biases, our social groups and upbringing, and our cultural values and norms. A study of urban space undertaken by architects and urbanists, therefore, will not be a purely scientific investigation of the subject within timeless laws of physics, but an interpretation of that space as developed and used by a particular society.[94]

All these different levels of perceptions and conceptions are intensively interlinked. We represent the things with the means – including patterns, structures and words – already existing in our life-world, while our representations reciprocally become part of that world. The material experience of spatial and temporal ordering is mediated by the way space and time are represented, whereas the spaces and times of representation affect both our direct experiences and the way we interpret and understand representations.[95]

The term 'labyrinth' has been applied as a means to order the environment of the city, but it is a tool that was produced in a specific, largely Western life-world. When imagining the city as a labyrinth, the procedure is a combination of physical movement within space, going back and forth, looking through, stopping and continuing. And it is also a continuous mental movement: a simultaneous interchange between what is being immediately experienced and what is being imagined or interpreted. The interpretation influences the experience of space while the experience consolidates or alternates the emergent mental image. The concept of labyrinth constructs a symbolic frame in which the spatial relations and urban significations of cities are reset and rearranged based on collective Western interpretations. The resetting is embodied, conceptually, in the symbolism of the labyrinth and constituted a reality by the cultural practice of signification.

Moreover, interpretations of space are always real – and we cannot say if they are true or false. The city of imagination and perception is part of the reality of the city: 'The soft city of illusion, myth, aspiration, nightmare, is as real, maybe more real, than the hard city one can locate on maps, in statistics, in monographs of urban sociology and demography and architecture.'[96] The representations contain 'truth claims' about a space, though perhaps not 'scientific' claims, that reveal different aspects and dimensions of the city and urban space.[97] So perceiving a city or a category of cities – like Islamic cities – as a labyrinth or as labyrinthine cannot be dismissed as a 'false' interpretation as the attribution is now a part of the reality of the cities. It can even hint at particular urban dimensions – although not in a scientific way. The multiple layers that the term brings to our understanding of space have already been discussed; certainly it engages sensual perception and offers a comprehensive, though vague and metaphoric, interpretation. Yet it is still a reductionist representation of Islamic cities as it hides some key characteristics of urban space. These can be discussed under two main points:

(a) The labyrinth as a *means* for representation of the space and for production of knowledge is socially and politically embedded. Through discourses, symbols and metaphors culturally specific meanings are assigned to the urban environment and urban life which are the loci of intense struggle over the significance of place. As Shields also notes, this 'differential social spatialisation is the basis of our geographical sense of the world as a space of distinctions, difference and distance.'[98] The labyrinth metaphor, which belongs to the category of 'uterine images and symbols,' attaches symbolic associations to a given space.[99] Such symbolic, imaginary or archetypical elements 'have their source in history – in the history of a people as well as in the history of each individual belonging to that people,'[100] and, as discussed, the notion of the labyrinth is rooted in the thought and traditions of Europe. It is a spatial leitmotif in this context, which has received different meanings, implications and applications during the course of history, while still retaining close metaphorical associations with its specific historical and cultural context. Therefore, thinking of cities as labyrinths decontextualizes and dehistoricizes the cities that have originated and developed outside this context.

(b) 'Spatial metaphors are epistemological statements.'[101] Representations that highlight pre-determined sets of characters, principles and values while repressing others that are connected with different practices, feelings and rationales contain specific definitions of space which arrange, order, include and exclude.[102] As discussed previously, the labyrinth as a spatial model constructs an image of a city based exclusively on a set of spatial characteristics that the term emphasises and highlights: movement, routes, geometry and feelings of being lost. Thus the widely disseminated image of the labyrinthine city focuses on form and geometry, which should be intriguing enough to make the space be felt as a labyrinth in every realm, including the virtual, the material and associated practice.

Using the term 'labyrinth' prioritises the path as the spatial unit of understanding, and movement as the spatial practice. This way of understanding involves the passage of time and a traversal of space, because it is constituted based on the displacement of an object from one point to another.[103] By foregrounding the displacing, as well as networks of moving and flows, expressions like 'the labyrinthine city' put the 'spaces of place' (to use Manuel Castells's terminology) in the background. For instance, Wilson expresses the character of 'spaces inside spaces' in connection to the impression of labyrinth when she describes urban spaces depicted in the novel, *Into the Labyrinth*, by Christine Mallet Joris, in which a schoolgirl's sexual experiences took place in diverse urban spaces: in the bedrooms, hotels, the theatres and cafes of a great city. For Wilson, this labyrinth city is 'like a magic set of boxes, with, inside each box, a yet smaller and more secret one.' The structure that inspires her to see the city as a labyrinth is 'boxes in boxes.' Yet, in other parts of her book, she defines a labyrinth-like or labyrinthine city as a city with elements like a 'circular journey': (not) having a secret centre, the retracing of the same pathways, and so on. Therefore, in fact, the boxes which are the main elements of her labyrinth lose their significance and independent existence within this usage of the concept.[104] The places, centres, voids, and sections of space which are ignored in this context have, however, significant roles in creating (urban) space in all realms of the material, social and virtual. They are also key elements in the construction of phenomenological perceptions of the city. In Islamic cities, for instance, not openly accessible interior spaces contribute to perceptions of mystery. Flow is an inherent part of urban life in the modern city, and seeing a city as a labyrinth imposes the modern(ist) way of thinking onto a non-modernist phenomenon and ignores the most important spatial practices of 'nuclei' and 'halting' in the city. On the other hand, being so dependent on pattern and form excludes the social practices, cultural values, and definitions that are historically connected to the space of the Islamic city, reducing it to a material and physical entity, and seeing it merely as a network of lines and linkages, whereby the assimilations to the labyrinth are not direct but rather metaphoric.[105]

Paradoxically, however, employing the term labyrinth plays down those phenomenological characteristics that originally played a part in generating the view of (Islamic) cities as labyrinthine. When a city is perceived as a labyrinth, multiple senses or rationalities are involved which go beyond the mere pattern of movement; features such as blank, windowless walls also play a part and yet are not represented in the term, which principally conveys information about patterns of paths and feelings such as 'getting lost.' Thus labyrinth is a metaphor that lacks methodological clarity and does not offer a productive analytical framework for understanding the specific character it attributes to a city because it does not finely delineate what that character subsumes. Therefore, although application of the notion of labyrinth gathers diverse metaphorical, physical and practical spatialities, it reduces the experience of space: 'Itself visible, it has the effect of making invisible the operation that made it possible. These fixations constitute procedures for forgetting.'[106] In other words, it transforms 'action into legibility, but in doing so it causes a way of being in the world to be forgotten.'[107] New concepts are needed to put the focus on the spaces of place as the most articulated spaces, with highest intensity of everyday life activities.

Metaphors and understanding cities

The human mind perceives the world by conceptualising and categorising, and, likewise, we conceive of urban space using abstract representations which include words, graphs, maps, diagrams and pictures in which 'imaginations, fears, emotions, psychologies, fantasies and dreams' also have a part.[108] A concept is an understanding of what something in the world is like, and it can relate to a single entity or a set of entities and stem from an individual or be globally shared; such abstractions provide us with frameworks to categorise our experiences of the world. To understand phenomena, we break them down into their constituent parts, and then reconstruct them so that they make sense to us. This process is embedded in the linguistic process of providing accounts wherein we recurrently use words, images and gestures as our tools of communication.[109]

The concepts produced while experiencing the world, which in turn shape the conceptual world of groups and individuals, are mediated by linguistic signs that, besides enabling us to communicate, dictate a certain way of understanding the world.[110] The signs that we use to understand space filter our perceptions and conceptions of it by defining our mental frameworks, which then produce the meaning transmitted when we communicate our spatial experience.[111] Language as a primary framework for meaning and as a system of communication, like other communication systems, uses signs that include and exclude values, facts and realities. Consequently, any given account selects and prioritises. As Madanipor observes:

> [an account] is always a narrative, told from one perspective, and delivered in different forms . . . [it] includes some words and sentences and not others, refers to some facts and events and not others, draws on some values and not others, includes some viewpoints and interests and not others.[112]

Naming a path a 'cul-de-sac,' for instance, describes a single spatial quality of the object by focusing on pattern of movement, meanwhile concealing social, functional and phenomenological characteristics.

The lack of vocabulary can result in overlooking elements for which there are not words, often resulting in the exclusion of one language group from the common knowledge of another. Amin and Thrift underline this problem of description when they write that 'we do not seem to have the vocabulary to make the everyday life of the city legible; so much seems to pass us by.'[113] As a solution, they go on to build a new sociospatial vocabulary based on understanding the city as a collection of systems or networks that evolve continuously, or machinic assemblages which intermix different categories such as the biological, technical, social and economic. Using the metaphor of propinquity to critique and extend the new urbanism, they note 'by reworking this notion, we are able to demonstrate the multiple forms that community now takes in the city; forms which cannot be encompassed by old-style notions of community based on repeated face-to-face interaction.'[114] With this insight as a motif they envisage propinquity through the city and the city through propinquity.

Using fresh metaphors or vocabularies to grasp further dimensions of urban phenomena can provide access to new aspects of cities and encourage a democratic epistemology – a trend which is favoured in contemporary urban studies: new urbanism deploys metaphors to explain its agendas, for example. Amin and Thrift believe in theorising the (modern) city by pivoting on the banality of everydayness and a phenomenality of urban life that 'cannot be known through theory or cognition.'[115] This is a project that should be executed by going 'beyond the powers of cognition, venturing into the realms of poetic invocation and sensory intimation.'[116] The essence of such dimensions cannot be grasped by traditional tools, they note, adding that in order to access the layer of phenomenality of a city 'one possibility is the use of metaphors.'[117] With this advice they echo Walter Benjamin who suggests diverse metaphors – such as transitivity, rhythms and footprints – by which an individual may understand a city and decipher its hidden meanings, thereby transcending the existing body of knowledge.[118] Transitivity may be used to grasp the spatial and temporal openness of a city and is a term first used by Benjamin in 1924, in a flâneur's take on Naples, to suggest it as a place of blending and spontaneity as a result of its porosity to the past and varied spatial influences.[119] For Benjamin porosity lies in the way buildings and human activity permeate the courtyards, arcades and stairways and create unanticipated urban constellations. It is the crucial part of the city – that is, Naples' urban life – which constantly reappears.[120] The tradition of everyday urbanism has also read the city as place of manifold rhythms that are created by daily encounters and diverse experiences of time and space, including the repetitive activities, sounds and even smells that punctuate life in the city; this is a metaphor that highlights 'neglected temporalities.'[121] Finally, viewing the city through the prism of 'the footprint' brings to it to light as a contained space with a spatial and temporal porosity that opens it to impacts from the past and contemporary links elsewhere: a city *imprinted* by the past and relations beyond the city.[122]

The use of metaphor increases when observed features reach the margins of an individual's experience; people use metaphors to write about places or characters they do not know. There have been debates about the reason and way metaphors produce the creative spark, with the most common approach, as Barnes and Duncan confirm, known as the 'interaction view'; this is based on the idea that words do not have fixed meanings but, rather, encompass a range of associations and kindred concepts. This fluidity in meaning enables ideas associated with one thing to be transferred to something else.[123] Yet Rorty notes that we should not talk about the transmitting of meaning in metaphors in order to keep them mystical; indeed, it is by being literally nonsensical that metaphors provide the jolt, the frisson that 'makes us see the world in a different way; a way that could not be imagined before the metaphor was used.'[124] Debate over the function of metaphors has a long history. Many have viewed them as 'frivolous and ornamental or . . . obfuscatory and logically perverted,'[125] while Harvey believes that metaphors hinder objective judgements.[126] Yet metaphor can tap into a city's virtuality and represent it as 'beyond the powers of cognition, venturing into the realms of poetic invocation and sensory intimation.'[127] It can create new perspectives on the world. As Buttimer suggests, 'metaphor . . . touches a deep level of understanding . . . for it points to the process of learning and discovery – to those analogical leaps from the familiar to the unfamiliar which rally imagination and emotion as well as intellect,'[128] while Amin and Thrift use metaphors for capturing the phenomenality of everyday spaces and recurring practices that, according to them, has been neglected in urban studies.

The next chapter introduces the concept of Hezar-tu as a spatial metaphor suited to new explorations of urban space, particularly that present in Islamic cities. I developed the concept by rethinking the attribution of the metaphor of labyrinth to the Islamic city. Hezar-tu has recently been used in the sphere of Persian language studies as synonymous with the term labyrinth. Yet I argue that the two notions hint at significantly different spatial structures, with Hezar-tu casting a clearer light on characteristics of Islamic urban space that have been misleadingly described due to the lack of proper terminology – resulting in the notion of labyrinth being applied as the closest explanatory concept or terminology.

Notes

1 Patrick Conty, *The Genesis and Geometry of the Labyrinth: Architecture, Hidden Language, Myths and Rituals* (Rochester: Inner Traditions International, 2002), 5.
2 Ulrich Conrads, 'Zeit Des Labyrinths', *Bauwelt* 20 (1980): 830–6.
3 Hermann Kern, *Through the Labyrinth, Designs and Meanings over 5,000 Years* (Munich, New York: Prestel, 2000).
4 Norman Bancroft-Hunt, 'Labyrinth and Maze', in *The Dictionary of Art*, ed. Jane Turner, vol. 18 (New York: Grove, 1996), 584.
5 James Stevens Curl, *Encyclopedia of Architectural Terms* (London: Donhead, 1992), 195, original emphasis.
6 *Random House Webster's Unabridged Dictionary* (New York: Random House, 2000), 1072.
7 Bancroft-Hunt, 'Labyrinth and Maze', 584.
8 Curl, *Encyclopedia of Architectural Terms*, 208.
9 *Random House Webster's Unabridged Dictionary*, 1189.
10 Penelope Reed Doob, *The Idea of the Labyrinth from Classical Antiquity through the Middle Ages* (London: Cornel University Press, 1990).
11 William Henry Matthews, *Mazes and Labyrinths, a General Account of Their History and Developments* (Detroit: Singing Tree Press, 1969).
12 Janet Bord, *Mazes and Labyrinths* (London: Latimer New Dimensions, 1976).
13 Kern, *Through the Labyrinth, Designs and Meanings over 5,000 Years.*
14 Ibid.; Nigel Pennick, *Mazes and Labyrinths* (London: Robert Hale, 1990).
15 Kern, *Through the Labyrinth, Designs and Meanings over 5,000 Years.*
16 Ibid.
17 Ibid.; Doob, *The Idea of the Labyrinth from Classical Antiquity through the Middle Ages.*
18 Kern, *Through the Labyrinth, Designs and Meanings over 5,000 Years.*
19 Histories, second book cited in ibid.
20 Ibid.
21 Ibid.; Pennick, *Mazes and Labyrinths.*

22 Kern, *Through the Labyrinth, Designs and Meanings over 5,000 Years*, 106.
23 Ibid.; Pennick, *Mazes and Labyrinths*.
24 Sig Lonegren, *Labyrinths. Ancient Myths and Modern Uses* (Glastonbury: Gothic Image Publications, 1996).
25 Until the modern age the term 'labyrinth' was used for uni-path patterns with only one path leading from an entrance to the centre, while the maze was employed for multi-path patterns whose complexity is established by posing choices among multiple routes of which some are deliberate dead-ends. The term 'maze', which had only occasionally been used in Christian times, became popular during the Renaissance.
26 Doob, *The Idea of the Labyrinth from Classical Antiquity through the Middle Ages*, 75.
27 Ibid., 66.
28 The weakening of metaphorical implications along with the disappearance of Christian labyrinth designs led authors to label this stage the secularisation of the concept of labyrinth. Kern, *Through the Labyrinth, Designs and Meanings over 5,000 Years*.
29 Ibid.; Pennick, *Mazes and Labyrinths*.
30 Pennick, *Mazes and Labyrinths*.
31 Kern, *Through the Labyrinth, Designs and Meanings over 5,000 Years*.
32 Pennick, *Mazes and Labyrinths*, 145.
33 Doob, *The Idea of the Labyrinth from Classical Antiquity through the Middle Ages*.
34 Ibid., 96.
35 Ibid., 97.
36 Ibid.
37 Ibid.
38 Doob, *The Idea of the Labyrinth from Classical Antiquity through the Middle Ages*.
39 Ibid., 98.
40 Ibid.
41 Ibid.
42 Ibid.
43 Ibid.
44 Physical structures with patterns similar to premodern labyrinths or mazes have recently been used for creating spaces designed for meditation and relaxation.
45 See Diana Agrest, *The Imagined and Real Landscapes of Piranesi* (New York: Columbia University Graduate School, 1992); Manfredo Tafuri, *The Sphere and the Labyrinth: Avant-Gardes and Architecture from Piranesi to the 1970s*, trans. Pellegrino d'Acierno and Robert Connolly (Cambridge, MA, London: MIT Press, 1990).
46 Sergio Roncato, 'Piranesi and the Infinite Prisons', *Spatial Vision* 21, no. 1–2 (2007): 3–18.
47 Teresa Stoppani, 'Voyaging in Piranesi's Space: A Contemporary Re-Reading of the Beginnings of Modernity', *Haecceity Papers* 1, no. 2 (2006): 32–54.
48 Ibid.
49 Sergei M. Eisenstein, 'Piranesi, or the Fluidity of Forms', in *The Sphere and the Labyrinth: Avant-Gardes and Architecture from Piranesi to the 1970s* (Cambridge, MA, London: MIT Press, 1990), 87.
50 Gerhard Hoffmann, 'The Labyrinth', in *From Modernism to Postmodernism: Concepts and Strategies of Postmodern American Fiction*, ed. Gerhard Hoffmann (Amesterdam: Rodopi, 1994), 415.
51 For more discussion on the architecture in and of Borges's fictions, see Sophia Psarra, '"The Book and the Labyrinth Were One and the Same" – Narrative and

Architecture in Borges' Fictions', *The Journal of Architecture* 8 (2003): 369–91, and part two in Sophia Psarra, *Architecture and Narrative* (London, New York: Routledge, 2009).

52 Jorge Luis Borges, 'The Garden of Forking Paths', in *Collected Fictions*, trans. Andrew Hurley (New York: Penguin Books, 1999), 113.

53 Beno Weiss, *Undesrtanding Italo Calvino* (South Carolina: University of South Carolina, 1993); see Italo Calvino, 'La Sfida Al Labirinto [The Challenge to the Labyrinth]', in *Una Pietra Sopra*, ed. Italo Calvino (Milan: Mondadori, 1995), 99–117.

54 Dani Cavallaro, *The Mind of Italo Calvino* (North Carolina: McFarland, 2010), 6. He structures his stories with complex patterns and with no beginning or end to emphasise the importance of the joy of reading and the way through it.

55 Aimable Twagilimann, 'Italo Calvino's If on a Winter's a Night, a Traveler and the Labyrinth', in *The Labyrinth*, ed. Harold Bloom and Blake Hoppy (New York: Infobase Publishing, 2009), 83–4.

56 Stefano Rosso, 'A Correspondence with Umberto Eco', trans. Carolyn Springer, *Boundary 2* 12, no. 1 (1983): 7.

57 Umberto Eco, *Semiotics and the Philosophy of Language* (Bloomington: Indiana University Press, 1986), 81, original emphasis.

58 Eco, *Semiotics and the Philosophy of Language.*

59 Rosso, 'A Correspondence with Umberto Eco'. Guglielmo is a fictional character in the novel *The Name of the Rose* by Umberto Eco.

60 Gilles Deleuze and Felix Guattari, *A Thousand Plateaus, Capitalism and Schizophrenia*, trans. Brian Massumi (Minneapolis, London: University of Minnesota Press, 2000).

61 See, for example, Jody Kolter, 'Abductive Reasoning as an Aesthetic of Interpretation and a Logic of Creativity in Umberto Eco's The Name of the Rose', *Res Cogitans* 2 (2011): 165–73.

62 Gilles Deleuze, *The Fold, Leibniz and the Baroque*, trans. Tom Conley (London: The Athlone Press, 1993), 3.

63 Gilles Deleuze, 'The Fold', trans. Jonathan Strauss, *Yale French Studies* 80 (1991): 231.

64 Deleuze, *The Fold, Leibniz and the Baroque.*

65 *Semiotics and the Philosophy of Language.*

66 Ibid., 81.

67 Eco, *Semiotics and the Philosophy of Language*; Rosso, 'A Correspondence with Umberto Eco'.

68 For example, in the symbolic labyrinth (i.e. pictorial-graphical depictions), the path symbolises a difficult threshold between two extremely different places or conditions – between, for instance, the world and the underworld in prehistory; adulthood and childhood in ancient Roman; and sinfulness and being guided by Christ in the Christian era.

69 Bernard Tchumi, *Architecture and Distinction* (Cambridge, MA: MIT Press, 1996), 43.

70 Rob Shields, *Spatial Questions, Cultural Topologies and Social Spatialisations* (Los Angeles: Sage, 2013).

71 Michel de Certeau, *The Practice of Everyday Life* (Oakland, CA: University of California Press, 1988), 92.

72 Walter Benjamin, *The Arcades Project* (Cambridge, MA: Harvard University Press, 1999).

73 Stephen Spender, *World within World* (London: Hamish Hamilton, 1951), 120; quoted in Elizabeth Wilson, *The Sphinx in the City: Urban Life, the Control of Disorder, and Women* (Oakland, CA: University of California Press, 1991), 90.

74 *The Sphinx in the City: Urban Life, the Control of Disorder, and Women.*

75 See ibid.; Alexis de Tocqueville, *Democracy in America* (New York: Harper & Row, 1966); Gustave Le Bon, *The Crowd* (Harmondsworth: Penguin, 1981).
76 The nineteenth century city was seen as comprising two contrasting groups of characteristics: on the one hand, the solid triumphal features which were related to the towers, vistas and industrial zones in the city, and, on the other, as in the control of the urban crowd. While the former was attributed the masculinity, the latter was described using feminine terms to refer to its instability and irrationality. Wilson, *The Sphinx in the City: Urban Life, the Control of Disorder, and Women.*
77 Ibid., 3.
78 Ibid., 7.
79 Ibid., 136.
80 Ibid., 157.
81 Ernst Cassirer, *An Essay on Man* (New Haven: Yale University Press, 1944); cited in David Harvey, 'Space as a Key Word', in *A Critical Reader, David Harvey*, ed. Noel Castree and Derek Gregory (Malden, Oxford: Blackwell Publishing, 2006).
82 Harvey, 'Space as a Key Word', 279.
83 See Harvey, 'Space as a Key Word'; Walter Benjamin, *The Arcades Project*, ed. Howard Eiland and Kevin McLaughlin (Cambridge, MA: Harvard University Press, 2002); Henri Lefebvre, *The Production of Space*, trans. Nicholson-Smith (Oxford: Basil Blackwell, 1991).
84 Harvey, 'Space as a Key Word', 279.
85 Deborah Stevenson, *Cities and Urban Cultures* (Maidenhead: Open University Press, 2003).
86 Cassirer, *An Essay on Man.*
87 Lefebvre, *The Production of Space.*
88 Harvey, 'Space as a Key Word', 279.
89 Trevor J. Barnes and James S. Duncan, 'Introduction, Writing Worlds', in *Writing Worlds: Discourse, Text and Metaphor in the Representation of Landscape*, ed. Trevor J. Barnes and James S. Duncan (London, New York: Routledge, 1992), 1–17.
90 James Clifford, 'Introduction: Partial Truths', in *Writing Culture: The Poetics and Politics of Ethnography*, ed. James Clifford and George E. Marcus (Oakland, CA: University of California Press, 1986), 1–26.
91 See Barnes and Duncan, 'Introduction, Writing Worlds'; Clifford, 'Introduction: Partial Truths'.
92 Barnes and Duncan, 'Introduction, Writing Worlds', 2, 3. See also Derek Gregory and Rex Walford, 'Introduction: Making Geography', in *Horizons in Human Geography*, ed. Derek Gregory and Rex Walford (London: Macmillan, 1989), 1–7.
93 Barnes and Duncan, 'Introduction, Writing Worlds'. Tyler, for example, argues, 'although most ethnographic accounts are portrayed as objectivist descriptions based on field research, they are better described as intertextual works, highly mediated by a traditional corpus of anthropological monographs and theories.' Stephen A. Tyler, 'Ethnography, Intertextuality, and the End of Description', in The Unspeakable: Discourse, Dialogue and Rhetoric in the Postmodern World (Madison: University of Wisconsin Press, 1987), 89–106; cited in Barnes and Duncan, 'Introduction, Writing Worlds', 7.
94 Lefebvre, *The Production of Space*; cited in Ali Madanipour, 'Public Spaces of European Cities', *Nordic Journal of Architectural Research* 18, no. 1 (2005): 8.
95 Harvey, 'Space as a Key Word'.
96 Jonathan Raban, *Soft City* (London: Hamish Hamilton, 1974), 2.

97 Kevin Hetherington, 'In Place of Geometry: The Materiality of Place', in *Ideas of Difference*, ed. Kevin Hetherington and Rolland Munro (Oxford: Blackwell, 1997), 189; Lefebvre, *The Production of Space.*
98 Shields, *Spatial Questions, Cultural Topologies and Social Spatialisations*, 32.
99 Lefebvre, *The Production of Space*, 41.
100 Ibid.
101 Jane Rendell, 'Introduction: "Gender, Space"', in *Gender, Space, Architecture, an Interdisciplinary Introduction*, ed. Jane Rendell, Barbara Penner, and Lain Borden (London: Routledge, 2000), 107.
102 Hetherington, 'In Place of Geometry: The Materiality of Place'.
103 Tim Cresswell, *On the Move, Mobility in the Modern Western World* (New York, London: Routledge, 2006).
104 Wilson, *The Sphinx in the City: Urban Life, the Control of Disorder, and Women*, 3.
105 This is a similar response to that encouraged by modern cartographic maps.
106 de Certeau, *The Practice of Everyday Life*, 97.
107 Ibid.
108 Harvey, 'Space as a Key Word', 279.
109 Ali Madanipour, *Designing the City of Reason, Foundations and Frameworks* (Abingdon: Routledge, 2007); René Driven and Marjolijn Verspoor, *Cognitive Exploration of Language and Linguistics* (Amsterdam: John Benjamins Publishing Company, 1998).
110 Driven and Verspoor, *Cognitive Exploration of Language and Linguistics.* Based on this view, language is part of a larger sphere of conceptual world and only covers part of the world of concepts which humans have.
111 Wilson notes that authors used feminine terms in describing their paranoid fear of urban crowd in the nineteenth century city: 'the crowd was increasingly invested with female characteristics, while retaining its association with criminals and minorities. The threatening masses were described in feminine terms: as hysterical, or, in images of feminine instability and sexuality, as a flood or swamp. Like women, crowds were liable to rush to extremes of emotion.' Wilson, *The Sphinx in the City: Urban Life, the Control of Disorder, and Women*, 7.
112 Madanipour, *Designing the City of Reason, Foundations and Frameworks*, 233.
113 Ash Amin and Nigel Thrift, *Cities, Reimaging the Urban* (Cambridge: Polity Press, 2002), 5.
114 Ibid., 37.
115 Ibid., 9.
116 Ibid.
117 Ibid.
118 Fran Tonkiss, *Space, the City and Social Theory, Social Relations and Urban Forms* (Cambridge: Polity Press, 2005).
119 Amin and Thrift, *Cities, Reimaging the Urban.*
120 Walter Benjamin, *One-Way Street* (London: Verso, 1997).
121 John Allen, 'Worlds within Cities', in *City Worlds*, ed. Doreen Massey, John Allen, and Steve Pile (London: Routledge, 1999), 17; quoted in Amin and Thrift, *Cities, Reimaging the Urban*, 17.
122 Amin and Thrift, *Cities, Reimaging the Urban.*
123 Barnes and Duncan, 'Introduction, Writing Worlds'.
124 Richard Rorty, *Contingency, Irony, and Solidarity* (Cambridge: Cambridge University Press, 1989); cited in Barnes and Duncan, 'Introduction, Writing Worlds', 10, 11. Compare this with the general agreement on the meaning of metaphor that it states a similarity between two or more different things.
125 Barnes and Duncan, 'Introduction, Writing Worlds', 9.

126 Ironically the increased interest in metaphor partly originated because of the critique mounted on objectivism. David Harvey, 'Models of the Evolution of Spatial Patterns in Human Geography', in *Integrated Models in Geography*, ed. Richard Chorley and Peter Haggett (London: Methuen, 1967), 551; quoted in Barnes and Duncan, 'Introduction, Writing Worlds', 10.

127 Amin and Thrift, *Cities, Reimaging the Urban*, 9.

128 Anne Buttimer, 'Musing on Helicon: Root Metaphors and Geography', *Geografiska Annaler* 64 B (1982): 90; quoted in Barnes and Duncan, 'Introduction, Writing Worlds', 10.

3 Hezar-tu as an urban concept

Hezar-tu, a concept which is inspired by the phenomenological readings of cities, connotes a quality connected to a specific type of spatial organisation. Previous authors have also referred to this characteristic in their phenomenological descriptions of urban space, though with different terminology; Abu-Lughod, for instance, notes an overall feeling of enclosing, enfolding, involuting, protecting and covering that is experienced in structures, in neighbourhoods and in entire Islamic cities,[1] while Bianca observes that the walker experiences a feeling of spatial continuity that goes beyond individual buildings and connects the various realms of Arab public life. This provides the impression of being 'under one roof' as one meanders through a seemingly endless series of interconnected chambers within an articulated and homogenous urban space. This is a feeling that, according to Bianca, encourages a spatial experience characteristic of most traditional Arab cities: one always has the feeling of being at the centre of space, wherever one stands.[2] O'Meara, on the other hand, portrays the urban space of the Islamic city as ajar: simultaneously open and closed. For it is, visually, a liminal realm of multiple planes, 'shuttering and weaving the visual field, framing and reframing space, layering it into bays and arcades'.[3] To characterise the organisation of space in the Islamic city in qualitative terms, authors apply different terminologies, all lacking an analytical focus on the spatiality of thresholds as edges and boundaries of urban space.[4] We need words or, more precisely, concepts to explore, focus and highlight one of the key characteristics of urban space (in the Islamic city): the simultaneity of opposites in the space of multiple thresholds. Concepts are needed that provoke an understanding in which the boundary is a key element of space and, rather than solidly determined, is viewed as dynamic and spatial, with a specific quality as the meeting point of opposites. Hezar-tu fills this gap.

This chapter explores the potential of the term as a spatial metaphor, and how it might be used as a conceptual tool and theoretical framework to encourage a change in the ways cities are encountered and their (urban) space conceptualised. As noted at the beginning of this book, I borrow the term – which I argue has spatial connotations – from literature studies, and expand its operational meaning so as to diversify our conceptual vocabularies in terms of cities and provide fresh understanding of them. I do not apply this term as a solid or static idea, nor do I try to represent any city or group of cities with the single notion or use it to make generalisations. Hezar-tu, here, is applied as an attitude, a characteristic, a concept, an epistemological tool, rather than a form or an existential essence. So, its use is aimed at opening new perspectives rather than determining a clear-cut definition for any given city. As a skeletal framework, Hezar-tu produces different findings in different cities, thus keeping in sight the temporal and geographical variety of cities in the Middle Eastern and North African region, let alone more globally.[5] As is elaborated in this chapter, the purpose of Hezar-tu as an urban metaphor is to express and understand the relations, similarities and differences of urban space.

Hezar-tu as a vocabulary

Hezar-tu is used both as a noun and an adjective. As a noun, it refers to a structure, and as an adjective to a constellation of spatial characteristics. The term consists of two words: hezar [*hizār*] and tu [*tū*], each with their individual meanings and word families. In one of the oldest Persian-Persian dictionaries, Burhān-i Ghātiᶜ, dating back to 1641, *tū* is defined as (1) *pardih*, *tah* and *lā(y)*; and (2) interior (inside) in contrast to the exterior (outside).[6] In the same dictionary, *pardih* is defined as a curtain. In the juxtaposition of *tah* and *lā*, *tah* means beneath and below; in that of *tā* and *lā*, *tā* refers to a sheet (of paper) and *lā* to a layer.[7] To investigate the meanings of the words further, I refer to *Lughatnāmih-yi Dihkhudā*, a Persian-Persian dictionary compiled between the last years of the nineteenth century and 1945, while the editing and publication of all its sixteen volumes was accomplished in 1980. In this work there is a collection of different meanings for words that were used in older sources such as the Burhān (1641), Ānandirāj (1888), and Nāẓimulaṭibā (late nineteenth) dictionaries; in these, diverse words with interrelated meanings are mentioned as synonyms of *tū*, each of which is defined individually in other parts of the dictionary. Comparing all these definitions, we can summarise that a *tū* means: inside (*tūy*); curtain (*pardih*); screen (*pardih*); fold (*lā*); in-between (*lā*); wrinkle or pleat (*chīn*); ringlet (*shikan*); bend (*tā*); curve (*tā*); end (*tah*); beneath (*tah*); underneath (*tah*); bent (*kham*); and layer (*ṭabaghih*).[8] Thus, the term *tū* is associated with five groups of significance, inherently carrying references to:

(a) a mode of insideness, the inside of something, or an inside in contrast to an outside, such as inside a house; walls behind walls; porous rooms;
(b) a mode of being folded; it can denote a fold, wrinkle, pleat, ringlet, bend, or curve and also the act of folding;
(c) a mode of in-betweenness;

(d) a mode of sequential discovery – referring to the fact that a *tū* is beneath or underneath something;
(e) performing as a curtain; separating and hiding.

Two distinct types of spatial structures smoothly blend into the continuum of *tū*'s meanings. One structure, to which meaning (a) refers, is a three-dimensional figure that is constituted by three-dimensional inside spaces connected to each other. An 'inside' in this case is identified as being enclosed from its background or context, and thus in opposition to an 'outside.' The second type of structure, which is indicated in meaning (b), is a two-dimensional conformation that is made up of folds, bends, and curves. So the term *tū* refers simultaneously to both structures, as if a curve, bend or pleat is equivalent to an 'inside' or functions similarly to it. The meanings (c), (d), and (e), indicating (further) features of the *tū*, are in fact characteristics shared by the two structures (the inside and the fold). The features can be listed as follows: the inside or the fold (*tū*) acts as an in-between; it is a separating or hiding element and it can be accessed or discovered in a sequential process of revealing, that is, insides are positioned within each other, pleats behind each other.

The mingling of both structures in the concept of *tū* is also evidenced in two word combinations. The first is *tū-dar-tū*, which literally means a *tū* in a *tū* (an inside in an inside). It refers to compositions with many *tū*s connected to each other by doors and passages, or spaces with many rooms inside rooms.[9] The second word composition is *tū-bar-tū*, literally meaning a *tū* on a *tū* (a bend on a bend). The synonyms of *tū-bar-tū* are layer-on-layer (*lā-bar-lā*), end-on-end or end-over-end (*tah-bar-tah*), fold-on-fold (*tā-bar-tā*), and curtain-on-curtain (*pardih-bar-pardih*); in other words, anything that involves many interlinked *tū*s' impinging on each other in sequential, successive (*mutavālī*, *piy-dar-piy*) arrangements. In the poems of Hāfiz and Niẓāmī, for example, the *tū-bar-tū* evidently resembles the structure of an onion or a flower, while the terms 'fold-on-fold' (*tā-bar-tā*) and 'layer-on-layer' (*lā-bar-lā*) are offered as synonyms for 'inside-in-inside' (*tū-dar-tū*).[10]

Hizār literally means a thousand. It is a word of exaggeration implying multiplicity, plurality and infinity that is added to other words to intensify any indication that may be present of variety or infinity. For example, the words *hizār-dastān* or *hizār-āvāz*, both literally meaning 'a thousand songs', can be used to refer to a nightingale because of its multiple melodies. Similarly, a diplopod is called *hizār-pā*, or 'a thousand feet', while *hizār-rangh*, or 'a thousand colours', describes something highly coloured. *Hizār* is also employed to emphasise the size and dignity of an entity. Consequently, Hezar-tu denotes countless number of *tū*s positioned inside or atop each other. In the Lughatnāmih-yi Dihkhudā the term is defined as 'a thousand rooms' (*hizār-khānih*), 'a thousand layers' (*hizār-lā*), and 'the gut', which is seen as having numerous 'rooms'.

The English term 'labyrinth' has been imported into the Persian language as *lābīrint*. In the original version of the Dihkhudā dictionary it is defined as (a) a French word from the Greek *labyrinthus*; a building or construction with numerous parts whose entrance and centre can be found with considerable difficulty; (b) a large palace in Egypt with numerous dark rooms connected by corridors wherein foreigners could not find their way, for example, the tomb of Amenmehat; and (c) the *lābīrint* in Crete, which Daedalus built for the Minotaur. In these definitions, no connections are made between the terms *lābīrint* and Hezar-tu; they are clearly not considered related. Recently, however, this has changed and the term *lābīrint* has begun to be interpreted or translated as Hezar-tu. We can see traces of this new definition in recent Persian-Persian dictionaries, in scientific literature, and in popular usage of the terms in the Persian language sphere where Hezar-tu is also defined as a labyrinth (*lābīrint*).[11] Yet, despite this recent juxtaposition of the two notions, Hezar-tu and labyrinth connote significantly different spatial structures, thereby supporting Pandolfo's observation that some vocabularies and conceptual configurations 'resist translation and directly engage notions from a different cultural tradition.'[12] In the following, I will commence exploration of the structure of Hezar-tu and the spatial characteristics it denotes by reviewing its original application to critical understanding of classic Persian poems and the structure of the Quran.

Hezar-tu as a text

Hezar-tu and its synonyms have long been used in studies of mystic and Quranic texts and literature critiques, exemplified by ᶜĀshūrī's use of the term *tū-dar-tū* to describe and characterise the poems of Hafiz,[13] and Ahmadī's use of it to explain Sufi ideas (*ᶜirfān*).[14] When certain works of literature, which also present embedded spatial references, invoke an overall mode of delaying and suspense to achieve their core meanings, they are interpreted through application of the concepts. The elements contributing to this mode can be listed as follows:

(a) There is a coincidence and intersection of opposites. In the poems, for example, there are two layers of meaning: the inner (*bāṭīn*) versus the outer (*ẓāhīr*), wherein the former is articulated and hidden behind the latter.[15] ᶜAshūrī states that the mastery of poetry, as in the work of Hafiz, for example, lies in the use of double-level-ness: with having an outer and an inner level. He notes that while the outer level is generally understandable to anyone, the inner level can only be reached by sages or hakims.[16] Similarly, the key postulate of the Way (*ṭarīqa*)[17] is that there is a hidden truth in all things, meaning that every form carries within itself an inner reality which is its 'hidden, internal essence.'[18] So while there is an outer meaning – the sensible, quantitative form which is readily comprehensible, such as the shape of a building, the body of man or the colours of glazed faience – there is also an inner meaning in all things which comprises their essential and qualitative aspects. It is believed that one cannot know a thing in its completeness by seeking only its outward and ephemeral reality; rather, one should seek the essential and inward reality in which the eternal beauty of the object resides.[19] To quote al-Ghazālī, 'Know that the visible world is to the world invisible as the husk is to the kernel; as the form or body to the spirit; and darkness to light.'[20]

The simultaneity of opposites can also be traced in Quran and Sufi ideas. The doctrine of the 'unity of being' is the basis of Sufi metaphysics whose central postulation is that there is a hidden meaning in all things. This idea is based on another assumption that recognizes in God immanence and transcendence at one and the same time: 'At the same time as God is immanent, God is absolutely transcendent. At the same time as God is "nearer . . . than the jugular vein" (50:16), God is above every form, thought or thing in the universe.'[21] In Islamic metaphysics, according to Nasr, basic qualities are attributed to the ultimate reality, which are derived directly from the Quranic verse: 'God, the Ultimate Reality, is both the Inward . . . and the Outward . . . the Centre and the Circumference.'[22] A means for producing this coincidence of opposites has been the use of symbols right across the range of different types of texts, poems and mystical, religious works, because a symbol transfers its meaning by not-saying. As Ardalan and Bakhtiar write:

> The entire journey in God is a journey in symbols, in which one is constantly aware of the higher reality within things. Symbols reflect both Divine transcendence and Divine immanence; they refer to both the universal aspect of *creation* and the particular aspect of *tradition*.[23]

Sufis developed a language of symbols and associations in saying-while-not-saying and, through explaining the Quran, created a mystical, religious language in which words received new connotations and implications; hence the paradoxical *shatah* in Sufi speech, which is a short and compact utterance allowing a multiplicity of explanations and interpretations.[24] Similarly, Hafiz's book of poetry is a text which embraces ambiguity, and is filled with allegories, metaphors and symbols whose decoding is difficult, and which everybody understands according to his own perceptions and presuppositions.[25]

(b) Hiding the inner meaning takes place by creating multiple thresholds between the outer and inner levels, thereby deferring the achievement of understanding the internal 'ultimate reality'. To this end, poets use the tools of delay and suspense, of putting or keeping the subject in doubt, where she remains in a constant condition of not-exactly-comprehending-the-intended-meaning. The method for creating this condition includes the use of terms, expressions or structures that can have diverse meanings, with one being more common and obvious, and the others more distant and hidden. In Hafiz's poems, for instance, the structure of superimposition or interconnection between layers is not one-dimensional, nor is it linear with connections between meanings built only through superficial literal sequences; rather, the connections build a multilateral network in the mind of the reader.[26] According to Khuramshāhī, Hafiz's style has a circular or even spherical movement and structure, like a half-blown bloom, so his poetry can be read from any point and finished at any point.[27] The Quran has a similar structure,[28] as Corbin, a researcher of the Quran and Islamic philosophy, notes:

> The Quran possesses an external appearance and a hidden depth, an exoteric meaning and an esoteric meaning. This esoteric meaning in turn conceals an esoteric meaning (this depth possesses a depth, after the image of the celestial Spheres which are enclosed within each other). So it goes on for seven esoteric meanings (seven depths of hidden depths).'[29]

Thus a deeper meaning lies behind the words of the Quran and one has to penetrate to the hidden core. Schimmel calls it the 'never-ending meanings' of the Quran which have been sought across the ages, as it is believed the ultimate meaning of Quran is only known to God (an unachievable goal).[30]

The tactic of delaying movement from one point or layer of meaning to another through the creation of in-between thresholds leads us to another concept in the literature of the Islamic world: the *barzakh*. In *barzakh*, contraries come together in an indefinite, intermediary locus, giving rise to a mode of in-betweenness. According to Ibn al-Arabi, in whose work the *barzakh* is a key concept understood as a being-in-between, it summarises the condition of all existence.[31] In his book *muqaddima* he writes: 'There is nothing in existence but *barzakhs*, since a *barzakh* is the arrangement of one thing between two other things . . . and existence has no edges.'[32] A *barzakh* is something that separates two things without being a part of either, like the line that separates shadow from sunlight.[33] For Ibn al-Arabi a *barzakh* is synonymous with the *ᶜĀlam-i-mis̱āl*, that is, the Imaginal Realm. It is a virtual, yet concrete, meeting ground between the realm of invisible and undiscovered essences and that of sensual reality and, despite belonging to the sphere of the imagination, its forms, sounds and colours have an objective reality.[34] For Ibn al-Arabi, as Chittick interprets, the world of the imagination is not merely a theory of representation posited as being a mirror of the objective world. It is rather a real space, a parallel world of 'real images,' an angelic space, where bodies are dematerialized and spirits appear in sensual forms.[35] The Imaginal Realm, according to Islamic cosmology, is located in an intermediate region between the material and spiritual worlds in the hierarchy of cosmic existence;[36] the *barzakh* in Ibn Arabi's cosmological typology is thus an intermediate realm, a separating or obscuring element (like *tū*) between absence and presence, between spirituality and body, and between self and other. The locus of the boundary in which contraries come together, bodies are spiritualised and spirits are embodied comprises a partition, a barrier, a midland, an intermediate zone between two states or objects, or an intermediate degree of something. It is, therefore, both a limit and an *entre-deux*: something that stands between two things, both separating and joining them, and combining the attributes of both sides.[37]

Hezar-tu as a space

From the discussion above and fieldwork research in the cities of Fez, Isfahan and Tunis – whose descriptions follow in the ensuing chapter – we can define Hezar-tu as a concept that is about the organisation of space and an order of differences, and as an idea that indicates the constant openings of *tūs* inside each other, thereby generating a state of transition, intermediacy, suspense, and in-betweenness. The exaggeration of 'a thousand' suggests countlessness, innumerability and infinity, while the opening of *tūs* inside each other creates a state of intermediacy where opposites coincide. Some key features of Hezar-tu-ness in relation to features of space can thus be summarised in more detail under five points:

(a) *In-betweenness, in-between spaces and boundaries*: The structure of Hezar-tu is based on multiple *tūs*: *tū*-in-*tū* or *tū*-on-*tū*: transitions of space taking place by virtue of innumerable *tūs*' opening in/on each other, thereby constructing transitional boundaries. In this structure the in-between elements or spaces function as boundaries as they defer access to the inner realm, meditating relations between the spatial nodes in a dynamic manner. Furthermore, they are transformers and connectors which are spaces in themselves: a mid-place between inner and outer realms. So Hezar-tu is about space and its boundaries at the same time, giving both a distinctive spatial character and significance and explaining a quality or mode of spacing and placing.[38] It affords spaces, and spaces in-between, the same level of significance, whereby liminal zones are ambiguous mediators of spaces.[39] The idea is that the in-betweens construct boundaries by being produced continuously and transitionally. More precisely, Hezar-tu is about the spatial conditions of the edge, while a *tū* acts as a *barzakh* – as defined by Ibn Arabi – and 'frontier', of which de Certeau writes:

> This is a paradox of the frontier: created by contacts, the points of differentiation between two bodies are also their common points. Conjunction and disjunction are inseparable in them. Of two bodies in contact, which one possesses the frontier that distinguishes them? Neither. Does that amount to saying: no one? The theoretical and practical problem of the frontier: to whom does it belong? The river, wall or tree *makes* a frontier. It does not have the character of a nowhere that cartographical representation ultimately presupposes.

> It has a mediating role . . . But this actor, by virtue of the very fact that he is the mouthpiece of the limit, creates communication as well as separation; more than that, he establishes a border only by saying what crosses it, having come from the other side. He articulates it. He is *also* a passing through or over. In the story, the frontier functions as a third element. It is an 'in-between' – a 'space between,' *Zwischenraum* . . . A middle place, composed of interactions and interviews, the frontier is a sort of void, a narrative symbol of exchanges and encounters. Passing by, an architect suddenly appropriates this 'in-between space'. . . Transformation of the void into a plenitude, of the in-between into an established space.[40]

(b) *Spatial depth*: *Tūs* positioned inside or behind each other delay access to the internal realm, indicating a sequential experiencing of layers of meanings or spaces in the notion. Hezar-tu often also indicates depth, as the discovery of layers or spaces in-between (*tūs*) is supposed to lead to the inner meanings and realms, that is, *towards* something. Movement is as much a part of the spatial and visual experience of the Islamic city as if an itinerary were being followed. As Le Corbusier observes:

> It is appreciated by walking, on foot; it is by walking, by moving, that one sees the order of the architecture developing. It is a principle contrary to that of baroque architecture, which is conceived on paper, around a fixed theoretical point . . . In this house it's a question of a real architectural promenade, offering constantly changing views, unexpected, sometimes astonishing.[41]

The concept of Hezar-tu bears in itself the spatial practice of a sequential experiencing of *tūs* – which can be hierarchical or preparatory. In a *tū*, symbolic, spatial or social relationships intersect and come together. It is a node of, or a locus for, relationships that generates belonging, embracing, holding within, and including. A *tū* indicates inclusion: a *here* in relation to a there, familiarity in relation to foreignness, or an inside in relation to an outside. In this constellation, a *tū* can be conceptual, spatial, visual, material, social, metaphorical, or a mix of some of these. For instance, a network of social relationships that promotes a feeling of belonging can socially construct a *tū* – which appears as a node in the wider context of the city. Or a *tū* can be defined as an established physical place – a void or a courtyard – which assembles a number of other spaces around itself, creating a mode of spatial interiority. Symbolically, the *tū* is the higher, inner meaning hidden in, for example, poems or ornamentation.

(c) *Revealing but hiding – that is, deferring*: In-betweenness is a space of absence-presence, a space of opposites, at once impenetrable and offered to the gaze: a simultaneous implication and estrangement which might create unreadability. The different arrangements and articulation of in-betweenness creates an overall character of revealing but hiding which defers access; this can play the role of separating and dividing.

(d) *Containment*: The boundary, here, creates a mode of containment, yet not necessarily a closed form, as the boundary may be porous. Based on this feature and according to empirical research in cities across the Middle East and North Africa discussed in the following chapter, different types of *tūs* can be observed in terms of urban space: (i) the spatial *tū* refers to the spaces that promote architectural and physical interiorities and includes elements like courtyards which are at the centre of a number of spaces that can be accessed after traversing diverse preliminary stages; (ii) the social *tū* refers to nodes of relationships, gatherings, groupings and social meanings, like family names and neighbourhood-based connections; (iii) the conceptual *tū* touches on the notional meanings hidden in ornamentation and words (It is a *tū* because it is an abstract thing hidden behind layers of meanings: the innermost concept that is hidden behind layers of meanings.); (iv) the visual *tū* expresses visual layers as thresholds that act as in-between boundaries and defer access; and (v) the symbolic *tū* which includes symbolically coded zones, territories and places.

(e) *Ambiguity*: Finally, as Hezar is used for exaggeration to refer to an infinite, numerous number of something, it retains and foregrounds a logic of ambiguity, exaggerating the number of in-between spaces and elements. This characteristic transforms Hezar-tu into a metaphor which highlights an indeterminacy that is both ontological and spatial.

Notes

1 Janet L. Abu-Lughod, 'Preserving the Living Heritage of Islamic Cities', in *Toward an Architecture in the Spirit of Islam*, ed. Renata Holod (Philadelphia: Aga Khan Award for Architecture, 1978), 61–75.

2 Stefano Bianca, *Urban Form in the Arab World, Past and Present* (New York: Thames & Hudson, 2000).

3 Simon O'Meara, *Space and Muslim Urban Life: At the Limits of the Labyrinth of Fez* (London: Routledge, 2007), 70.

4 Eugen Wirth uses terms such as 'to-be-inside' (*Innrehalb-sein*) – in contrast to 'to-be-outside' (*Außerhalb-sein*) – and 'including-by-enclosing' (*eingrenzen*) – in contrast to 'excluding-by-keeping-outside' (*ausgrenzen*). He believes that urban space in the Islamic city emphasises, and has a tendency to create, a mode of insideness and inclusion by through enclosure. Although these terms hint at the sensual characteristics of Islamic urban space, yet in none of the terms – *innerhalb, außerhalb, eingrenzen* or *außgrenzen* – is the idea or concept of boundary been given any spatial existence. *Innerhalb* and *außerhalb* literally mean, consequently, the half (of something) that is inside and the half (of something) that is outside. It is as if a place or space is divided into two, and the space is either in one or the other; there is no intermediary sphere. Similarly, in the verbs *ausgrenzen* and *eingrenzen*, the boundary (*die Grenze*) is only a limit, a boundary according to which the included-excluded is defined and embodied. The terms do not give a spatial existence or characteristic to the concept of boundary. That is, neither of the words spatialise or characterise the boundary.

5 Yet, as works in urban studies also show, it is obviously possible to theorise without generalising. Ash Amin and Nigel Thrift, *Cities, Reimaging the Urban* (Cambridge: Polity Press, 2002).

6 Muḥammad Ḥuṣiyn Bin Khalaf Tabrīzī, *Burhān-i Qāṭiᶜ*, ed. Muḥammad Muᶜīn (Tehran: Ibn Sīnā, 1951). The same meanings appear in ᶜĀṣif-ul-lughāt, authored by Khān Bahadur Shams-ul-ᶜulamā Navāb ᶜAzīz Jang, which is an unfinished work compiled between 1907 and 1921.

7 The definition of *lā* appears in an additional note to the meaning of *lā-bar-lā*. There are other definitions for *tū*, unrelated to our discussion, including, for example, similarity or individual.

8 The meanings of each of the synonyms to *tū*, in the same dictionary, are as follows: *tūy* means inside (*darūn*) or an in-between (*dar mīān*). *Lā* means fold (*tā. tah. tū. tūy*); and in-between (*lā*). *Tā* means fold, wrinkle, pleat, bent, to bend, curve, to fold, to ply (*lā, shikan, chīn*). While *tah* means under, underneath (*zīr, pāīn*). Except for bend (*kham*) and layer (*ṭabaghih*) that are added by Dihkhudā, all the definitions of *tū* are compiled from older dictionaries such as Burhān (1641), Anandirāj (1888), Fahrang-i Jahāngīrī (1608) and Nāẓim-ul-aṭibā (1884). The term *tū* was used in several poems – for instance, Salman Savoji (1288–1358) writes: *chun ghunchi bastam sar-i dil rā bi sad girih / tā būy-i rāz-i ᶜishgh nayāyad bi tūy-i dil.*

9 ᶜAlī Akbar Dihkhudā, *Lughatnāmih* (Tehran: Tehran University Press, 1980).

10 Quoted in ibid.

11 Nujūmīān's interpretation of *hizār-tū* as equivalent to labyrinth instantiates this recent fusing of terms not previously related in the intellectual discourse. Nujūmīān, a linguist, uses hizār-tū as a synonym to 'labyrinth, web, maze', to discuss postmodern semiotic structures, the role of space, the role of the concept of labyrinth in postmodern discourse, and to explore the use of labyrinthine space as a semiotic structure and the relation between intertextuality and *hizār-tū*-ness (*hizār-tū-ī*). The labyrinth, web or maze (*hizār-tū*), according to Nujūmīān, is one of the most significant semiotic structures in postmodern discourse, and has multiple roles in this context. The postmodern city keeps its inhabitants in a permanent bewilderment. A *hizār-tū* space, in contrast to map-based knowledge, does not determine the person's position in the city, according to Nujūmīān's interpretation. The inhabitant of a *hizār-tū* is thus trapped in corridors that have similar value and quality; there is no from-above view into the space and movement within it is not inevitably towards development / achievement. Postmodern literary and cinematic texts that encourage a kind of intertextuality demonstrate a similar type of *hizār-tū* space. In defining the labyrinth or maze, he refers to the standard definitions of the (European) labyrinth discussed in the previous chapter: a network of tunnels in which one can easily get lost that are complicated, intricate, *tū-dar-tū*, *pīch-dar-pīch*, and *mārpīch* (winding); an anatomy with connected chambers; a complicated construction of rooms and ways that are usually built to bewilder people; an Egyptian labyrinth-like temple; and Daedalus's Cretan labyrinth. According to him, the labyrinth (i.e. *hizār-tū*) has two main forms: (a) it refers to the maps that one needs in order to find the right route from an entrance towards a centre or exit point; (b) it refers to walled or hedged structures that one enters with no idea or image of the overall pattern, and whose exit routes can only be discovered by trial and error. He adds *hizār-tū* is one of the most significant spatial structures of postmodern discourse. Above all, it refers to the spaces of the cities we inhabit where there is no image from above but, rather, circular movement, a lack of corresponding value for selected routes or rational and discursive implications of choices, and disorientation of the human mind. There is no apparent difference between the routes and thus the individual cannot reach the centre of

hizār-tū, which symbolises the truth, using sensual or rational means. The only rule of *hizār-tū* is coincidence. The textual structure of *hizār-tū* is not linear but rather has a centre which can be where the truth resides, or a place from which a prisoner should escape. The Internet, for example, has this structure, because each web page can lead us to many other pages. Amīr Alī Nujūmīān, 'Hizār Tū-Yi Shahr Dar Hizār Tū-Yi Matn, Yik Barasī-Yi Nishānihshinākhtī (City's Hizār Tū in Text's Hizār Tū, a Semiotic Investigation)', in *Maghālāt Duvumīn Hamandīshī Nishānihshināsī Hunar (Second Symposium of Semiotics of Art)* (Tihrān: Farhangistān Hunar Press, 2006), 213–30.

12 Stefania Pandolfo, *Impasse of the Angels* (Chicago: The University of Chicago Press, 1997), 5.

13 Dāryūsh ᶜĀshūrī, *Hastīshināsī-yi Ḥāfiẓ (Ontology of Hafiz)* (Tehran: Markaz, 1998), 9.

14 Bābak Aḥmadī, *Chāhār Guzārish Az Taẕkiratululīa (Four Reports of Attar's Taẕkiratululīa)* (Tehran: Markaz, 1997).

15 Bahāidīn Khuramshāhī, *Ẕihn va Zābān-i Hāfiẕ (Mind and Language of Hafiz)* (Tehran: Sidā-yi Muāsir, 1999).

16 ᶜĀshūrī, *Hastīshināsī-yi Hāfiẕ (Ontology of Hafiz)*.

17 *Ṭarīqa* or the Way is the esoteric dimension which contrasts with the exoteric dimension of Islam that concerns the Divine Law (sharia).

18 Nader Ardalan, 'Color in Safavid Architecture: The Poetic Diffusion of Light', *Iranian Studies* 7, no. 1–2 (1974): 166.

19 See, for example, Ardalan, 'Color in Safavid Architecture: The Poetic Diffusion of Light'; Seyyed Hossein Nasr, 'Contemporary Man, between the Rim and the Axis', *Studies in Comparative Religion* 7, no. 2 (1973): 113–26; Seyyed Hossein Nasr, 'Foreword', in *The Sense of Unity*, ed. Nader Ardalan and Laleh Bakhtiar (Chicago: University of Chicago Press, 1973), xi–xv.

20 Translated in Margaret Smith, *Al-Ghazzālī the Mystic* (London: Hijra International Publishers, 1944), 174; See also Henri Corbin, *Creative Imagination in the Sufism of Ibn Arabi*, trans. Ralph Manheim (Princeton: Princeton University Press, 2016).

21 Nader Ardalan and Laleh Bakhtiar, *The Sense of Unity* (Chicago, London: The University of Chicago Press, 1973), 9, original emphasis.

22 Nasr, 'Contemporary Man, between the Rim and the Axis'.

23 Ardalan and Bakhtiar, *The Sense of Unity*, 25 original emphases.

24 Aḥmadī, *Chāhār Guzārish Az Taẕkiratululīa (Four Reports of Attar's Taẕkiratululīa)*.

25 ᶜĀshūrī, *Hastīshināsī-yi Ḥāfiẓ (Ontology of Hafiz)*. There is a belief that the imagination of the traditional artist in the Islamic city was constantly influenced by Islamic cosmology, and of course more directly by the Quran. As a result, the Way permeated science and the crafts, and was embodied in the traditional craft guilds, the creators of traditional art and architecture. The guilds were invariably directed by masters who, as practicing Sufis, instilled in themselves spiritual knowledge. See Seyyed Hossein Nasr, 'The Contemporary Muslim and the Architectural Transformation of the Islamic Urban Environment', in *Toward an Architecture in the Spirit of Islam*, ed. Renata Holod (Philadelphia: Aga Khan Award for Architecture, 1978); Corbin, *Creative Imagination in the Sufism of Ibn Arabi*; Ardalan, 'Color in Safavid Architecture: The Poetic Diffusion of Light'; Laleh Bakhtiar, *Sufi: Expressions of the Mystic Quest* (London: Thames & Hudson, 1976).

26 Khuramshāhī, *Ẕihn va Zābān-I Ḥāfiẕ (Mind and Language of Hafiz)*. See also Arthur J. Arberry, ed., 'Introduction', in *Fifty Poems of Hafiz* (Cambridge: Cambridge University Press, 1970), 30–1.

27 Khuramshāhī, *Ẕihn va Zābān-I Ḥāfiẕ (Mind and Language of Hafiz)*. We also have a type of 'topological ambiguity' in miniature. Pandolfo states that, in

miniature, historical events are illustrated in real places in the form of perspectival representations of cities or villages, in which successive times and actions are represented on different planes or spaces. The illustrated scenes are shown side by side and are structured by a superimposition of planes and a multiplicity of spaces. Thus the boundaries in these representations blur to indeterminacy: '[I]n these miniatures the perimetric walls of cities and the facades of buildings are oriented in different directions, forcing the viewer to move along with the drawing and adjust to shifting frontal projections. Separate and independent spaces are grafted onto the main picture frame, indicating narrative and conceptual multidimensionality (what appears as topological ambiguity).' Pandolfo, *Impasse of the Angels*, 35.

28 The Quran's structure has been the inspirational source for poets like Hafiz. Khuramshāhī, *Ẓihn va Zābān-I Ḥāfiẓ (Mind and Language of Hafiz)*. Terms like *tū-dar-tū* also have been used to describe similar characteristics in the structure of Quran. See, for example, ibid.

29 Henri Corbin, *History of Islamic Philosophy* (London: Routledge, 1993), 7.

30 Annemarie Schimmel, *Islam, and Introduction* (New York: State University of New York Press, 1992), 48; See also Seyyed Hossein Nasr, *Islamic Life and Thought* (London: Taylor and Francis, 2007).

31 Pandolfo, *Impasse of the Angels*, 188, 189. Khurramshāhī notes that there is a close similarity between Hafiz's Sufi ideas (*ᶜirfān*) and the Ībn-Arabī's. Khuramshāhī, *Ẓihn va Zābān-I Ḥāfiẓ (Mind and Language of Hafiz)*.

32 Translated in William C. Chittick, *Ibn Al-Arabi's Metaphysics of Imagination: The Sufi Path of Knowledge* (Albany: State Univeristy of New York Press, 1989), 14, original emphasis.

33 Chittick, *Ibn Al-Arabi's Metaphysics of Imagination: The Sufi Path of Knowledge.*

34 Seyyed Hossein Nasr, *Islamic Art and Spirituality* (Albany: State University of New York Press, 1987).

35 Chittick, *Ibn Al-Arabi's Metaphysics of Imagination: The Sufi Path of Knowledge*; see Pandolfo, *Impasse of the Angels*.

36 Nasr, 'The Contemporary Muslim and the Architectural Transformation of the Islamic Urban Environment'; Corbin, *Creative Imagination in the Sufism of Ibn Arabi*.

37 Pandolfo, *Impasse of the Angels*. Ibid., 5, original emphasis, uses the notion of *barzakh* to refer to the 'heterological space of intercultural dialogue,' where languages and cultures, genders and categorisations come together in a postcolonial subject from the village of Qsar in Morocco.

38 This is what Shields calls 'spatialisation.' Rob Shields, *Spatial Questions, Cultural Topologies and Social Spatialisations* (Los Angeles: Sage, 2013).

39 According to Pandolfo, in classical Arabic geographical descriptions, boundaries are assumed as the 'places of the uncanny, *al-gharîb*' Pandolfo, *Impasse of the Angels*, 24, original emphasis.

40 Michel de Certeau, *The Practice of Everyday Life* (Oakland, CA: University of California Press, 1988), 127, original emphasis.

41 The original quote reads as 'L'architecture arabe nous donne un enseignement précieux. Elle s'apprécie à la marche, avec le pied; c'est en marchant, en se déplaçant que l'on voit se developer les ordonnances de l'architecture. C'est un principe contraire à l'architecture baroque qui est conçue sur le papier, autour d'un point fixe théorique. Je préfère l'enseignement de l'architecture arabe. Dans cette maison-ci, il s'agit d'une veritable promenade architecturale, offrant des aspects constamment varies, inattendus, parfois étonnants.' Le Corbusier and Pierre Jeanneret, *Oeuvre Complète*, ed. Willi Boesiger, vol. 2 (Zurich: Grisbeger, n.d.), 24; translated in Beatriz Colomina, *Privacy and Publicity* (Cambridge, London: MIT Press, 1996), 6.

4 City as Hezar-tu

Fez, Isfahan and Tunis

This chapter rereads the spatial relations in three urban fabrics using Hezar-tu as a conceptual tool. The case study sites are parts of the historic cores of Fez, Isfahan and Tunis, henceforth referred to as 'medinas'. I have chosen those parts of the cities whose form has remained largely unaffected by the common impacts of industrialisation and modernization although, admittedly, in these surviving historic structures, the urban fabric and 'urban structures . . . represent a late stage in the evolution of urban form, stretching over the last three or four centuries.'[1] The three cities have been selected because, firstly, each has been named an example of a typical Islamic city in multiple sources, and, secondly, they represent three different types of Islamic city, as they developed in diverse historico-cultural contexts. Fez provides an extreme example of the use of *tūs* in creating its urban space. Its urban fabric is also relatively coherent in terms of the juxtaposition of its historical layers; that is, different parts of the urban fabric evolved in, and belong to, certain distinct periods. Tunis, in contrast, is representative of less *tū*-based structure, one in which *tūs* are exteriorised to a certain extent. It is also, in contrast to Fez, an example of a city in which buildings from diverse historical periods assemble around a single passage, creating multiple, superimposed, historical layers in an urban block. Isfahan, on the other hand, exemplifies the use of *tūs* outside the Arab world.

Some epistemological points should be made prior to analysing and describing the cities:

(a) Studying the medina involves a constant oscillation between different temporalities, necessitating the use of diverse sources of knowledge, as its space is somewhere that eras intersect, by virtue both of its materiality and the activities conducted within it. Recent global theorisation conceptualises urban space in ways that transcend the homogenising dynamics of modernity and globalisation by acknowledging the multiplicities as well as peculiarities of space in different urban and social settings and local identities. Urban space, in this view, is perceived as comprising the co-presence of multiple temporalities and spatialities in which, it is suggested, different times fuse together to make cities

> places where multiple time-spaces are intensively superimposed.[2] In this sense, each part of the city is considered a 'contained space' in which the 'temporal porosity of the city opens it to footprints from the past.'[3] This porosity generates a multiplicity of histories and a syncretism of traditions that play a considerable part in producing the spatial, making the contemporary city a scene of the simultaneous presence of diverse temporal layers.[4] Studies reveal that the present is affected by impacts from the past in three forms: built space, the practices of individuals and symbols. The juxtaposition of different built forms generates interconnections across time, and transfers orders and building practices from one era to another.[5] The individual is also a container for blending periods when she internalises processes, inherits rituals, habits, values and beliefs, and re-articulates them in a set of practices and performances.[6] In addition, verbal and non-verbal representations of space, such as imaginaries, symbols and spatial notions, retain previous spatial arrangements in their conception and inception, and thus influence present-day spatialisations.[7]

In medinas, too, the fusion of times is evident and distinctive; however, their material urban fabric – at least the parts that have been selected as case study areas here – remains largely in the sphere of the late premodern past, despite the small-scale appropriations people have undertaken. That the main street routes have endured relatively unchanged is clear when comparing the first cartographic maps drawn of the cities with their current layout, while some of key historical buildings have also been preserved. Details might be missing, but the general outlines represent the original structures in most cases, as pointed out by architectural historians. My main data source when studying the form and physical space of the contemporary medinas is, therefore, the existent architectural fabric, while further knowledge has been gleaned from a range of documents casting light on the cities' historical evolution.

Historic sections of the case study cities, particularly in Fez, also bear witness to the survival of premodern traditions and behaviours – such as cultural values, sociospatial practices and symbolic meanings – which have been transmitted from the distant past to combine with modern flows and dynamics. As will be discussed in the following sections of this chapter, this longevity is mostly evident in the ways the spaces are used, named, symbolically signified and valued. Therefore, in order to understand the sociocultural dimension and context of the spaces, research has moved back and forth between historical and modern analysis, using secondary sources to gain information on the past functions of spaces and rules and norms of everyday life. Other sources include on-site observation of behaviour in private and public urban space, and interviews with residents that explore the way they use space on a daily basis, a combination that provides a rich context for the meaning of spatial practices such as, for example, the separation of the public and private spheres.

(b) I narrate the space of Fez, Isfahan and Tunis while walking a number of routes through their medinas which were selected after on-site investigations and interviews with local experts established that they have, to a certain extent, retained their premodern urban physical form. Each route also has characteristics and architectural elements and functions that make it representative of the fabric in general.[8] Field research had two main steps: using the data sources listed previously, I began by collecting diverse types of information on the elements, details, structures and daily rhythms of each of case study route, and its surrounding neighbourhoods and city; I also walked the routes with various local residents who were familiar with the site, its stories, symbolic meanings and inhabitants and could describe them to me. During this stage, I gained fragmented knowledge of different urban architectural elements and sociocultural aspects of the spaces around the routes. Then, with the background of understanding achieved in the first step, I walked the route alone and narrated it. The goal was to piece together the fragmentary knowledge gained in the first stage, and to combine it with the (subjective) sensual experience of walking through the space.[9] The second, solo walk brought together the diverse physical or non-physical characteristics which are presented as 'a narration of the path.' The main focus of my observations and narrations is the transition of space through the cities' in-between-spaces, their in-between-ness: reading the Hezar-tu-ness of the cities while negotiating them on foot.

This has been one of the key tools for interpreting a city and experiencing its space in contemporary urban studies which have, for example, renewed the tradition of the *flâneur* to read the city through street-level inference. The idea behind this is that traditional tools, based on maps and description, do not provide a comprehensive understanding of urban space. We need a reflexive walker, a flâneur, who, through sensory, emotional and perceptual engagement with the passages of the city, involves herself in a 'two-way encounter between mind and the city' resulting in 'knowledge that cannot be separated from this interactive process.'[10] The flâneur's sensibility is links space, language and subjectivity in a series of reflexive wanderings, underpinned by particular theorisations of urban life: a methodology that reveals the social meanings that are embedded in the fabric of a city.[11] She is a walker who is a 'theorist', purposefully lost in a city's spaces and daily rhythms; she possesses 'a poetic sensibility,' 'a poetic science' and a 'transcendental speculative philosophy' that allow the 'theorist' to select, order and interpret the sensory experiences of her urban surroundings.[12]

Moreover, the corresponding mobility on the part of the witness enables her to grasp the mutability and porosity that exists in urban life and space. On observing the transitive juxtaposition of elements and activities in city space while in the flâneur mode, Walter Benjamin, who helped revive the tradition, writes: 'building and action interpenetrate in the courtyards, arcades and stairways,' and constantly build 'new, unforeseen constellations' so that 'the stamp of definitive is avoided'.[13] Benjamin's wanderings as a meditative walker in the corners and spaces of different cities capture this layer. He believes that the diverse temporal and spatial flows that intermingle in everyday interactions are what allow a city's continual transformation into new forms and conditions. According to Benjamin, porosity to the past and to spatial influences reappears everywhere in the urban milieu.[14]

In order to understand urban space, de Certeau also suggests changing from a map view, a totalising perspective of the whole, to walking in the streets. He believes 'ordinary practitioners' of the city are 'walkers, *Wandermänner*, whose bodies follow the thicks and thins of an urban "text" they write without being able to read it.'[15] The experience of walking derives from being in a series of spaces that are traversed one after the other. The resulting sensual perceptions are thus partially the result of a spatial practice based on a sequential experience of spaces – that is, a tour or movement whereby the city is spatialised through a set of actions.[16] It is about direction, movement and velocity.[17] De Certeau writes:

> The networks of these moving, intersecting writings compose a manifold story that has neither author nor spectator, shaped out of fragments of trajectories and alterations of spaces: in relation to representations, it remains daily and indefinitely other . . . Walking affirms, suspects, tries out, transgresses, respects, etc., the trajectories it 'speaks'. All the modalities sing a part in this chorus, changing from step to step, stepping in through proportions, sequences, and intensities which vary according to the time, the path taken and the walker. These enunciatory operations are of an unlimited diversity. They therefore cannot be reduced to their graphic trail.[18]

Each individual's experience of space and city, on the other hand, is fashioned by her perceptions, mental maps and spatial practices which, together, generate a myriad of narrative maps unique to individuals, which can be mythological, imaginary and partial.[19] In walking, each person reads her own world in the city, producing what de Certeau terms 'spatial stories'. Pedestrians insert their own history into the streets which they fill with their desires and goals. The reader's world slips into the built place and the city is read by being assimilated into previous memorable spaces or words.[20]

De Certeau, citing Linde and Labov, points out two categories of descriptions of places which, according to him, often coexist in a single description: the 'map' and the 'tour.'[21] These are two 'poles of experience' and, in passing from one to the other, one passes 'from "ordinary" culture to scientific discourse.'[22] The map is of the type: 'The girls' room is next to the kitchen.' It is based on '*seeing* (the knowledge of an order of places)' and presents a '*tableau* ('there are . . .').'[23] In contrast, the tour is of the type: 'You turn right and come into the living room.' Descriptions of the tour type are made in terms of operations. Based on this approach the path is 'a series of units that have the form of vectors that are either 'static' ('to the right,' 'in front of you,' etc.) or 'mobile' ('if you turn to the left,' etc.).'[24] The tour type is based on '*going* (spatialising actions)'; it 'organizes *movements* ("you enter, you go across, you turn. . .").'[25] The tour type is like an itinerary: 'a discursive series of operations.'[26] In maps,

> thick or thin curves only refer, like words, to the absence of what has passed by. Surveys of routes miss what was: the act itself of passing by. The operation of walking, wandering, or 'window shopping,' that is, the activity of passers-by, is transformed into points that draw a totalizing and reversible line on the map. They allow us to grasp only a relic set in the nowhen of a surface of projection. Itself visible, it has the effect of making invisible the operation that made it possible. These fixations constitute procedures for forgetting. The trace left behind is substituted for the practice. It exhibits the (voracious property that the geographical system has of being able to transform action into legibility, but in doing so it causes a way of being in the world to be forgotten.[27]

Thus, on the one hand, we have the space of visual, panoptic or theoretical constructions, which, similar to the panorama-city, misunderstands people's practices in and interactions with the space. On the other, we have an 'anthropological, poetic and mythic' experience of space which emerges from specific forms of activities in it.[28] This latter '*migrational*, or metaphorical, city . . . slips into the clear text of the planned and readable city.'[29]

This categorisation accords with the distinction de Certeau makes between two phenomena, the first of which is related to the order in which the elements of a space are located in relation to each other; stability, located-ness and pattern are dominant here. De Certeau refers to this as 'place': the solid distribution of elements in a given locus that is geometrically defined by urban planning. Here the order defines how the elements should be distributed in relationships of coexistence.[30] The second phenomenon, in contrast to 'place,' is about directions, velocities and time variables. Termed 'space' by de Certeau, this is seen to be 'composed of intersections of mobile elements. It is in a sense actuated by the ensemble of movements deployed within it . . . *space is a practiced place*.'[31] Thus a 'place' is transformed into a 'space' by walkers or practitioners of space – just like an act of reading a written text about a place which is constituted by a system of signs.

Barthes, on the other hand, believes we need to combine multiple personal histories of cities to provide a basis for understanding them. As Stevenson notes, for Barthes, too, it is through acts of wandering and looking that one reads and interprets the urban landscape, although his approach is more psychoanalytic than social. Barthes suggests, however, a shift from interpreting and reinterpreting urban texts through personal histories to more scientific, knowledge-based readings of the landscape. To achieve this shift, he believes insights into the language of the city should be gained by accumulating the urban stories of multiple city users and bringing their readings together to create a collective.[32]

The flâneur's poetic of knowing, however, can be insufficient to grasp urban phenomena adequately. It might, for example, fall into the trap of remaining limited to a distinctive subject position where the emphasis is only on the primacy of personal readings and sensory experiences.[33] To overcome this weakness, Amin and Thrift suggest using additional tools to apprehend the city's transitivity, some of which, as they note, can draw on 'now routine technologies of knowing, historical guides and photographs charting change over time, imaginaries which illustrate the city in motion (such as airborne video-shots).'[34] Developed at one remove from the street and flâneur, the tools help provide a combination of different means of study to provide a rich framework for research.

(c) The urban form in the medina was the result of the superimposition of a number of *nīẓāms*. I use the term *nīẓām* here to highlight the multi-layered relationship between, on the one hand, elements such as water, trade-related structures and social institutions, and, on the other, local life-worlds in Islamic cities, a relationship which affected the meaning and role of urban elements. The urban form in all organic cities, in general, is shaped under the strong influence of factors such as water, topography and sociocultural organisation.[35] Although these factors do not impose a rigid geometric order, like top-down planning systems, they determine urban geometry to a large extent.[36] Furthermore, in an Islamic city there is another aspect to the presence and function of some of these urban elements due to the role of the religion. As Bianca notes, '[i]n the traditional Islamic context, the divine order was a commonly accepted reality' and, accordingly, the given system of daily rituals had its particular meaning.[37] Islamic ordering in urban life was twofold: (i) As a sharia, Islam determined daily practices and routines because the system of sharia laws provided a comprehensive body of guidance which was concerned with regulating all facets of private and social life in its earthly forms.[38] From this perspective, Islam touched the exoteric dimension of life, determining, for example, cleanness in relation to water or, more precisely, to flowing water: the absolute (religious) cleanliness which is a necessity for every Muslim can only be gained by cleansing the body in water that has a current; still water does not suffice. Water is, in addition, necessary for many ceremonies and ritual purifications including ablutions for daily prayer. Its usage in daily religious urban life gives water a role beyond its influence in shaping a city merely as an ecological physical element. (ii) As the Way (*ṭarīqa*), Islam gave spiritual dimension and meaning to the elements regulating the esoteric dimension of life, with water once again of central significance.[39] From the philosophical-religious point of view (*hikmat*), water is understood to be a significant element in the Imaginal Realm (*ʿĀlam-i-miṡāl*) which, in Islamic cosmology, stands in an intermediate position between the material and spiritual worlds, in the hierarchy of cosmic existence.[40] The World of the Imagination, as Nasr notes, is believed to have an ontological reality based in the human imagination that goes beyond profane imagination as it is understood in the modern world.[41] According to Islamic philosophy, as Bianca declares, water enables man's mind 'to open a window into the realm of timeless existence.'[42] Paradise is also always represented in connection with water, in that water is an element present in all the descriptions of paradisial scenes in the Quran. So, from a philosophical-religious point of view, water is sacred element belonging to the World of the Imagination whose limpidity can reflect infinity, paradise and purity.

Beyond doubt water was also physically important to Islamic urban development. Environmentally, the cities of the Middle Eastern and North African region mostly have a hot dry climate. In this context, water has always been a significant element in increasing humidity, improving microclimates and tempering the heat of summer days, thereby promoting thermal comfort in hot arid lands.[43] Thus it was physically important, not only because water is an ecological element which is valued in all cities, but also because its scarcity transformed it into something that represented more than just a normal prerequisite. Its ecological and symbolic aspects defined how it was understood and used in the Islamic city, which subsequently determined how buildings, mahallas and routes were shaped to meet the city's needs for it. Each of these fields – the environment, religion, and philosophy – has a part in determining the importance, function and application of water, and affects the way the city has to embrace water, use it and interact with it; thus it is connected to the local life-world in multifarious ways with diverse meanings and functions in urban life.

Islam's influence on daily social practices, in this view, gave the constituent urban elements mentioned above – from water and topography to trade and sociocultural structures – further symbolic and religious dimensions. In the multiplicity that emerged from this concatenation, each factor which was influential in shaping the city constituted a distinctive framework of urban relations, and each was dependent on the element's diverse meanings and functions in daily urban life, which determined how the city might embrace and interact with it. To highlight this characteristic, I use the term *niẓām* (versus *naẓm*). *Niẓām*, in both Arabic and Persian, points to a kind of logic, perhaps better described as a character, attitude or linking element.[44] It is cognate word of *naẓm*, which refers to regularity and order and is manifested in regular, geometric patterns such as those characterising Islamic ornamentation; *niẓām*, on the other hand, connotes a kind of hidden order that does not necessarily produce a regular, geometric pattern. In other words, *naẓm* always has *niẓām* but *niẓām* does not necessarily present *naẓm*. *Niẓām* indicates a framework which connects the elements of a complex whole to each other. It has a sense of logic, but not necessarily a clearly determined regular order on the surface. Each factor that impacts on the urban form enters the framework of the city as *nīẓām*, which is, in fact, the framework determined by that factor's many-layered relationship to the local life-world.[45]

In premodern Isfahan, for instance, the river and water canals impacted on the form and functional-spatial structure of the city at different scales, ranging from architectural to city-wide. Isfahan's water was provided by a river passing to the south of the city called Zāyandihrūd ('life-giving river'), in addition to its qanat system. It is believed that Isfahan, founded on the Zāyandihrūd, endured over the centuries due to this natural source, and indeed, owes its life to it.[46] The river had a key part in determining more than just the location of the city, defining city axes and (southern) edges;[47] it also created a physical barrier between minority neighbourhoods and the city,[48] forming a natural boundary in the religious segregation of residential quarters whereby religious minorities were located on its southern shore. For instance, Julfā, a Christian neighbourhood, was located south of the river, while the centre of the city was to the north. The river's water was disseminated throughout the city through a wide system of canals. From the eleventh to the fourteenth centuries, the Saljuqid era, the canals (*mādī*) derived from the river were expanded but they were not brought into the city until the seventeenth century, the Safavid era, when the network of water canals became part of the urban infrastructure and one of the elements of urban organisation.[49] In this new system, a second group of smaller canals (*jadval*) branched from the main *mādī*s, and runnels (*jūy*) forked from the *jadval*s, which were used for household purposes.[50] Access to water and its distribution throughout the city was regulated on the basis of special rights (*ikhtiṣāṣ*), joint rights (*ishtirāk*) and rights by rotation (*tanāvub*), and each of these was divided according to three further principles: by city districts, by streams and by villages.[51] The person controlling this system (*mīrāb*) appointed supervisors (*mādīsālār*) of the irrigation canals, to keep them clean and to ensure water was conducted to all of Isfahan's neighbourhoods according to the rights and shares in it, preventing, for example, the powerful from trespassing on the weak in this regard. If any conflict arose between the landowners and the commoners of a district over water shares (*imtīyāz* and *takhsīs*), the *mīrāb* was responsible for proceeding with investigations and settling disputes. In every case he had to seek the confirmation and approval of higher authorities (*vazīr*, *kalāntar* and *mustufī*).[52]

Fez, too, had rich water resources, besides being located at the intersection of important regional trade routes.[53] In addition to wells inside the city walls, the water of the Middle Atlas Mountains constitutes an immense subterranean reservoir for Fez, which emerges as multiple springs that combine to form rivers with significant roles in the life and growth of the city.[54] The abundance of water has led to the construction of major systems of canalization in Fez since its earliest days. Basins, tanks, water jets, rooms for ablution and fountains, whose presence was regularly noted by contemporaries and historians, were spread throughout the city. These facilities equipped private or public architectural spaces with running water, yet, despite its ready availability, its distribution among houses and public buildings was strictly regulated by the *muhtasib*, and maintenance of its supply systems was controlled by experts. As Ferhat notes, there is a rich vocabulary in this field in the Moroccan language. The symbolic significance of water is further reflected in the fact that key persons and patrons of the city endowed the quarters, the alleys and public buildings with fountains which were not simply designed to provide water, but were also architectural masterpieces faced with colourful ceramics decorated with geometric designs.[55]

At another urban scale the water network system impacted on the emergence and distribution of certain spaces across the city, such as ice or water reservoirs which, along with mosques or schools, were most often located on the main watercourses (figure 4.1).[56] This impact on functional distribution subsequently had effects on the development of semi-cores like neighbourhood centres. The pattern of canals also accorded, in some parts, with the main routes, city walls, and boundaries between neighbourhoods. At the architectural level, the aesthetic aspects of the presence of water in urban settings have been widely discussed. In most Islamic cities, the flow of water was celebrated in a sophisticated way through the many types of fountains, channels, ramps and pools. Bianca notes that water is displayed in a subtle and intimate manner through the 'soft bubbling of a spring in a pool, the rhythmical trickling of an overflowing basin, or the silver-like veil of water coating the stone surface.'[57] Islam, always enamoured of water, made

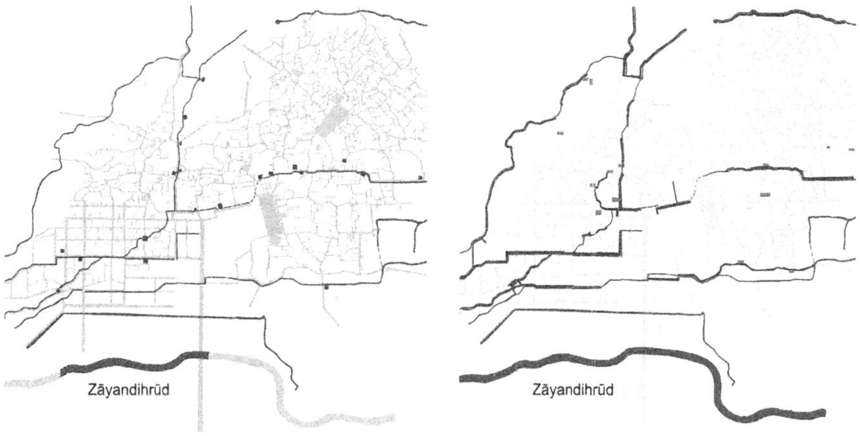

Figure 4.1 The distribution of mosques or schools (left) and some main routes (right) along the water network system

Note: The base map is modified from the Dārulsalṭanih-yi Isfahan map.

playful use of bridges, and deployed them in the cityscape as something to enjoy aesthetically, thus exploiting water's picturesque aspects.[58]

Trade constituted another *niẓām* in the city. A vital component in Islamic cities, and playing a leading role in their establishment and development,[59] the embodiment of the presence of trade and commerce was the bazaar and all related spaces throughout a city. Islamic rules for trade as well as social norms governing commercial professions and their location (*ᶜurf*s) were practiced in the commercial spaces of the city, while the form of the bazaar was adapted to climatic conditions, as well as pre-existing routes and connections between cities. The structure of the commercial space influenced the nature of the city, both in its parts and as a whole, by foregrounding specific pathways as important routes for trade, shaping the centre of the city and influencing the situation of the micro-cores (neighbourhood centres) and subsequently city divisions. In Isfahan the structure and the function – which interacted with, and mutually shaped each other – of the commercial space changed over time, evolving from an open market in the early eighth century to an extensive linear structure in the seventeenth and eighteenth centuries (the Safavid era).

In sum, the materiality and meaning of the urban character and space in the region's cities is the result, of and formed by, the interaction of *niẓām*s – and more precisely, by the simultaneous presence of multiple *niẓām*s, none of which was notably dominant.[60] Cities not only had to facilitate the operations of trade and commerce, but also had to take into account religious requirements, cultural values such as privacy, and the segregation of different ethnicities and professions; meanwhile, practical response to climatic and ecological issues was also required, which, because of the heat and aridity, necessitated special solutions. Consequently, all the *niẓām*s played significant roles in urban development, and none was so dominant as to overshadow all others and impress its framework on the whole.

Based on the assumptions discussed here, in the next chapter, I describe urban space along the case study routes in Fez, Isfahan and Tunis with a particular focus on borders, thresholds and boundaries. Prior to this exploration, however, a brief history of the evolution of the three cities will be presented to outline the backbone and structure of the urban fabric in their historic cores, and the diverse angles and dimensions of the study. These are different in each city: for example, while in Fez I elaborate largely on the sociospatial aspects of alleys and neighbourhoods, in Isfahan I expand on the interior space of a mosque and the phenomenological characteristics of the bazaar, while in Tunis, I explain the juxtaposition of elements that belong to diverse historical periods and the tendency towards exteriority that emerged in the Ottoman period.

Fez

The historic core of Fez has been one of main referents for studies of the Islamic city since the early twentieth century. With different parts developed in accordance with particular historic periods and events, the city is an agglomeration of diverse elements. A visible difference in its sociospatial structures and evolutionary periods has led to the emergence of two major urban sectors: those in keeping with modern developments during and since the twentieth century, such as Ville Nouvelle; and the historic areas dating back to the tenth century that were gradually constructed in the character of the typical Islamic city and present two principal cores, Fez al-Bālī and Fez al-Jdīd. The old sector of the city has been interpreted as an 'urban duality that has its own melody,'[61] while the modern sector is seen as comprising 'heterogeneous components.'[62]

The focus of this section lies on the historic fabric of Fez, more precisely the core of the Fez al-Bālī, the oldest part, which represents a typical Islamic city – even being regarded as a 'model Islamic city'[63] – which I refer to as 'the medina', as it is called locally. The planning and building that define the medina took place primarily from the eleventh through the fourteenth centuries and has been largely preserved, particularly since efforts by UNESCO to protect Fez's cultural heritage began in 1972 and culminated in the master plan of 1978.[64] The medina covers an area of approximately three by two kilometers and is marked by a number of key urban elements, including the al-Qarāwīn mosque, the Mūlāy Īdrīs sanctuary (*zāwīya*)[65] and a specialty market (*qiysarīyya*), which shape the medina's core, and two main public arteries which connect the core to one of the gates. A large number of madrasas, residential houses and sanctuaries are dispersed across the city, also constituting the dominant cityscape of the medina, which, it is believed, has preserved its medieval configuration.[66]

A history of urban evolution

Located in a shallow valley at the crossroads of trade routes, and the fertile receptor of natural watercourses, Fez, according to common account, was founded at the turn of the ninth century under the Īdrīsīds dynasty.[67] In 789 AD Idris I (Īdrīs bin Abdallāh) began to build a city on the eastern shore of Fez's principal river, which he named Madīnat Fās. About twenty years later, his son, Īdrīs II, founded a second settlement on the western bank, named al-ᶜĀlīya.[68] The population of Fez at that time probably consisted of three groups: Arabs associated with the Īdrīsīd family, Berbers of the region and Jews. Between 818 and 825, large migrations of people from Andalusia and Kairouan also moved to the area: the Andalusians settled in the eastern-bank city, named the Andalusian Bank; the people from Kairouan settled in the western-bank city, or Kairouanian Bank. In the middle of the ninth century, an important mosque was built on each of the banks to replace the primitive sanctuaries: the Kairouanian (Jāmiᶜ al-Qarāwīn) and the Andalusian (Jāmiᶜ al-Andalus) mosques.[69] The al-Qarāwīn served as the Friday mosque for the western side, and is believed to have accommodated mainly Arabs, while the Andalusian mosque filled the role on the eastern side which was mainly populated by Berbers. The cores of the twin cities, each with its own city wall, were separated by the river. No archaeological evidence remains of their layout, but there is evidence that the two mosques and their minarets, still called the al-Qarāwīn and Andalusian mosques, date back to the Īdrīsīd age.[70] Up until the eleventh century the two settlements existed beside each other in a state of duality and rivalry. They attained urban status only very gradually, and there can have been few monuments built during this period.[71]

Fez, as a united single city, like most of cities at the western end of Mediterranean basin in North Africa, was built after the rise of Islam in the seventh century, meaning that the influence of Islamic laws contributed to the unique development of its urban space.[72] In the eleventh century the al-Murāvīds seized the city, ran a single wall around both the east and west cores, established a unified city and provided it with economic and religious impetus.[73] This marked the start of a very important stage in the history of Fez when it bloomed as centre of art and culture; consequently, the al-Murāvīd dynasty has been called the 'second founder of Fez.'[74] It is assumed that a citadel was built in the place of today's Būjlūd kasbah (citadel) and, subsequently, the main line of development of the core of the city defined a connection between the location of the al-Qarāwīn mosque and the citadel that crossed the two main arteries, Ṭālaᶜ Saghīra and Ṭālaᶜ Kabīra, still extant today. The al-Murāvīd, Alī bin Yūsif, destroyed the original mosque apart from its minaret, which still stands, and built a replacement of vast dimensions, sumptuously ornamented by Andalusian artisans. An important fortress, no longer standing, was also built on the west bank, stimulating the growth of new quarters in that direction, while during the period, the eastern bank held a secondary position, accommodating less important trade and crafts.[75] Fez had one of its most prosperous periods under the al-Murāvīds, which lasted for almost three-quarters of a century.[76]

Almost a century later, the al-Muvaḥidūn dynasty, Berbers from the High Atlas, overthrew the al-Murāvīds in Marrakesh but Fez remained an 'important commercial, administrative, and military city.'[77] Between the twelfth and thirteenth centuries a new city wall with eight gates was built which has survived until today. Wirth believes we can draw some assumptions about the layout, structure and spatial arrangements of the city from this age: its centre consisted of the al-Qarāwīn mosque and the market area, including the specialty market (*qiysarīyya*) and suqs. The secondary eastern city core, containing the Andalusian mosque, was linked to the western side by a number of bridges and the two centres, together with the eight city gates in the west, north and southeast, were connected in a star-shaped pattern by alleyways. The fortress was destroyed and again reconstructed, while empty spaces, gardens and orchards once existed within the enclosure of the settlement. Apart from the latter, the medina of Fez has retained these proportions until the present time.[78]

From the mid-thirteenth until the sixteenth century the al-Mārīuns kept Fez as the capital of Morocco.[79] They built the new palace city of Fez al-Jdīd in 1276, although the religious and commercial centre of the city still centred on the al-Qarāwīyīn mosque and the specialty market (*qiysarīyya*). The grave of Mulāy Īdrīs was rediscovered in the vicinity of al-Qarāwīyīn and became a place of pilgrimage.[80] In this period, the area within the boundaries marked by the al-Muvaḥidūns' walls was gradually filled with numerous madrasas, mosques and other urban facilities.[81] The madrasas included: Ṣaffārīn (1321), Sbāyīn (1323), ᶜAṭṭārīn (1346), Miṣbāhīyya (1346) and Bū ᶜAnānyyia, Fez's largest madrasa, which was built at some unspecified date after 1351 by Abū ᶜAnan.[82] The urban culture of Fez experienced the summit of its flowering under the al-Mārīuns, and its position was enhanced as a major commercial centre at the junction of important trade routes.[83] After 1492, with the fall of Granada, Fez absorbed another wave of refugees who brought with them Andalusian traditions which were absorbed into the life of the city.[84]

The new royal and administrative town built by the al-Mārīun dynasty in the thirteenth century, Fez al-Jdīd, mainly consisted of the palace, various administrative buildings, a great mosque, a number of sanctuaries and barracks, and the homes of important al-Mārīun dignitaries. This part of the town was surrounded by a double city wall with a few gates.[85] In the al-Mārīun period Fez was divided into a number of neighbourhoods – for instance, in the fifteenth century, a Jewish quarter was established in Fez al-Jdīd – yet the details of this division are not precisely known. Le Tourneau writes:

> It may be inferred, however, that it was probably not very different from that existing in the nineteenth century: at that time the old city was divided into eighteen quarters, twelve on the Qarāwīnian [Kairouanian] bank, six on the Andalusian . . . the important fact is that the quarters existed, whatever may have been their number and boundaries in the Marinide [al-Mārīun] period.[86]

From the fourteenth century beautiful houses were erected both in Fez al-Bālī and Fez al-Jdīd. The floors and facades of their courtyards, like the madrasas, were decorated with colourful mosaics, plaster and carved wood. Bosworth notes:

> The same decorative style prevailed in sanctuaries, palaces and rich homes. The masonry, also very homogenous in style, is less beautiful but almost as delicate as the ornament . . . Cedar wood plays a large part in all the architecture of Fez . . . This wide use of wood, the frequency of pillars and the rarety [*sic*] of columns, are the only characteristics which distinguish the Marīnid [al-Mārīun] monuments from contemporary . . . buildings.[87]

Le Tourneau describes the al-Mārīun Palace in Fez al-Jdīd as a structure of great elegance:

> The furnishings consisted of mattresses covered with rich materials, thick-pile Berber carpets, and a few pieces of simply carved wooden furniture. The reception rooms opened on courtyards enclosed on all sides; these were floored with little paving stones of painted faïence, interspersed with beds of flowers and fruit trees. In at least some of these courtyards a fountain fell back into a pool gracefully placed in the center.[88]

After a century of life under the Saᶜdī dynasty in the sixteenth century, the ᶜAlawīd dynasty, under Mūlāy al-Rashīd, took power in the city in 1666 and kept it until 1912.[89] Under the ᶜAlawīds further mosques, madrasas and sanctuaries were added to Fez's fabric, although the centuries following al-Mārīun prosperity did not leave any special traces in the cityscape and the urban structure of the medina' the imprints that date back to the Middle Ages remain intact, in fact.[90] Even though most of the houses of Fez date from the ᶜAlawīd period, they continued to be built in the al-Mārīun tradition.[91] In the second half of the nineteenth century, another period of active construction began. However, this time the construction did not include religious buildings – madrasas and mosques – but rather private residential buildings and courtyard architecture. The area between the two medinas, Fez al-Bālī and Fez al-Jdīd, began to fill with princely gardens and pavilions and two palaces, Dār al-Baṭḥā and Dār al-Biyḍā, were constructed in the western part of Fez al-Bālī.[92] It is during this period that the merchants of Fez began to make contact with European and African markets and the city gradually engaged in international trade, introducing a new era of development.[93]

After years of unrest and disturbed conditions in the nineteenth century, Morocco and France signed a contract in the palace of Būjlūd in 1912, establishing Morocco as a protectorate of France. This marked the start of constructing a new, European town called the Ville Nouvelle.[94] The strategy of urban development and planning between 1912 and 1945 was to keep the old medina and the new European sector separate, preserving the Moroccan heritage while founding European quarters based on modern urban planning agendas. In the course of this project, the principle of isolating the medina and forbidding any new construction in and around it was encouraged and adhered to.[95]

A change of population took place in the medina during the twentieth century. Rural immigrants replaced previous residents, leading to a high degree of densification during which the built environment, including residential houses and urban spaces like madrasas, began a process of physical decline. The social fabric also changed considerably; the new population had a different life-world.[96] After independence in 1957 the problem of densification and the lack of residential space and accommodation became a major focus point in urban development strategies for the medina. In the 1970s and 1990s different aspects of the city were studied, mapped and documented, mainly under the auspices of UNESCO,[97] which principally focused on the material culture of the city rather than the daily life and life-worlds of residents.[98] In 1980 UNESCO decided that the medina of Fez should be rescued from its decline and be restored, and in 1981 it was listed as a World Heritage site.

The urban *intra muros* of Fez had long had open spaces – including cemeteries, gardens, meadows and groves – still present to a large extent at the beginning of the era as a French protectorate in 1912,[99] but during the twentieth century a large portion of the green belt was progressively built upon. In the 1960s and 1970s four to five-storey apartment blocks were constructed without providing compensatory open space in the form of interior courtyards.[100] The result is that today the urban structure of Fez consists of four main centres: (a) the medina, Fez al-Bālī, which dates back to the eighth century; (b) Fez al-Jdīd which itself is divided into three parts: the Muslim town, the Jewish quarter of Mellah and the palace; (c) the Ville Nouvelle, founded in 1916 by a French resident-general; and (d) new developments to the northwest of the palace which were developed based on modern planning standards.[101]

The tour

The route I have chosen in order to explore Fez presents the main characteristics of its urban space, casting light on how boundaries are delineated and expressed and the social practices which are associated with *dirb*s[102] of different characteristics: some exclusively residential (like al-Shurafā and Bin Zīān) and some offering a complex of diverse functions (like Sīdī Muḥammad al-Ḥāj and Sīāj). The locations along the route are shown in Figure 4.2 It starts from Sīdī Muḥammad al-Ḥāj at Ṭala[c] Ṣaghīra and ends in the Shāwī *dirb*, with a reference to Saba[c] Lūyāt *dirb* to the east of the al-Qarāwīyīn mosque (figure 4.2).

Sīdī Muḥammad al-Ḥāj is one of the numerous pathways diverging from the main route of Ṭāla[c] Ṣaghīra.[103] Located in one of the oldest neighbourhoods of the Fez medina, Sīdī Ṣāfī, it is situated almost midway between the al-Qarāwīyīn mosque at the centre of the medina and the Bujlūd gate (Bāb Būjlūd) at the medina's westernmost side. Sīdī Muḥammad al-Ḥāj is the name of the sage who founded one of the *zāwīya*s of the alley.[104] The transition from the main, mostly commercial route, Ṭāla[c] Ṣaghīra, to Sīdī Muhammad al-Ḥāj occurs via a narrow path lined by shops. Currently most of these have modern functions but among them there is a small grocery (*ḥānūt*) and a an oven to cook domestically prepared doughs (*farrān*), which are traditional features of urban life that have survived into the present. This short transitional space brings one onto a pathway which widens slightly

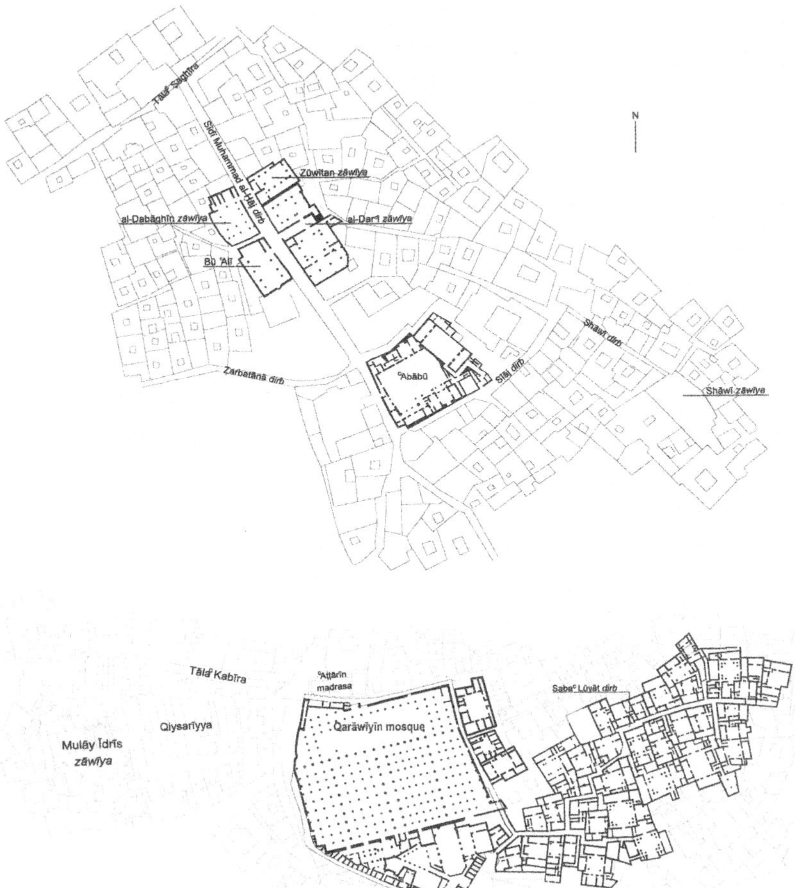

Figure 4.2 Urban fabric on the walking routes, Fez al-Bālī (2015). Above: Sīdī Muḥammad al-Ḥāj, Sīāj and Shāwī *dirbs*. Below: Saba^c Lūyāt *dirb*

Note: Based on my on-site observations with basic data adopted from *Urban Form in the Arab World* (Bianca, 2000), the digital map of medina of Fez (L'Agence pour le Développement et la Réhabilitation de la ville de Fès [ADER-Fez], accessed 2015) and Schéma Directeur D'urbanisme de La Ville de Fès (Royaume du Maroc, 1980).

and immediately changes its visual character, as if announcing the beginning of a new type of space: the garish colours of the retail outlets segue into a comparative monochrome in which cream is dominant; the number of people decreases; and the bustle of buying and selling is swapped for children playing amongst small gatherings of women. The change in sensual perception blurrily marks the crossing of a boundary or virtual delineation and entrance into a new type of urban space – the *dirb* of Sīdī Muḥammad al-Ḥāj. People may perceive different perimeters for the area – as interviews with residents demonstrate – but, while the boundaries are blurred, its core is understood to be shaped by all the houses, *dirb*s and religious buildings which have access to or from the pathway, that is, whose doors open onto the passage of Sīdī Muḥammad al-Ḥāj.

While still among the shops, two alleys branch off from the route: the path on the left leads to a medium-sized house through a short, roofed corridor onto which the door of another house also opens; this is a transitional space which belongs to neither house. Passing through this buffer, one negotiates the boundary space of the second house's gate area before entering its central space, the courtyard; then there are a few corners before the inside of the house is finally reached: the typical typology of an average medina house.[105] The courtyard constitutes a key space in the urban fabric of the medina in which multiple layers of interiority and exteriority overlap, and where people practice exteriority and interiority simultaneously. As there is visual access to the central space through the windows of adjacent rooms, the courtyard functions as the exterior for the interior of the house, although the inside of the rooms around the courtyard are not visually exposed to the void due to the height of the windows and their ornamentation. The courtyard facades are, in fact, the facades of the building as a whole, although only visible after one has actually entered the building. In the space of the courtyard, the family members experience exteriority within the family environment, since it is in this space that they gather, spend their daylight hours, receive their guests and do some of the kitchen work – simultaneously practicing interiority, as the space is closed to uninvited outsiders.[106]

The *dirb* on the right side, al-Shurafā, is approximately three meters wide and separated from the alley of Sīdī Muḥammad al-Ḥāj by a lintel, previously a gate, which marks where the *dirb* begins.[107] There is also an arched roof (*sābāṭ*) at this point where the spatial character starts to change significantly: the width of the path becomes narrower, the atmosphere dimmer, and passers-by rarer. This accelerates perceptions of the transition from the space of Sīdī Muḥammad al-Ḥāj into the more private and smaller *dirb* of al-Shurafā, and thus the navigation of another sociospatial boundary. Deeper into the *dirb*, its spatio-sensual characteristics consist of sequences of spaces which are defined by curves, bends and turns which transition into each other smoothly and continuously. Each turn constitutes a stage of spatial discovery and a definition of depth en route to the last house of the *dirb*, like opening a series of nested insides beginning from the outer limit of the *dirb* and ending at the cul-de-sac of its core. The core is not materially defined as located at the centre of the area of the *dirb*; rather, it indicates the final sociospatial 'inside' of a *dirb* – which is generally the space within houses.[108]

Back to our route along the alley of Sīdī Muḥammad al-Ḥāj: shortly after al-Shurafā the pathway is framed by a brickwork arch which roofs a lintel that used to have a gate. This element once more marks – and more concretely perhaps than the brief retail stretch with the bread oven – the border and beginning of the area of the *dirb* of Sīdī Muḥammad al-Hāj. Passing under the roofed arch one enters a quieter area of the passage (*zanqa*) lined by a concentration of religious buildings and cemeteries dating back to different periods. The former include four *zāwīyas*: Zūwītan (pre-eighteenth century) and al-Dabāghīn (d.n.); Sīdī Muḥammad al-Ḥāj (1390); the *zāwīya*-mosque of Sīdī Ahmad bin Nāṣir al-Darᶜī (eighteenth century, dated 1717 on the gateway); and the mosque of Bū ᶜAlī (d.n.) (figures 4.3, 4.4).[109] The walls of the *zāwīyas* are plain, like those of the houses, while their double sets of gates are finely ornamented and, rather than facing each other – to allow a view of what lies within – they are 'staggered: one begins where the other ends.[110] The pathway space between the gates is also subdivided by arches, creating further sub-spaces along the way. Neither walls nor gates reveal the functions of the buildings within with names or signage. The Bū ᶜAlī, for instance, is a mosque which is indistinguishable from other three

Figure 4.3 The courtyard, al-Dabāghīn *zāwīya*, Sīdī Muhammad al-Ḥāj *dirb*, Fez al-Bālī (2015)

Figure 4.4 The courtyard, Zūwītan *zāwīya*, Sīdī Muhammad al-Ḥāj *dirb*, Fez al-Bālī (2015)

buildings which are *zāwīya*s. Only the transcriptions from the Quran and the poets worked into the ornamentation of the gates indicate that they are religious places.

The gates providing access to the buildings are transitional links which ritualise the connection between the pathway and inside spaces, while the opening of several in-between spaces or elements into/onto each other takes place in a rather condensed area. Approaching the entrance of each of the four buildings, there is a tiled threshold with several recesses, which creates the first sub-space; this is followed by one or two steps, sometimes along with a stoop (in, for example, al-Darᶜī), which together comprise another sub-space immediately after the door. The ceiling of this sub-space is ornamented to define more concretely that it is a halt point; in al-Darᶜī there is even an arch to close and finish the area. Then one either enters an arcaded space (in, for instance, the *zāwīya*s of Bū ᶜAlī, al-Dabāghīn and Zūwītan), or a staircase space followed by the arcades (in, for example, al-Darᶜī *zāwīya*) (figure 4.5).[111] After the arcades, one passes into the courtyard(s), some steps lower than the arcaded area. Thus the act of entering is ritualised by the fractioning of space – often provided by this addition of steps to create, or control, the different levels of the approach – resulting in a series of elements, each of which constitutes a threshold. Combined, they celebrate the door as the boundary, along with

Figure 4.5 Steps at the entrance of al-Dar^c^ī *zāwīya* – view from interior, Sīdī Muhammad al-Ḥāj *dirb*, Fez al-Bālī (2015)

the very act of entering a space – or, more precisely, moving from one space to the other, that is, traversing spaces. Articulating the space of the pathway to the space of the entrances (and their rituals) highlights the paramount roles of both, particularly in comparison with the walls. The ornamentation and the Quranic or poetic calligraphy of the gate façades, along with the different layers of apsis, niches and recesses circumscribing the threshold of the entrance, constitute its transitory space. The assemblage of these elements portrays a spatial incident within the walls of the pathway which signalises the celebration of the act of 'entering into' the space located behind the walls. The entrance sub-spaces here are in fact in-between spaces where both outside and inside, mundane and sacred, as well as interior and exterior, coincide and coexist.

Inside each of these four buildings – al-Darᶜī, Bū ᶜAlī, al-Dabāghīn, Zūwītan – there are several visual layers. The arcades, for example, create a visual layer around the courtyard, partially blocking the view into the interior walls of the core space while still providing some limited glimpses. As in the medina houses, such devices produce the effect of layers behind – or upon – layers. There are also diverse symbolic signs: names on graves, for instance, carry history and meaning, indicating religiously or spiritually respectful persons among a group of people (a Sufi order or brotherhood). The geometric ornaments, as always, have their own significance, infusing meaning and ideology into a given space. At the same time, multiple spatial interiors are constituted by several rooms, sub-spaces, apsis, niches and recesses, as is typical in this kind of typology and which is repeated all over the medina.

Between the al-Dabāghīn *zāwīya* and the Bū ᶜAlī mosque on the passage of Sīdī Muḥammad al-Ḥāj, there is another opening to a *dirb* called Bin Zīān. The boundary is marked by an arched lintel, also once a gate, and like the previous *dirb*s, narrower and darker with fewer people. In some *dirb*s the dress code can also be a signifier of delineations in the practice of space.[112] After the religious buildings, there are two cemeteries, one on either side of the passage; one belongs to the al-ᶜAmrānī family and the other to the family of Sīdī ᶜAlāl al-Baqalī. The cemeteries have lower walls than the religious buildings and the tops of a number of green trees are visible from the pathway.

The next incident along the way is the appearance of a new name, Zarbaṭānā, depicted on a fountain (*saqā*) that marks a new spatial boundary and associated with the alley in front of it. There is an oral story among the locals that the people from the Zarbaṭānā alley endowed the fountain, which is set in an alcove carved out of the wall. It is not the wall, the material, however, that makes the fountain sculpture-like, but rather the creation of negative space in the carved-out wall. Thus the fountain is the void in the wall, both spatially and visually. By taking the Zarbaṭānā pathway, one enters a new sociospatial area and also a different historical realm.

Meanwhile, after the fountain, the Sīdī Muḥammad al-Ḥāj *dirb* seems to be preparing to come to an end. Here there is a transitionary space in which all sides coexist and intersect: the Sīdī Muḥammad al-Ḥāj *dirb*, the Sīdī Muḥammad al-Ḥāj *zāwīya*, the Zarbaṭānā fountain (*saqā*), the Zarbaṭānā *dirb* and an open area in the passage (*sāḥa*). That the elements are named constitutes a virtual containment of the zones, introducing and attaching associations to the various spaces, and thereby creating nodes of relationships. The virtual boundaries are reinforced sensually by the changes that take place in the space, particularly the arched roof that covers a part of the passage and ends in an open area (*sāḥa*), which meanwhile frames and adds signification to the path under, or entrance into, the roofed passage (*sābāṭ*).

On both sides of the passage, a number of plainly decorated doors open into the roofed space (*sābāṭ*), which belongs to the large bourgeois house of ᶜAbābū, built in the nineteenth century and influenced by imported architectural elements. For example, inside the house there are elements such as decorative wrought iron balconies; the proportions of the ornamentation around the courtyard are asymmetrical; the entrance has fewer bends and there are some small windows overhanging the outside (with sight obstructions). However, the general spatial concept, in which a core void space (here the courtyard) arranges and collects all other spaces of the house around it, is still the dominant logic within the house. There are in fact two courtyards each, with a number of balconies and rooms lining and facing onto them.

At this opening in the passage (*sāḥa*), four roads intersect: Sīdī Muḥammad al-Ḥāj; Wād Ṣarrāfīn, which local residents believe to have received its name from a canal; the ᶜAqba Sabāᶜ; and the Sīāj, which continues until reaching al-Rum *dirb*. At the corner of the intersection stands the Bū ᶜAlī mosque, with two doors each facing the convergence of the two roads. The entrance to the mosque from both gates shapes intermediary spaces in the change-over from the passage to the mosque. Like the four religious buildings already discussed, these spaces are constituted and differentiated by a number of steps and a sub-space immediately after the door marked by a dome. At the beginning of the Sīāj alley, a gate with a door in it announces the entrance into the 'area' of the Shāwī *zāwīya*, although it is still quite a long way from this point to the actual *zāwīya*;[113] it appears that the importance and precedence of the *zāwīya* justifies this early notification (figure 4.6). Here, the naming – comprising a written text celebrated and emphasised with a gate and an ornamented arch – constitutes another sphere in the urban space that encircles and is impacted by the existence of the Shāwī *zāwīya*. After this point we are in the domain or vicinity of Shāwī, which creates a vast virtual containment zone centred on the *zāwīya*. Meanwhile, the ornamentation and structure of the gate manifests the direction of entrance and exit: ornamented on one side and pale on the other, it indicates entrance and departure in the movement between Sīdī Muḥammad al-Ḥāj and the Sīāj. Thus, not only is it a marker that one has entered the sacred, spiritual zone of Shāwī; it also punctuates entrance into the Sīāj area.

Figure 4.6 The gateway and sign that mark the beginning of the Shāwī zone and Sīāj *dirb*. Left: shows the side of the gateway when entering the Sīāj alley from the Sīdī Muhammad al-Ḥāj passage; right: the sign and the other side of the gateway, Fez al-Bālī (2015)

After the gate the *dirb* of Sīāj begins. As one continues along the way, different combinations and sequences of spaces, elements and events that resemble those already passed continue to emerge: the walls are plain, with gates their only features; few windows are visible; and a further *dirb* – a short, nameless cul-de-sac – with its own gate branches off from the Sīāj alley (Sīāj *zanqa*). After that *dirb* one encounters a roofed passage (*sābāṭ*) with the Sīāj fountain (*saqā*), under it which again draws one's attention to being in the Sīāj *dirb*. The Shāwī *dirb* starts with a narrow, dark, sloping alley, gated by a door, which is roofed in many parts by *sābāṭ*s; the alley rises until the Shāwī *zāwīya* at the corner and then goes down into another *dirb*. On the way, different smaller culs-de-sacs branch off it to enter further residential *dirb*s, each with its own exclusive characteristics (figure 4.7).

Figure 4.7 Shāwī *dirb*, a residential alley, Fez al-Bālī (2015)

These features can best be seen in an old, exclusively residential *dirb* in Fez medina, Saba^c Lūyāt, located at the southeastern corner of the al-Qarāwīyīn mosque. Saba^c Lūyāt literally means 'seven bends', a name residents believe stems from the seven turns in the *dirb*. This *dirb* is a large residential cluster, with many historically important houses, which is accessed from the pathway that surrounds the al-Qarāwīyīn mosque, a busy route in the city. The beginning of the *dirb* was once functionally marked by a gate of which now only a lintel remains. The threshold to the *dirb* is, once again, made apparent by the sudden change in the phenomenological characteristics of the space: it is significantly dimmer and quieter, consequently appearing more mysterious than the busy thoroughfare beyond it. Its space is characterised by a number of bends, roofed passages (*sābāṭs*), variations in light and shade and the numerous house doors that open onto it. Each turn in the *dirb* blocks the view and thus frames each section as a sub-space of the pathway, thereby constituting a series of visual layers which are traversed sequentially, as if positioned one behind the other. The entrances to the diverse residences of the *dirb* connect its space to that of the houses whose typologies principally date from the fourteenth century, although they have been modified to some extent in that time.[114]

Isfahan

Although surrounded by new developments and modern urban growth, Isfahan's central historic core, which largely evolved and developed during the Islamic period, is considered an important case study in Islamic city research. The third largest city in Iran, Isfahan is located halfway between the Caspian Sea and the Persian Gulf – approximately 340 km south of Tehran – in desert and semi-desert terrain, with a water supply sufficient for agriculture and urban growth provided by the Zāyandihrūd river. Its historic core has two centres: the old and the 'new'. The old, located in the northeast, took shape in the era before the rule of the Safavid dynasty, while the newer section developed mainly under the Safavids, from 1501 to 1736. Together, they have been described as a vital representative of an Iranian-Islamic city,[115] as 'the quintessence of Iran'[116] and as a 'typical premodern Iranian city'.[117] Habibi likewise notes that old Isfahan, as 'the ideal, typical Iranian traditional city,' excellently reflects the ancient life-world.[118] Furthermore, there is a common belief among scholars that the principal foundations of Persian architecture and urban planning, studied under the rubric of the 'Isfahan Urbanism School', flourished and took shape in Safavid Isfahan; at the same time, in a tendency referred to as the 'Divine Isfahan School', philosophy and mysticism also flowered.[119] Despite retention of many historic elements, however, the form of the premodern core has been strongly influenced by the street network and other new construction work imposed on the historic fabric after modernisation, during the first decades of the twentieth century.

A history of urban evolution

Although the first documentary records of the district were only provided by historians and geographers who lived in 660 AD, the history of human settlement in the Isfahan region is said to date back to 550–330 BC.[120] According to the seventh-century historians, at that time there were two main settlements, lying about four kilometres apart, in the present-day location of Isfahan: Yahūdīyyih and Jiy.[121] Jiy was a circular settlement divided into four parts by its two principal axes, with four gates whose locations were determined by astronomical consultation.[122] Inspired by Zoroastrianism, the division, which was based on the cardinal directions, was one of the important characteristics of Iranian cities before Islam.[123] According to Blunt, the founding of Jiy was the result of an imperial order, most frequently attributed to Fīrūz who reigned from 459 to 483 BC.[124] Golombek cites the story told by Abū Nuᶜaym, an early Islamic geographer-historian, about the selection of the site for this town:

> The Sassanid king wished to move his capital to a healthier climate and wrote to the Byzantine emperor, asking him to send a capable physician. The physician was asked to tour the realms and find a place where the elements, water, earth, air and fire, were free from blemish. After traveling the length and breadth of the Sassanid kingdom, the physician chose Isfahan and wrote to the king. He found the land so much to his own liking that he asked permission to settle here.[125]

Yahūdīyyih, on the other hand, was the work of a Jewish colony and is supposed to date back to 605–562 BC.[126] It is narrated that a Jewish community settled in Isfahan, as they thought its soil was similar to Jerusalem's.[127] In the eighth century, an Abbasid governor started another settlement in the region between Jiy and Yahūdīyyih, which moved the centre of the area from Jiy to the new location of Khūsīnān.[128] A new mosque, a bazaar and a palace complex were built.[129] Soon after, however, the governor was removed from Isfahan and development of the new urban core was continued by Arabs settled in nearby villages. In 772 they constructed the initial parts of the present-day old Friday Mosque (*Masjid Jāmiᶜ*), which became the most important mosque of the area.[130] Over time Khūsīnān and Yahūdīyyih spread towards each other, and in the eighth century, a combined settlement with a new administration was formed.[131]

Between the eighth and tenth centuries, in common with the other cities of Iran, Isfahan did not face major developments;[132] but in the tenth century Iran achieved political autonomy. The resulting political stability and commercial improvement produced a prosperous period that facilitated the nurturing of various arts, including architecture, throughout the whole of the country; Iranian cities also began to absorb Islamic ideals and principles into their traditional culture. This provided the impetus to steer cultural creativity in a new direction that endured over the following centuries, a synthesis particularly evident in the flourishing of the arts, science, literature and urban development and life.[133] During the tenth century Isfahan was ruled by a powerful Iranian government called the Ālibūyih dynasty (932–1055), under whom a part of the town was encircled by a defensive wall and a citadel built in its southwest quarter; subsequently the area inside the walls was divided into neighbourhoods, mostly reported as four in number, three of which were most commonly referred to as Jūbārih, Kārān and Dardasht. Jūbārih is still the name of one of quarters in the northeast of Isfahan corresponding to the ancient settlement of Yahūdīyyih. Kārān occupied the southeast quadrant and Dardasht – incorporating the villages of Yāvān and Chumulān (also known as Sunbulān) – covered the large area of the northwest quadrant and was divided into several sub-districts. The remaining southwest quadrant of the walled city, which later became the Safavid quarter of Duwlat, bore the name Kūshk. It is also listed by historians like Qazvīnī along with Jūbārih, Kārān and Dardasht as one of four original villages that, combined, formed Isfahan. The city gained its initial structure in this era; the four quarters constitute the quadrants of a circle or oval, the centre of which was located on a square just south of the old Friday Mosque.[134] There was an axial street running between Kūshk and Kārān which was a bazaar in the period, and the four main intra-urban axes – converging on the square at one end and terminating in four main gates at the other – were lined for long stretches with shops and workshops, forming the arterial bazaars of the city.[135] Each of the quarters also contained a series of major arteries which radiated from the central point of the city outward toward the gates in the city walls. In the course of extensive building activities taking place in the eleventh century the old maidan became and remained the most important commercial, religious and administrative centre and heart of the city until the sixteenth century.[136]

At the beginning of sixteenth century, during the rise of the Safavid dynasty, Isfahan was rebuilt by the first two Safavid kings, Ismāʿīl (1502–1524) and Ṭahmāsb (1524–1576), who integrated further constructions into the existent plan of Isfahan. Their main concern was the reconstruction and embellishment of the old square around which they constructed five major urban buildings: a madrasa/caravanserai complex, a shrine, a mosque and a further caravanserai.

In the winter of 1597, when the Safavid, ʿAbbās I, established Isfahan as his kingdom's capital, he began strongly encouraging international trade, and merchants seeking trading privileges, along with ambassadors and representatives of foreign monastic orders, came to Isfahan.[137] In consequence, Isfahan gradually reached its highest point of development. According to Ehlers:

> Esfahan's urban growth and economic upswing from 1600 onwards is documented by an impressive sequence of architectural as well as

> industrial/manufactural developments: the construction of the royal quarters, the embellishment of the central square with its mosques, madrasses and caravanserais, the design of Chahar Bagh or of a new bazaar, shops and caravanserais of [*sic*] which were [the] private property of the ruler.[138]

Over a short period of time, the basic concepts of enlargement and reformation of the city were laid out, directing the developments of Isfahan along new paths. ᶜAbbās I decided not to live in the old city and built his court on the southwestern edge of the city as it was in those days.[139] Lockhart notes, ᶜAbbās I 'felt it essential to carry out drastic changes in Isfahan in order to make it a fitting metropolis.'[140] Deciding not to reconstruct the existing city except in minor respects, the main feature of the new scheme involved moving the central square of the city two kilometres to the south and constructing magnificent buildings around it.[141] In the sixteenth century this part of the city, southwest of the walled city, was rather removed from the main urban centre, the old maidan, and largely undeveloped, containing the retreats of urban nobles since the tenth century and the garden palaces of emperors since the eleventh.[142] Yet the north-south axis was the busiest in Isfahan, taking all the traffic to and from the south of Iran, especially Shiraz.[143] Moving the main square of the city from its previous location near the Friday Mosque to its present location at Naqsh-i Jahān is understood by some scholars as an expression of the physical and symbolic separation between the clergy and the ruler.[144]

Safavid constructions, redevelopments and beautifications took place in two major stages between 1598 and 1722: the years between 1598 and 1602 witnessed the construction of some major buildings such as the Naqsh-i Jahān square and the buildings around it, that is, the ᶜĀlī-Qāpū, the Shiykh Luṭfullāh mosque, the Shāh mosque, and the entrance to the royal bazaar (*qiysarīyya*), together with the Chāhārbāgh street and the Allāh Virdī Khān bridge across the river, which formed the skeleton of the new part of the city;[145] fleshing it out took place during the remainder of the seventeenth century. By its end, the imperial bazaar overflowed with workshops, caravanserais, markets, retail shops, mosques and madrasas. Over the century, the population of the city increased, the hinterland villages grew in size and the garden retreats of the emperors and great men reached farther and farther into the suburbs. In about 1722 Isfahan acquired its final form after this slow process of construction and expansion.[146]

The centre of this new capital was Naqsh-i Jahān, one of two key features, along with Chāhārbāgh, of the plan ᶜAbbās I had for Isfahan. Naqsh-i Jahān was a huge multifunctional open space, approximately 507 meters in length and 158 meters in width, which lay to the east of the northern end of Chāhārbāgh and at a slight angle to it. It was surrounded by a uniform portico screen of two storeys with a commercial function.[147] Other uses for the maidan varied from polo and the performance of festivals to the accommodation of entire caravans.[148] Chāhārbāgh was originally designed and built as a garden avenue for the residences of nobles and the wealthy;[149] a paved pathway for pedestrians that contained rows of trees and water channels, it stretched for about two kilometres to the north of the river and three kilometres to the south, ending in the garden of Hizārjarīb.[150] Later, it was flanked by the garden palaces and mansions of princes and grandees which were separated by water runnels and rows of plane trees;[151] some of the pavilions were places of public retreat and used as coffee houses.[152] New residential quarters were also erected: ᶜAbbāsābād, to the west of Chāhārbāgh, for immigrants from the city of Tabriz; and New Julfa to the south of the river.[153]

With the end of the Safavid dynasty in 1722, a depressing vacuum occurred, accompanied by considerable destruction of the city; quarters that had once contained around six hundred thousand inhabitants suddenly became empty, while the remaining population of a hundred thousand continued a meagre life in the urban sectors that had survived.[154] After 1896, during the reign of Muẓaffar al-Dīn, there were various outbreaks of violence in the city as the changes that came with modernity also started to affect Isfahan, along with other Iranian cities; industrialisation, for instance, began in Isfahan in the early decades of the twentieth century with the production of different textiles such as carpets, cotton fabrics and silk. Later, due to its large number of historic monuments, it became a major tourist centre. In 2005, when the city had an estimated population of 2,540,000, it was designated a World Heritage City by UNESCO.[155]

The tour

The route that I have chosen in Isfahan is located behind the Shāh mosque at the southeastern side of the Naqsh-i Jahān square. The route starts from inside the bazaar and ends in a house in Tārīkīhā alley in the Pusht-i Masjid neighbourhood (behind the mosque), traversing the diverse spaces of mosques, neighbourhoods and alleys on its way; furthermore, the urban fabric around the route is one those in the historic centre of Isfahan that has been successfully preserved. The two features – diversity and a good level of preservation – mean that the route offers an appropriate case study for this project (figure 4.8).[156]

The space of the bazaar is publicly accessible while, architecturally, it is an interior (figure 4.9). The shops lining it, its open areas and its roof define and enclose the route, constituting it as an inside void surrounded by diverse spaces. While in the bazaar, one is in a physically enclosed space which is given its character by the linear juxtaposition of a number of spatial cells opening into each other, providing the effect of a series of layers. Each cellular unit is a vaulted space – consisting of two shops on each side of the way, four columns and an arched ceiling – offering the experience of a particular combination of colour, sound, smell and movement. Thus each cell constitutes a spatial containment zone separated from its neighbour by a brief, liminal link. What we see, as our eyes are drawn down the passage

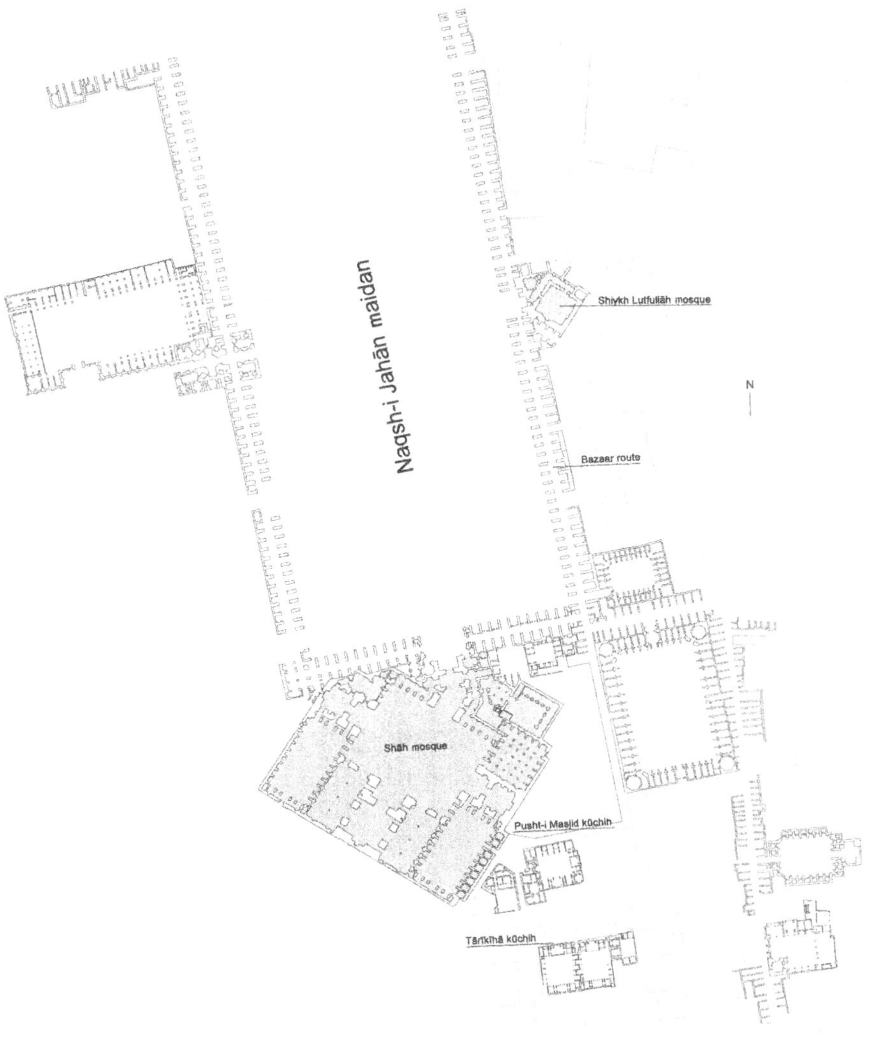

Figure 4.8 Urban fabric on the walking route in Isfahan (2013)

Note: Based on my on-site observations with basic data adopted from documents provided by the Naqsh-i Jahān Pārs Consultation.

of the bazaar, is a string of similar, small, vaulted units, lined consecutively along the route until reaching a fountain of natural light. The repetition of the cells creates a space that is continuous and fluent.

The flow of layers continues at different scales from the overall ambience down to the finer details; for instance, the geometrical patterns of the rugs and

Figure 4.9 The bazaar, Isfahan (2013)

carpets, which are among the main items sold in the bazaar, are made up of the superimposition of various geometrical or flower-shaped lines, which likewise present multiple layers of meaning. Then, at the level of social practices, the bazaar is a constellation of socio-commercial connections which create nodes of relationships that spread throughout it. Different groups of artisans or craftsmen – carpenters, dealers, shoemakers – form groups on the basis of their common occupation that then develop particular rights, practices and relations, constituting them as nodes in the social dimension of the bazaar. Spatially, too, they gather in the same or nearby areas whose boundaries are marked by naming and alterations in sensory aspects like smell, colour and sound. Thus, reflecting its physical qualities, the space of the bazaar also has a non-material layer where nodes of relationships flow from one to the other.

Continuing within the bazaar, the repetition of vaulted sub-spaces takes place in a dimness in which the single incursion of light along the way is visually startling, and promises a different spatial event. Approaching the light source, the contrast between darkness and brightness increases, indicating an access to Naqsh-i Jahān. The square has the typology of a courtyard, though on a larger scale. Surrounded by rows of two-storey shops behind arches, and with a central void, it has the character of an enclosed space. The facades act to divide the inside space of the maidan from the outside space of the surrounding urban fabric – or, more precisely, to protect and beautify its inside space to highlight the contrast with what lies outside. The elements of space emphasise the centre of the maidan, yet this is a void. The central void is not only emphasised; it is also celebrated. Using multiple arches and abstract geometric ornamentation as architectural features to cover the facades of the four interior walls of the maidan obscures the space by obscuring perception, since the geometric patterns do not explicitly transfer knowledge about the function, meaning and urban context of the space. They only implicitly express the principles and values of the society through the ornamental lines and the words of the calligraphy. The simplicity and repetition of the arches and the units of the ornamental element and layer together produce this obscurity, as the information the surface of the space reveals remains limited to a pre-determined extent:

> This repetition and similarity in shape, in both bazaar space and maidan's partition, plays the role of a cover for understanding the space, although the space has been manifested through it. It is something between revealing and, at the same time, concealing a concept. The space, our view . . . is arranged by the layers and in this order we see the similar geometric shapes on different surfaces which frame the sky, the space, and our view.
>
> (Falahat 2014)

The composition gives the walker information only to the extent that he or she can just understand there is something different there, in another part, not so distant from the route, but it is not completely clarified. The result is that the space implies but does not reveal.

Stepping back into the roofed area, the bazaar continues with the same spatial order, the combination of arches, vaulted sub-spaces, and contrasts of darkness and brightness. The sub-sectioning of space by the contrast of darkness with brightness results in its gradation; and then another source of light cuts the repetition of sub-spaces along the bazaar route. Approaching it, an alley branching out of the bazaar appears and leads into the residential section where the spatial atmosphere changes dramatically. This significant alteration in ambience marks the boundary of a neighbourhood or *kūchih*,[157] and the entry into a new social and spatial containment zone. The sounds, smells and vibrant colours of commerce are swapped for the silent monochrome of a residential alley – a different world. The alley is narrow and flanked by tall walls that curve with its turns. Each bend creates a visual layer and the series of bends which must be traversed in turn create the visual structure of layer-on-layer. The turns prevent the walker from seeing,

Figure 4.10 Isfahan (2013)

perceiving or guessing the end of the route, thus making the way unclear and obscure. The walls are plain and high with doorways and occasionally small windows as their only openings. Thus they do not inform the walker of what is happening behind them, which contributes to the creation of an atmosphere of ambiguity and mystery in the space of the alley. This gives rise to questions in the mind of the walker about how and where the route might end and what awaits. On one side of the alley, a blue dome towers above a tall brick wall, suggesting some undisclosed potential or event (figure 4.10).

Returning to the main walking route, namely the bazaar space, and getting closer to its destination, the doorway of the Shiykh Lutfullāh mosque appears. Its portal, with its *muqarnas* and a surface filled with coloured geometric lines, floral ornaments and texts, is a visual contrast along the way.[158] Its highly ornamental surface has a layer-on-layer structure, both visually and conceptually, which is perceivable only consecutively. As Graber states:

> The implication is that the *muqarnas* represents a whole which subsumes an almost infinite number of parts which are visually independent

> of each other. And as one looks at a *muqarnas*, it is possible to begin with the completed form and then lose one's self in an array of different shapes or else to begin with the smallest leaf on one panel and end up with a vision of the full unit.[159]

The multiple combinations of the diverse visual or conceptual layers produce multiple levels on the surface of the portal; these include, for example, the layer of geometric lines, of floral ornaments, of colours, of external lines of *muqarnas* and of words (calligraphy), or, alternatively, a combination of the layer of geometry and that of calligraphy. Each of these has its own pattern, concepts and meaning, and thus develops nodes of conceptual connections and meanings which take the viewer from the two-dimensional field of motifs and colours, to a three-dimensional world of associations and connotations. The patterns symbolise, for example, the verdant lushness and ideality of paradise through the flower motifs and the blueness of the colour. Similarly, the calligraphy – artistically written and tiled Quranic words narrating the original context of the holy text – opens up another layer, leading the individual into a spiritual realm. Here, attention not only moves over the lines of the text, but delves into the semantic matrix of words and meanings. Thus the surface of the portal becomes matrices of layers with revealing/concealing associations, a journey of semantics.[160]

Passing through the portal, one enters the space of the mosque with its numerous visual, conceptual and spatial containment zones. An ornamented wall which stands directly beyond the door blocks the view immediately after one steps into the mosque, presenting a sharp contrast to the beguilingly inviting power of the portal. The wall is pierced by an interlaced window, presenting colour and geometry that is significantly different from its background. The contrast with the background and the simplicity of the geometry of its ornamentation in contrast with the detailed ornamentation of the other walls makes the vision-impeding barrier stand out. This time it is the simplicity of the structure and colour that attracts attention. The lattice of the interlaced window frames a view to another space, that of the dome. Despite this small revelation, it remains unclear where the space is, and whether it is a part of our way. It signifies an existence but does not reveal much about it.

The continuation of the way is a corridor with a number of spatial cells, similar to those of the bazaar, consisting of a vault and with walls on either side; these are so full of the lines and colours of ornamentation that that taking them in with a single glance is impossible. At the end of the view, a curve can be seen in the route which is emphasised and illuminated by the invasion of light through the lattice window in the curve. The consecutive position of vaulted sub-spaces, their multilayered ornamentation and the light source constitute multiple visual layers that create a fluidity of view. Tracing the sub-spaces one after the other, the two-dimensional visual layers change to a number of three-dimensional spaces. These cells transform smoothly into each other and thus the space gradually metamorphises while it is walked. Approaching the light source, another space opens up, which also includes consecutive vaulted cells, although with a door at the end. Here the ninety-degree turn is mitigated by the smooth transformation of arches, ornamental lines and figures, and the enlightening of space with a lattice. A large door opens onto the vast domed area at the end of the way. The meanings and significations of the space are alive in the words on the walls, in the sacredness of centrality and unity and in the endeavour by lines to present abstract geometric shapes. Here, the depth of the space is readable and may be experienced, not through physical movement, but through spiritual progress and by penetrating its inner layers. It is the celebration of spiritual multilayered-ness (figure 4.11).

Exiting the mosque and returning to the bazaar lane, the same previous characteristics are revealed: the cellular units which are arranged in a row with occasional glimmers of light which invite the walker to continue along the way, to pass, to discover, to walk through these spatial cells one after the other. This prospect also culminates in a dazzling band of natural light. On the left side of the way, another interruption appears: a brick wall which makes the walker aware of the beginning of a subsidiary road on that side. At the end of the bazaar route, at the intersection of three ways,[161] one enters a residential area orally known as the Pusht-i Masjid (behind the

Figure 4.11 Ornamentation, Shiykh Lutfullāh mosque, Isfahan (2013)

mosque) neighbourhood, and therefore associated with the Shāh mosque. Its boundaries are fuzzy. The alley's spatial features differ from those of the bazaar and there are none of its colourful goods; instead it is surrounded by tall brick walls with small doors in it, but rarely a window. The bazaar is a place of presentation; in marked contrast, the alleys are not, so in the bazaar the space, although roofed, is more open and therefore more easily comprehended. Entering the alley, the colour and flavour of the bazaar once again switches suddenly to monochrome tones. The wall height is relatively uniform, making an unbroken line of shadow along the ground. The first view and perspective of the route is blocked by a tall mud wall curving to the right. To discover the space, one has to follow the alley at least until this curve where a new view opens to be terminated once again by the next curve: a view whose beginning and end is actually two curves. Approaching each curve, even when right upon one, it is impossible to guess what will happen next and what actually lies beyond. Other alleys that branch from this route have similar features: the monotone line on the ground, the same wall height, the rare small windows here and there, the occasional treetops visible above the walls, a space constituted by numerous bends. With each curve the walker gets farther from the bazaar as the centre of the movement, farther from a mental city plan, as the way becomes more obscure. The single colour and similarity of all the walls creates and increases the spatial obscurity.

Each curve can reveal an unexpected discovery. For example, on our way, approaching one of the bends, suddenly an unexpected sight is revealed: a blue dome and an ornamented portal come into view at the end of the alley with its high mud walls. The dome and portal are indicators of the existence of a space behind the walls, though they do not reveal what type of space. They make the walker aware of its presence with two signs – the dome and the portal – yet the building itself remains introverted, hiding what lies inside. The space, therefore, notifies or symbolises but does not reveal. Beside the curves and bends that are constituent elements of the visual layers and spatial cells, there are also other thresholds and boundary-makers in the space of the alley, such as *hashtī*s.[162] In one of these *hashtī*s there are three doors, each of which opens into a house. The *hashtī* is a space with doors within doors and openings within openings.

In front of the portal there is an opening in the space of the alley which is a meeting of ways: Kūchih-yi Masjid (Mosque Alley) follows the wall of the mosque into the public area; a second pathway penetrates the residential sphere more deeply, approaching the semi-private realm of the neighbourhood. It is roofed, meaning that the space is surrounded on four sides by plain monochrome walls without any openings; appropriately, it is called Tārīkīhā (darknesses) alley. At its final curve, where a dim light indicates the continuation of the way, it branches into two routes, piercing the private sphere of the neighbourhood. One is a narrow, blind alley with some house doors on the left-hand side. The silence, the introversion of the buildings and the narrowness of the route make the space feel very private. The second is also an alley and at its first bend a new view opens up; it is roofed for a short distance and then open for another short distance. What can be seen is a tripartite assemblage of darkness, brightness and then darkness again. The atmosphere of the space is particular: the tall mud walls, small high windows, the treetops, the two simple doorways which are signs of the houses behind them and the opening and closing from brightness into darkness and from darkness into brightness (figure 4.12).

Figure 4.12 Tārīkīhā alley, Pusht-i Masjid neighbourhood, Isfahan (2013)

Approaching the last dark area, its space reveals that here there is also a roofed alley with a light source at the end, but it seems as if there is another space in the middle of it. To verify this surmise we must walk through it – as always. At its midpoint it divides into two very narrow, low-roofed alleys: in the one to the right there are two doors, to the left there are four and at the end of each alley is another door. That means that both alleys end in doors, or borders of new realms: houses, the spaces of which encompass many concepts and principles. Entering one of the houses of the *kūchih*, the Najafī house, one has to pass through a *hashtī*, which is a small, roofed, intermediate space between the alley and the two doors inside it which belong to two houses. The Najafī house is a typical, traditional, middle-class Iranian house. One passes through the first door at the alley – the door of *hashtī*; then the second door which is the house door *in* the *hashtī*; and then a long corridor to reach the main courtyard of the house around which the spaces of the house are arranged. The courtyard, as the core of the private life taking place in the house, is reached after traversing multiple, successive thresholds of curves, alleys, doors and corridors. The border-to-the-outside walls – which divide inside from outside – do not have a part in constructing the characteristics of the space of the house. Their irregularity is solved by positioning the less important rooms at the furthest point from the central core.

Tunis

The Tunis medina, located in the centre of a growing modern city sloping down to the Lake of Tunis, is being preserved within an administrational structure of safeguards and relevant management under the National Institute of Patrimony (Institute Nationale du Patrimoine [INP]) and the Association for the Safeguarding of the Medina of Tunis (Association de Sauvegarde de la Médina de Tunis [ASM]). Locals call it the *al-bilād al-ᶜArabī* (the traditional town)[163] and the first time the term 'medina' was used to refer to the older part of Tunis was in 1954 in a new piece of legislation compiled by a group of architects to protect the traditional buildings of the city.[164] The medina is a residential quarter housing approximately one-sixth of the population of Greater Tunis.[165] There was a major change in the population after 1956 (the start of the postcolonial period), when the old residents left the medina and immigrants from outside the city, mainly from rural areas, replaced them; however, the population flow had already begun during France's colonial occupation when the *bildīya* (noble) families became attracted to other areas of the city under the impact of colonial changes.[166] At the time, the medina became an identifying symbol for Tunisian people, a centre for resistance against foreign (French) forces that was seen as an icon for the resistance to colonialism.[167]

The medina's overall structure consists of a central core area with two newer 'suburbs' to the north and south of it; together they constitute the medina of Tunis and contain a large number of historical buildings, at the very centre of which is the Zaytūna mosque surrounded by suqs, hammams and madrasas. Scholars regard the medina of Tunis as 'the best, scientifically researched Arab old town.'[168] There have been a series of proposals for interventions in the medina and its planning and preserving has long been a topic of Tunisian national interest, also attracting the attention of Western countries since the mid-twentieth century. In 1979 the medina of Tunis was one of the first Arab historic city centres to be designated by UNESCO as a World Heritage Site.[169]

A history of urban evolution

There is a common account of the origin of Tunis, according to which the ancient city of Carthage, founded in 814 BC, was the first main settlement in the region of today's city.[170] Carthage created a powerful maritime empire on the west coast of the Mediterranean Sea, which, towards the end of the sixth century BC, extended from Tripolitania to the Atlantic. The settlement became a leading producer and exporter for the Mediterranean region, whose economy relied mainly on the cultivation of cereals, vines, olives and fruit trees. Indeed, the prosperity of Carthage sparked rivalry with Rome which ended in the outbreak of the Punic Wars – three wars fought over a period of nearly 120 years that culminated in the destruction of Carthage in 146 BC. During the Roman era, the city was completely razed to make space for a new urban structure, whereupon it became the principal city of the Roman Empire in the province of Africa.[171] After the fall of Rome the region remained under Byzantine domination until the middle of the seventh century when the Arabs took the control of the area.

The Arab conquerors founded Arabic Tunis during the last years of the seventh century and the early years of the eighth century, at a time when they were also undertaking the development of other cities in Ifriqiya.[172] Al-Marākishī notes that a community of Christians had been settled in the present-day location of the medina of Tunis. After a definitive victory, Hassan Ibn Nuᶜmān decided to build a mosque to replace the Christian sanctuary and medieval Tunis developed from this core.[173] In the ninth century a fortified enclosure was built around the medina and Ibn Nājī reports that the construction of a casbah in the medina dates back to the same time.[174] According to al-Bakrī and Ibn Khaldūn, Tunis was endowed with fortifications during the eleventh century, ensuring its security.[175] Access to the medieval medina was through a number of gates, most of which are indicated in al-Bakrī's book, where he writes that Tunis had five in number: Bāb al-Jazīra; Bāb Qarṭājina, Bāb al-Saqqāīn, Bāb ʾArṭā and Bāb al-Baḥr.[176] Situated at the centre of this first nucleus of the Tunis medina was the al-Zaytūna mosque, a project undertaken by the al-ʾUmawīyya governor, ᶜUbayd Allāh Ibn Habhāb, in 732 AD. Gradually the medina began to be arranged around the mosque: firstly the suqs of the city and then the residential district which extended beyond the nucleus and enveloped it on all sides. Not far from the gates of the medina, places (*fūndūqs)* were built to accommodate travellers and merchants from the hinterland.[177]

According to al-Bakrī, the eleventh-century medina survived until the al-Muvaḥidūn conquest of the twelfth century. From the twelfth century to the sixteenth century, an increase in population was accompanied by urban extension, leading to a diversification of industrial and commercial activities but retaining the old urban structure around the al-Zaytūna Mosque.[178] With the advent of the al-Ḥafṣīyūn kings (1229 to 1574) a number of major new buildings were constructed, enriching the architectural content of the medina. At the beginning of the thirteenth century the al-Ḥafṣīyūn king, Abū Zakarīyā, rebuilt the casbah, and a number of new suqs were added, including the Suq al-Aṭṭārīn (for perfumers) and the Suq al-Qumāsh (for the fabric trade).[179] In addition, several mosques and other buildings with pious purposes were completed during the era; for example, the first madrasa of the medina, the Madrasa Shamāᶜiya, was also built during the thirteenth century by Sultan Abū Zakarīyā.[180] A consequence of medina growth, two important suburbs developed to the north and south of the original nucleus: (a) The northern suburb, al-Suwayqa, was built in the twelfth century and developed mainly under the al-Ḥafṣīyūn when a number of mosques were built including the Abī Muhammed mosque in the street of al-Ḥalfāwīn, erected by Abī Muhammed bin Abī Ḥafṣ (early thirteenth century). At the end of the thirteenth century, the population of the northern suburb was augmented by the many families expelled from Spain by the Christian reconquest who came to settle here.[181,182] (b) The southern suburb, Bāb al-Jazīra, was where people from the hinterland originally resided. In the al-Ḥafṣīyūn period, several structures were erected in its quarters, with the al-Tawfīq and al- Ḥuluq mosques providing exemplars of al-Ḥafṣīyūn work. Subsequently, a second fortification was built, enveloping the casbah, the medina and the two new suburbs, containing six new gates: Bāb al-Khaḍrā, Bāb Abī Saᶜadūn, Bāb al-ᶜUluj, Bāb Khālid, Bāb al-Falla and Bāb ᶜAlīwa.[183]

From the beginning of the sixteenth century, Tunisia under the al-Ḥafṣīyūn was becoming weaker. The fatal blow it suffered with the Ottomans put an end to a dynasty that had lasted a long time in the Maghreb. Ifriqiya, due to its geopolitical position, had aroused the desire of both the Spanish and Turkish empires and the confrontations between the two powers ended with the defeat of the Spaniards, the fall of the al-Ḥafṣīyūns and the final capture of Tunis by the Ottomans in 1574.[184] From this date, Tunis became a province attached to the Ottoman Empire, enjoying an upsurge in commercial activity, restoration of the al-Ḥafṣīyūn heritage, increased expansion of both the medina and the suburbs, and several development projects in the course of which it acquired some beautiful architectural achievements, making a new city of it.[185]

Many urban architectural projects were realized in Tunis between 1591 and 1702, the period of the deys and the beys – by sovereigns as well as important persons under their ruling administration.[186] Throughout the

Ottoman reign, its government did not ceased to promote the commercial and artisanal activity of the new province by building specialized spaces set into in the arteries of the city.[187] The architectural complex built by Yusuf Dey (1610–37), for example, was an unprecedented urban intervention in the medina of Tunis during the first half of the seventeenth century. During his reign, four new suqs were built in the medina: the suq al-Bāshāmqīya which specialized in the making of *bāshmāq*, or Turkish court shoes; the suq al-Bīrka which specialized in the sale of black slaves from Africa; the suq al-Jarābī, held by Djerbian community[188] and specializing in the sale of textile products from the island of Djerba; and the suq al-Turuk (Market of the Turks), specializing in the making of Turkish cloth.[189] During the reign of Ḥammūda Pāshā Bey (1631–1659), a second architectural complex was founded near the first. In the era of Muhammed Bey (1675–1696), the medina of Tunis experienced a second important urban intervention between the casbah and the great al-Zaytūna Mosque, which consisted of the construction of the al-Shāwāshīn complex or the suq of the Shishīās.[190] Situated in a strategic position in the heart of the commercial centre of the medina of Tunis, Muhammed Bey's complex stretched between several complexes built during the first half of the seventeenth century.[191]

After Ḥusayn bin ᶜAli came to power in 1705, both the northern and southern suburbs began to receive more attention; a number of architectural structures were erected by the Ḥusaynid sovereigns, who developed Tunis enormously. The Ḥusaynids built on what they had inherited from their predecessors in the heart of the media, renovating a few existent suqs and adding some new markets; religious architecture in the form of new mosques likewise appeared, especially in suburbs. The founder of the dynasty, Ḥusayn bin ᶜAli, built the first Ḥusaynid mosque in Tunis, locating it in the southern suburb of Bāb al-Jazīra. Commonly called Jāmaᶜ al-Jdīd, it was the main element of the complex built around it, and part of the renovation project aimed at beautifying the suburban district. During the nineteenth century, the medina continued to present the overall structure it had adopted throughout its history. The Ḥusaynid beys, who succeeded each other in Tunis, made the Bardo Palace, a fifteenth-century al-Ḥafṣīyūn palace, their ordinary residence. They did not build further mosques in the medina; rather, it continued to be served by those which had been erected during the preceding eras.

The French established Tunisia as a protectorate in 1881. Thereafter, adjacent to the medina, a second, new, Westernized city called the *ville nouvelle* or *ville européenne* started to evolve; inhabited largely by Europeans, it had a different morphology and style of construction to the medina.[192] Throughout the early twentieth century, the modern city, juxtaposed to the old medina, continued to develop without impacting on the latter's traditional urban forms. Local experts believe that today's medina is in fact the heritage of the Ottoman era, which sketched out its lines. In the years between 1881 and 1956 – the period of the French Protectorate – the built fabric of the medina of Tunis was preserved by heritage conservation plans,[193] although, after independence, major urban changes took place, so that the basis of the old town's economy shifted since the 1960s, and the historic neighbourhoods have received new roles.'[194]

Since 1979, the medina of Tunis has been registered as a world heritage site by UNESCO. It contains seven hundred historically important buildings and benefits from the national protection of five buildings, fourteen streets (plus three suqs) and a square, provided by Law 35–1994 concerning the protection of the archaeological, historical and traditional arts heritage and by urban development plans for the medina of Tunis.

The tour

In Tunis I chose a route starting from Sīdī bin Arūs passage (*nahj*), passing al-Qaṣba, Siyyida ᶜAjūla and Dīwān alleys, and ending in al-Āghā passage. Between the start and finish, we encounter an urban fabric that is mixture of residential, commercial, religious and other public and semi-public spaces (figure 4.13). The public buildings are dispersed throughout the route and there

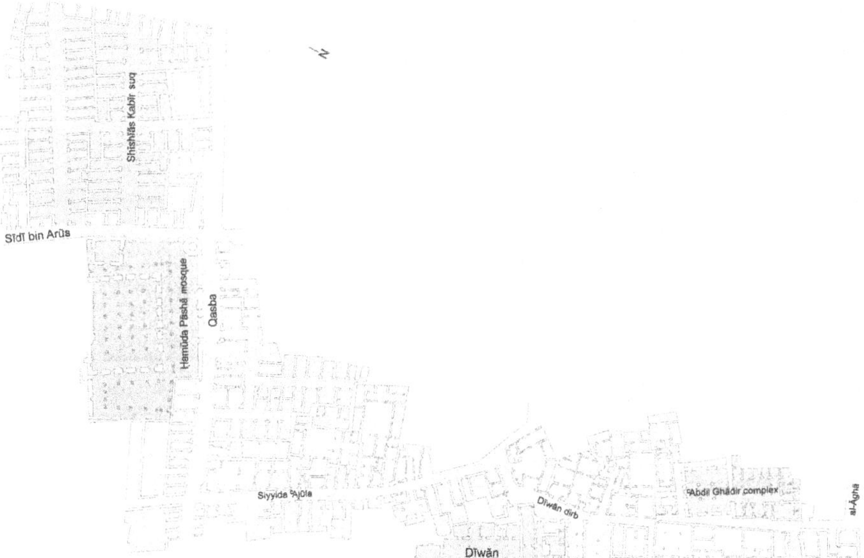

Figure 4.13 Urban fabric on the walking route: Sīdī bin Arūs, Qasba, Siyyida ᶜAjūla and Dīwān *dirb*s, medina of Tunis (2016)

Note: Based on my on-site observations with basic data adopted from documents provided by the Association de Sauvegarde de la Médina de Tunis (ASM).

is a fluid mixture of residential as well as public and semi-public spaces along the passages. These diverse typologies demonstrate how spaces are combined to create the experience of urban space in the city. In general, one can readily perceive that same concepts of edges and boundaries – the main constituent elements of urban space in the medina – are repeated here as appear in Fez and Isfahan. The difference lies in the borders of some public buildings that have a slightly different feature in that they are pushed towards exteriority. The route does not go deeply into the most private sphere of the city, though passages branch off the route that do so. A historical juxtaposition is highly evident, however, as we can see different styles and typologies of buildings and various conceptualizations of walls while walking along the planned way. Thus we experience the overlap or superimposition of containment zones, rather than penetrating deep into the private sphere as was the case in Isfahan and in the course of the Saba^{c} Lūyāt route in Fez.

Our Dīwān walk starts from in front of the Ḥamūda Pāshā mosque (*jāmi*^{c}) on the Sīdī bin Arūs alley, heading roughly north (figure 4.14).[195] At this point on the pathway, the walls of the Ḥamūda Pāshā mosque extend along the route on the walker's right. In contrast to previous experiences of public buildings and monuments in Fez and Isfahan, the walls surrounding and enclosing this building have large windows opening onto the pathway. The typology of the building also has a relatively different pattern. The difference in both cases lies in the fact that here we encounter a tendency towards exteriority, which, however, still cannot overcome the architectural characteristics that promote the physical interiority of the building and of its connection with the rest of the city. There is a mausoleum at the corner of the mosque complex, the resting place of Ḥamūda Pāshā and his family, which has an extrovert typology, with four ornamented walls surrounding and enclosing the inside space. It is a monument of a square plan, covered with a pyramidal roof in green glazed tiles. Its walls are decorated with ottoman texts and poems, arches, columns and blocked windows which are mainly carved out of the solid material; they are not extruded, but rather indented recesses. The windows on the outside walls are at a height that indicates that they are not necessarily aimed at creating transparency and communication between the inside and outside of the building. Their main purpose was probably to make the walls appear monumental, as they do not provide a proper view of the interior from the outside or the exterior from the inside; the technical reason for the obstruction of view, however, is that the ground of the yard of the mosque is higher than the passage. The walls also have decorations beyond the doorways and gates; for example, the windows are framed, and arches as well as columns ornament the walls.[196]

The Ḥamūda Pāshā mosque also deviates from the typical typology in that it does not have a courtyard. There is, however, a colonnaded yard in a corner of the complex (figure 4.15). When entering the mosque, one

Figure 4.14 In front of the Ḥamūda Pāshā mosque, Sīdī bin Arūs alley, medina of Tunis (2016)

Figure 4.15 Dīwān *dirb*, medina of Tunis (2016)

first steps into an intermediary space between the exterior wall and the area for prayer. The latter is the core space of the complex and is encircled by rows of arches that create another intermediary space between arches and walls. The centre of the building, this time, is an interior space – not the exterior of a courtyard – with multiple columns and bordered by walls on four sides. The space for prayer is divided into seven naves and four bays, covered with vaults – resting on forty-eight columns – that end in arches. The walls have numerous windows and doors that provide views only from the inside to the outside, and not vice versa. In this building, the doorway – constituted by multiple parts including a stoop, steps, recess and a halting space – is still an important punctuating element in the walls that marks and facilitates entry into the space. There is, however, no central spatial void with facades protected by putting elements such as stairs or doorways behind arches, as we encountered in the typical courtyard typology of buildings in Fez and in Isfahan. The space of the gateway here interferes in the space that one enters after passing the sub-spaces of the doorway.

Yet interiority is still dominant as the walls are not transparent enough to generate communication between inside and outside – although their monumentality tends to promote exteriority. This building cell is like a solid box in the urban fabric which oscillates between being and not being an enclosed interior. It is not architecturally an interior because (a) entrances to the space – that is, the door elements – are not framed as successive stages of traversing thresholds; (b) there is no element of unexpectedness, as we have some preview of the space through its windows; (c) the external walls that delineate the building cell in the urban fabric are monumental (and relatively transparent). Combined, this changes the relationship which characterises a spatial interior, wherein the central void plays the most significant defining role by gathering sub-spaces around itself. Here, it is the walls that form the borders of space, rather than the visual layers of buildings with a courtyard typology – such as those in Fez and Isfahan, for instance.

Continuing along the Sīdī bin Arūs passage, the walker is confronted by an archway that symbolises, or provides notification of, a spatial incident on the pathway, visually dividing it and creating a sub-space by (visually) enclosing a fraction of it. On this main route, on the left-hand side, there are a number of shops whose windows and doors open onto the passage. The practice of buying and selling takes place at the borders of the spaces: while the seller sits inside, buyers stand outside, communicating from the zone of the shop doorway which is open when the shop is open. Each of the shops is architecturally a void, an interior, carved out of the solid walls. The Shīshīās Kabīr suq is also located on the left, and consists of several shops lining three main passages that intersect at two points, which are connected to the surrounding network of streets through five doors – two of which open to the Sīdī bin Arūs passage. The suq – roofed, with shops placed as a series beside each other and with three doors closing off the suq to the outside – creates an interior. Its passages constitute its central space; gathering all the architectural elements around themselves to create a locus where the practice of commerce takes place. There are no designed or clearly-defined external walls here either; rather, it is the passages of the suq that are precisely shaped. The suq, like the space of the bazaar in Isfahan, is fractioned into domed sub-spaces which are positioned one after each other in the perception of a walker who has entered the suq through gates and doorways composed of the usual steps and obstacles. The suq as a whole is a sociospatial containment zone, where nodes of socio-commercial transaction intersect with, or take place in, an architectural interiority. Entering the space of the suq, one enters an interior ritualised by the elements of the doorway space, while walking inside the space of the suq also comprises the traversal of one zone after another, as the domed sub-spaces form visual layers as well as halting nodes.

Leaving the suq and returning to the original route, at the corner of the Ḥamūda Pāshā mosque the passage reaches the intersection of two routes – Sīdī bin Arūs and al-Qaṣba – where the minaret of the Ḥamūda Pāshā mosque stands. Taking the route on the right, the connection of the mosque to the urban fabric is observable from a different side whence it can be seen that the height of the windows is not adapted to the slopes of the pathway running beside them and that the building imposes its own pattern onto the cityscape. On the left side, one again encounters a door that opens into a suq. Like the Shīshīās Kabīr suq, this one also defines a sociospatial node in the urban fabric. It has four passages, intersecting each other at three points – thereby creating nine parts in the whole walkway system – which constitute halting zones in the interior space of the suq which are sequentially traversed and onto which the interiors of the shops open.

Returning to the planned route, the rest of the passage is lined mainly by shops whose patterns and heights follow the slope of the pathway and whose borders provide selling-buying zones. Other activities taking place in the passage space include sitting, chatting, watching, walking and waiting. At one point on the way, the passage becomes narrower which, along with the descending slope, creates a change in the atmosphere of the space, giving the feeling that we are drawing away from the public core of the city towards a denser – and perhaps less public – zone.

The right-hand pathway, al-Jilūd, gets narrower and fades into darkness, creating a sub-space which indicates that the route continues but at the same time is hidden by means of a semi-curve on the way and the contrast of brightness and darkness. The pathway directly in front (a continuation of the al-Qaṣba) also obscures the view by fading into a gloom produced by the narrowness of the way and the roofed arch (*sābāṭ*) that starts after only a few shops. What the walker might expect upon traversing this border is unclear, although probably a novel space might be anticipated after passing the visual and sensual border generated by the combination of roofed arch (*sābāṭ*), narrowness and darkness at the start of the path. At this point of the intersection of two routes, we are thus faced with three choices, in two of which the walker will enter a spatial zone characterised by changing sensory features. The third choice, the Sayyada ᶜAjūla alley, which our route follows, is straighter than the other two and gives a more extended view of what lies ahead. The space is divided into sub-spaces by the contrast of brightness-darkness created by the roofed parts (*sābāṭs*) along on the way. One encounters these roofed arches in different parts of the medina of Tunis; their purpose is to gather together a number of different spaces belonging to a residential complex which include the private house of the owner, the subsidiary residential places of the household, and shops or hammams with which the owner has endowed the city and people. Here, the concentration of shops starts to decrease and residential houses become more prominent while the walls follow the typical pattern, comprising blank canvases with small windows that do not communicate with the outside space.

Branching off the passage is the Dīwān alley, which gets its name from the Dīwān building located where it starts on the Sayyada ᶜAjūla alley (figure 4.15).[197] Like other neighbouring pathways, it was formerly bordered by numerous residential houses belonging to noble families but, during the eighteenth and nineteenth centuries, religious buildings and the Turkish Dīwān were constructed.[198] In contemporary Fez, three competing and overlapping layers of presence compete for dominance in this alley.[199] The first is the Dīwān building itself, whose physical presence in the passage is merely that of its gate, as the building is embedded and hidden within the urban fabric. Yet the whole passage is named after it, which broadens and deepens both its presence, and all the associations, meanings, functions and people that are connected with it, expanding its social zone to the whole passage; this produces a sociospatial containment area which provokes and embodies the nodes of meanings linked to this particular space.

There is also a residential complex, Silāmī, that has a bold presence.[200] The original owner, Muhammad Bāyrām Silāmī, or Bāyrām I, was of Turkish origin and came to Tunis during the first reign of Ottoman domination. In the eighteenth century, under ᶜAlī bil-Hussiyn, Silāmī was given the responsibility of the high office of Shaykh al-Islām,[201] which, in the Ottoman government system, was the title given to the Grand Mufti – the highest position in the hierarchy of the religious structure. It was his responsibility to issue the religious statements, derived from the Quran, which the community had to follow in their private and urban life, thereby representing sharia law, with concomitant power.[202] Mohamed Bāyrām's descendants were to retain this office until the end of the Protectorate, and the great house which they still occupy today, in the vicinity of the Dīwān, was where they received people in order to deal with their affairs.[203] The Silāmī house is marked in the passage by a roofed arch (*sābāṭ*), both sides of which belong to the complex, and the frontiers of its presence stretch deep into the Jabal alley, which is lined mainly by residential houses, defining a semi-public sphere. Thus, this corner both marks and embodies the relationships that were generated by the presence of the building, and also suggests the forces that led to its erection in the first place; for instance, there is a belief that the house was originally built here to be in the immediate vicinity of the Dīwān building.[204]

The third prevailing element in the Dīwān passage is the ᶜAbdil Ghādir complex. Consisting of a mosque and a *zāwīya*, it was built in 1735, as noted on its door, and is associated with a Sufi brotherhood (figure 4.16). The mosque is a domed space, with the largest dome positioned in the centre of the space and surrounded by a number of smaller domes resting on columns; it is connected to the *zāwīya* on one side. The (exterior) walls form the other three sides, each penetrated by two windows, or six in total, which provide exterior views of the Dīwān passage, and parts of the cul-de-sac.[205] Besides creating transparency between the inside and outside, the windows here are important architectural elements that accord the walls a specific character that is visible even from the outside space of the pathway.[206] The typology of the mosque – relatively similar to that of the Hamuda Pāshā mosque – evokes exteriority, which is in contrast to the typology of the *zāwīya* in the same complex and also to what we encountered in Fez and Isfahan. The *zāwīya* has the introverted courtyard typology. The walls do not have windows onto the outside and the rooms are gathered around the central space which is an (exterior) courtyard. We do not see, however, the multiplicity of visual layers of the *zāwīya*s on the Sīdī Muhammad al-Ḥāj *dirb* in Fez. There are only loggias (*īvān*) on two sides, and the central core is not architecturally emphasised as much as in buildings with similar function and of a similar historical period in Fez. Nonetheless, the central void is the key spatial element of the *zāwīya*, while the entrance space also carries the same feature: it is based on the concept of interiority, encountered in Fez and Isfahan, along with incipient tendencies towards exteriority, which are particular to Tunis (among our three case studies). The gate has a small space inside the building which connects the outside and inside, while the entrance staircase, located outside the building, interferes with and is part of the space of the Dīwān passage. So a part of space that in the other two case study cities is usually located in the interior is here found on the outside – thereby illustrating this different mode of incipient exteriority. The boundaries of the *zāwīya* are dynamic, differing according to day of the week, time of year, and various times of the day: during Friday prayers, for example,

Figure 4.16 The mosque (above) and the *zāwīya* (below) in the ᶜAbdil Ghādir complex, Dīwān passage, medina of Tunis (2016)

people also use the space of the Dīwān passage for listening to religious oratory and for praying (figure 4.17).

In addition to these principal spaces, there are two short culs-de-sac, containing a group of houses, which exhibit sensual features similar to the alleys in Isfahan and Fez: a width that is narrower than that of the main road, with more quiet space and less traffic (figure 4.18). Entering the Āghā

Figure 4.17 Friday prayer in the ᶜAbdil Ghādir complex, Dīwān passage, medina of Tunis (2016)

Figure 4.18 A residential *dirb* at Dīwān passage, medina of Tunis (2016)

pathway at the end of Dīwān pathway, for instance, one can see numerous arches (and *sabāts*) which comprise visual layers along the route. A very short cul-de-sac on the Āghā leads to a modest residential building, the al-ᶜIrfānī house, with the usual courtyard typology.

Seeing the city as a Hezar-tu

Investigations in the case study cities have brought to light the presence of multiple nodes of social or sociospatial relationships generating different modes of containment. This takes place in the form of being within an architecturally enclosed space, for instance, or being a part of a social grouping or community or being within (being included in) a virtual, symbolic zone. The *dirb* is an example of this kind of node, where people develop social connections which encourage the feeling of belonging to the community of the *dirb*. The bazaar is another example in which different craft groups generate socially close associations and cohere in designated, particular spaces in the bazaar. Walking in the city, one also encounters diverse boundaries that must be traversed, most of which mark the act of 'entering' a space or a (social/conceptual) zone. The Shāwī or Īdrīs sacred zones in Fez are examples in which the boundaries are set – mainly virtually – by their naming, although some small symbols mark them tangibly: a gate in the case of Shāwī *zāwīya* and wooden stake in case of Īdrīs *zāwīya*. The elaborated spatial arrangements of entrances to houses or other buildings can be identified as other instances giving rise to the need to traverse multiple in-between spaces to reach a destination. When negotiating Islamic cities on foot, one encounters a succession of thresholds that give onto each other and smooth and/or obscure the experience of space; in the passages, for example, bends and turns, as well as contrasts of light and shadow, create both spatial and visual thresholds.

In connection with all these features, two broad characteristics of the organisation of urban space in the (case study) cities[207] include: firstly, the existence of a 'tendency' towards enfoldedness (or containment); and, secondly, the 'instrument' of enfoldedness generated by the multiplicity of stages one traverses merely in order to move across urban space and access specific areas. The multiplicity mediates direct access and thus creates a mode of 'deferring and suspending,' which has a major part in generating the enfoldedness of spaces.

These characteristics and experiences of urban space can be explained, explored and consolidated in the body of knowledge about cities using the concepts of *tū* and Hezar-tu. Seeing the city as an assemblage of *tūs* helps highlight the characteristics of urban space and the network of relationships developed in it, meanwhile drawing attention to in-between spaces rather than walls. The concept of *tū* can represent the characteristic of containment. A *tū*, as explained in chapter 3, is connected to meanings that are associated with modes of insideness, enfoldedness, in-betweenness and sequential discovery, as well as the act of separating and concealing. As explained, the concept of *tū* refers simultaneously to two distinct types of spatial structures: a three-dimensional figure that is constituted by three-dimensional inside spaces, and a two-dimensional formation that is made up of folds, bends and curves. In these structures, the inside or the fold (*tū*) functions as an in-between; it is an element of separation and concealment which can be discovered only in the sequential process of revealing, which connotes that the insides or folds are positioned on/behind/after each other. Investigations in the case study cities demonstrated that their urban space is constituted by multiple virtual, phenomenological, social, symbolic and/or spatial *tūs* that overlap, intersect, superimpose and contest. That is, the experience of walking in the city is like walking in a Hezar-tu where diverse *tūs* – which are thresholds and in-betweens, generating boundaries – open onto each other and must be traversed one after the other. In some parts of the city – for instance in the residential passages (i.e. neighbourhoods) – the phenomenological *tū* and the spatial *tū* overlap, and intersect with the sociospatial *tū* which is broader than the former two.

The presence of different types of *tū* can be recognized at different scales. At the scale of the city, naming is a strong means of creating virtual, symbolic *tūs*, which mostly overlap with social and/or spatial *tūs*, and are marked by their names or a symbolic element like a doorway, gate, roofed arch or fountain. Each naming creates a symbolic boundary and a zone of attachment, particularly as the designation usually comes from an element, a characteristic or an incident within the area; subsequently the zone produces social difference between what lies inside and outside of it. The naming, therefore, brings together a group of elements and creates a new relationship dynamic in the context of city. When one is in a named area, one conceives that it is a specifically differentiated sphere (or territory). As all parts and zones of the case study cities are orally named, walking across them it is as if one is moving from one circle of containment or attachment to another: circles that overlap, intersect or smoothly give on to each other. We saw in Fez that the domain or vicinity of Shāwī *zāwīya*, marked by a sign-posted arch, creates a vast virtual *tū* centred on the *zāwīya*. This sphere overlaps with the *tū* of Sīāj *dirb*, so that the arched gate is not only an indicator of the entrance to the sacred, spiritual *tū* of Shāwī, but also marks the entrance to the Sīāj *tū*. We experience a relatively similar feature in the Mulāy Īdrīs zone in Fez and the ᶜAbdil Ghādir *zāwīya* and Dīwān *dirb* areas in Tunis. The naming of the neighbourhoods creates in their residents a sense of territory and of belonging to the space, and thus a zone of containment.

Physically the city consists of a large number of material, architectural *tūs*, like a porous mass pierced with numerous holes which are the courtyards of buildings. Due to the attitude towards interiority or enfoldedness, both public and private realms are materialized in the courtyard typology. At the physical level, both private and public buildings are centred on their courtyards, and building construction begins by first determining the sphere of the central area. This salience is emphasised by the fact that there is a decrease in status in the hierarchy of space the further towards the boundaries of buildings it is located; those spaces that are most used in daily life, and therefore the most important, are located around the courtyard or have openings onto it, while the rest are hidden at points further from the centre. The courtyard of a building constitutes a key spatial *tū* in the urban fabric of a medina. It is spatially a *tū* because it is an enclosed space where a central void has the significant role in defining the space by gathering sub-spaces around it.[208] Studying different spaces in all three case study cities showed that the courtyard is also spatially a *tū* in that it is the celebrated core of buildings.

Passages, the pathway of a bazaar and culs-de-sac are also architecturally *tū*s. The passages and culs-de-sac are architecturally enfolded by walls that are often opaque; they are also the central, void spaces that connect the houses whose doors give onto them, and thus act as connecting elements. Moreover, each of the shops along the route of a bazaar is architecturally a *tū*, as it is a void, an interior, carved out of the solid walls, while other spaces surrounding the route of bazaar – like caravanserais, madrassas and mosques – which adhere to the courtyard typology, are also *tū*s. All these architectural *tū*s across the city are the physical embodiment of the tendency towards enfoldedness or *tū*ness. Similarly, the fountains (*saqā*s) in Fez and Tunis can be interpreted as spatial and symbolic *tū*s as they are carved out of walls. It is not the wall, the material, that makes the *saqā*s like a sculpture, however; rather it is the negative space of the carved-out wall which provides this attribute. So the fountain is the void in the wall: a *tū*, spatially and visually.

The physical *tū*s in the city often have social meanings and connotations which result in the creation of sociospatial *tū*s at the intersection of social *tū*s and spatial *tū*s. Neighbourhoods act socially as centres in which diverse relationships and forces intersect, while in bazaar complexes the names of different craft groups symbolise diverse social groupings that physically mark their presence by occupying certain areas. A courtyard is also a space for social activity; socially a *tū*, as it is the locus of diverse gathering practices for family members and their relatives, separate from the rest of the city, which makes the space a node of social relationships. In public buildings, too, the courtyard is a place of social practices that are unique to each space/building. For instance, in a mosque, people practice being part of a community of prayers as well as a member of urban society. This overlap of social and material containments creates sociospatial *tū*s throughout the city. All these nodes – *dirb*s, *kūchih*s, courtyards and spaces in bazaars – behave as sociospatial *tū*s in the larger context of the entire city, thereby representing the practice of urban *tū*ness.

At the city scale, we can also talk about the existence of visual *tū*s (the visuality of *tū*ness) and phenomenological *tū*s (the phenomenology of *tū*ness). The space of passages and bazaars is characterised by the bends, *sābāṭ*s, light-shadow alterations and the numerous doors (of houses) that open onto it. Each bend blocks the view and thus frames a section of the space as a subspace of the pathway which constitutes a series of phenomenological *tū*s to be traversed sequentially, as if positioned one behind the other. Furthermore, as discussed when exploring the case study cities, changes in sensual perception often fuzzily mark the traversing of a boundary and the entrance into a new type of space. This creates a phenomenological *tū* that indicates the beginning of a sociospatial *tū*. Each curve or bend in a passage and each sub-space of a bazaar route is also a visual layer, and the series of curves create the visual structure of layer-on-layer (*tū-bar-tū*); this also applies to other visual layers in the city such as those produced by the screens around courtyards, as in the Naqsh-i Jahān, or in *zāwīya*s and the courtyards of houses. Inside each of the buildings or maidans, there are several visual *tū*s; for instance, the arcades create a visual layer around the courtyard, partially but not fully blocking the view of the interior walls of the core space, and as in houses, this presents the appearance of layers behind/on layers (*tū-bar-tū*). Ornamentation, too, provides visual and conceptual *tū*s: conceptual because notional meanings are hidden behind layers of geometrical or floral compositions, and are expressed in the ornate calligraphy. They are visually *tū*s because each layer of ornamentation acts as an in-between, a threshold, which defers access to the ultimate abstract meaning of the embellishment.

While the succession of sociospatial and virtual *tū*s create *tū-dar-tū*s (insides-in-insides), the visual *tū*s generate *tū-bar-tū*s (folds-on-folds) and *lā-bar-lā* (layers-on-layers), which are synonyms for *tū-dar-tū*. These different structures all blend into each other, moving between scales and types, and give rise to the Hezar-tu. While walking in the city, we traverse a range of different virtual and physical zones of containment as we pass through bazaars, passages and neighbourhoods. Large numbers of architectural spaces open onto these routes, including houses, mosques, madrasas and *zāwīya*s, each of which has an enfolded core void space (the courtyard). This core is connected to the route through a corridor, or the space of the gate, as seen in all three case study cities, which delays accessing the central void by virtue of multiple sub-spaces and thresholds so created. At a different scale, we encounter ornamented surfaces throughout the city; on doorways, inside spaces, on the walls of fountains. All these transitional spaces and elements ritualise connections in urban space and create separation and in-betweenness in the city.

Countering a myth

Much of the literature on the urban space of the Islamic city expounds the myth that its walls, as its primary boundary-makers, draw concrete and precise borders between spaces, and, further, that the urban fabric and structure are articulated in ways that strongly preserve the private sphere. I would argue against this claim: walls in Islamic cities cannot be indicators of the strong division between the public and private as the ordering of relations takes place mainly in terms of in-between spaces. Furthermore, there are also diverse sorts of boundaries in addition to walls, such as virtual, symbolic, and social edges.[209] The acts of setting boundaries 'between what we reveal and what we do not, and [maintaining] some control over that boundary' are among the most salient attributes of humankind.[210] The separation of public from private, and interior from exterior, is an essential part of the constitution of society and is utterly contingent on the creation and preservation of boundaries, activities which signify delimitation and protection while regulating concealment and exposure. People understand their world by connecting and separating things, by drawing distinctions and ordering relations, processes which leave their marks in space.[211] Indeed, the standard definition of a spatial boundary in the scholarly literature is based on public-private separations and interior-exterior divisions. A boundary is thus something that divides, regulates relations, separates the private from the public and removes interior from exterior. We often imagine a boundary as some form of element surrounding a space, or lying between two realms or spaces that are meant to be separated; then, we often associate boundaries with concrete barriers like walls and fences, yet they can be created by, for example, assigning a specific name to a space, thereby attributing vague symbolic or social edges to it, or by the pattern of movement that a path or a network of paths imposes on a walker and on space.[212]

In the first chapter it was observed that walls have been seen as the (most) determining constituent of space in the Islamic city in both phenomenological and rational readings. Moncef M'halla, for example, sees the wall as the basic component of the medina, calling it the medina's 'spinal column' and 'the key element of an architecture of which the house is the base module; the minimal unit of a ubiquitous composition that gives form to the medina.'[213] O'Meara states:

> [S]uch a generalized reduction holds true for Marinid Fez in specific. As just seen in the Almohad inventory of the city, the basic building block was the *dār* (pl. *dūr*): at its simplest, a walled enclosure, or cell; at its more elaborate, a house – an enclosure about an open courtyard. The *madrasas*, fonduks, a number of the neighbourhood mosques, and the houses followed the second pattern; the hammams, shops, workshops and factories, smaller houses (*maṣārī*), and ovens, none of which involved a courtyard, followed the first. Both patterns of enclosure were defined by walls. Given premodern Fez's and the generic Arab-Muslim medina's reliance on the *dār*, it is no wonder that the enclosure has been called "the fundamental concept of architecture in the Islamic world."[214] And given the *dār*'s reliance on walls, no wonder that M'halla should in turn consider them the 'Gordian knot' of Arab-Muslim urbanism: a very significant percentage of an historic medina's structure is defined by the enclosures' walls.[215] Its buildings are set out by them; its streets are delineated by them.[216]

Yet examination of the three case study cities, Fez, Isfahan, and Tunis, shows that the wall is not the key, and not the only boundary-maker;

rather, the *tūs* fulfil this role. Different arguments can be presented for this. First, the key boundary-maker is the numerosity of spatial thresholds – that is, the in-between spaces that defer access to spaces in the city. The thresholds, in general, play a role in regulating spatial relations and shaping the patterns of movement between spaces; in the case study cities, they act as *tūs*, creating points where movement is halted, so that the walker must traverse multiple edges and boundaries to reach a (target) space or even to traverse the city. Thresholds, including bends and turns in passages, for example, provide a mode of deferring that in itself acts as a dynamic boundary, constituting the space of pathways as a separating, as well as a linking element in the city.

It may be argued that the walls shape the pathways or in-between spaces and, on this basis, are still the key boundary-makers in cities. However, although walls contribute substantially to giving a path its particular spatial characteristic, they are not the only elements to do so. Walls in urban space are components of passages in that they put physical limits on the space, while their phenomenological characters (for instance, their opacity) impact on the perceptions of walkers. Yet the walls are not the only constituent features since there are other social, symbolic and visual layers (*tūs*) that overlap with, and are superimposed upon, the space of the path. The space of pathways is, for instance, the locus for, or constructed by, symbolic meanings and social practices which give each passage its particular characteristics, thereby creating nuances of publicness and privacy throughout an Islamic city. Meanwhile, the sensual experience of the space of the paths is affected by other elements that are present: landmarks like minarets, for example, function as visual and symbolic components of the passages (figure 4.19). Thus, the physical space of the path as the collector and regulator of all these diverse elements and layers has a more significant role in boundary-making and regulating relations than walls.

The *tūs* are urban markers and creators of boundaries in yet another way. The determining limit or border of a neighbourhood is not a wall; rather, the neighbourhood exists through the social, symbolic and physical relationships associated with the very physical space of the path (or the cul-de-sac), which is a spatial *tū*.[217] The path is the collector of diverse elements which together constitute a neighbourhood. Providing access to the houses of a neighbourhood, they cohere around it to produce a residential block. One feels one is in a certain neighbourhood when in the particular architectural space of a given path. It is the element that accords a name to a neighbourhood, thereby encouraging the feeling of community among residents;[218] furthermore, as a space shared by resident families, it hosts encounters among those who use it, who pass through it every day, crossing each other's paths as they do so. Thus the path generates a spatial proximity which promotes both social connections and feelings of territoriality. It is the physically void space of the alley that gives the neighbourhood its social

Figure 4.19 Landmarks like minarets function as visual and symbolic components of the passages. Right: Sīdī Muḥammad al-Ḥāj *dirb*, Fez al-Bālī (2015); left: Pusht-i Masjid *kūchih*, Isfahan (2013)

or sociospatial existence – its identity, existence and definition: something relatively separate and yet still part of the rest of the city by virtue of the connections of the various residents.[219]

Walls are not celebrated at the level of architectural scale, either, but rather the void, the *tū* and the inside of buildings, particularly in light of the fact that a large majority of buildings in Fez, Isfahan and Tunis are of a courtyard typology.[220] On the inside of a building, the spaces are gathered and ordered around the void locus of the courtyard.[221] The courtyard is a constructed space of refined facades with less important rooms positioned far from its purlieus, and the stairs leading up from it hidden so as not to destroy the beauty and precision of its ornamentation. It is like a room inside a house with picture-decorated walls, except that it has multi-dimensional access: it is open to the sky, it contains windows and doors onto important rooms, and there are corridors and stairs which provide access to back spaces or those on other levels. The vitality of this space, compared with the walls, is also confirmed by the fact that the central void, or *tū*, is carved out of the unity of the house, and has a significant role in constructing its space. The further we go from the *tū*, that is, the closer to the border walls – the solid barrier between the inside and outside of a building – the less important becomes the function of the spaces. It is as if the irregularity of the borders-to-the-outside (the walls of a house) is solved by positioning the least important rooms at the furthest point from the central core. These external walls thus do not have part in constructing the characteristics of the core space of the house. Sometimes they do not even represent legal borders or ownership limits. For instance, in the medina of Fez, there are two phenomena related to the construction and ownership rights that change walls from solid borders into dynamic dividers of space. The first is 'carrying and carried' or 'supporting and supported' (*ḥaml-maḥmūl*) referring to the situation where an upper room is built on top of part of a dwelling below it, which belongs to a different person.[222] The second is 'shared property' (*milk-mushtarak*), which refers to situations in which part of a building is property shared among different owners (a condominium). In the medina it is common to find a wall that is shared by two buildings. It is not for technical considerations. There is a belief among the locals that the explanation lies in a Hadith of the Prophet that asks people to allow their neighbours to put their wooden beams on their own existing wall to support the others' floors.[223] So according to these phenomena of shared property and 'carrying and carried', walls of buildings can be shared or the legal borders of ownership might be different on alternate levels of a single building, or a number of neighbouring buildings.

In terms of establishing boundaries between private and public spheres, the walls cannot be the main or only barriers. There is a common idea that there are two strongly contrasting zones in the city which are sharply separated: a public realm that is the city centre and the private sphere which belongs to the residential neighbourhoods or the interior space of houses. It has also sometimes been suggested that the house in an Islamic city is a 'box' or 'cell' of privacy.[224] Yet the most private cell of a city is rather one room or perhaps a number of rooms within a house. Privacy starts there and its contours gradually vanish as it moves out towards the neighbourhood and the city, for social nodes around a house take shape in multiple ways which go beyond its physical territory. Residents develop such nodes horizontally in *dirb*s and *kūchih*s through practices like allowing virtually free access to each other's houses, with the doors sometimes remaining open during the day and encouraging of the feeling of belonging to one community. Then there are the terraces of the roof tops, where people, especially women, develop literally vertical social nodes, experiencing socially constructed networks and practicing collective identities based on encounters in areas which transcend the boundaries of the *dirb* yet remain associated with its space and social meaning. Solid social relationships are established between women in nearby homes – even though they might physically belong to another *dirb* – given that the houses of a medina are attached to each other back to back. Discussions with some of the female residents of the alleys of Saba[c] Lūyāt, Sīdī Muḥammad al-Ḥāj, Ibn Ḥayūn, and Bin Zīān in Fez confirm that they consider their terrace-based connections part of their (sociospatial) *dirb* – further evidence that the walls of the house are not as socially impermeable as they are materially and visually solid, and thus not categorical boundary-makers.[225] Furthermore, despite the considerable body of literature on the importance of privacy and the claim that the private space of houses is strongly preserved against the public realm, it appears the suggested scale and extent of preservation is exaggerated.

There is, therefore, no clear physical marker for the concept of urban neighbourhood-based either on any specific public functions, or a defining physical barrier like a surrounding wall. Although most of the houses have access to essential local institutions such as the neighbourhood oven, the hammam and the mosque, the 'area' of a neighbourhood is not delineated on the basis of such facilities. The different layers of sociospatial networks across the medina generate multifaceted and complex meanings for 'neighbourhood' because the nodes of relationships to which the concept gives rise, though centred on the physical zone or territory of the alley, are not limited to it. There are other layers of connections and social relations, like those developed on the terraces or around the phenomenon of shared walls. These expand the residentially based sociospatial relations that extend beyond the alley, confirming that walls, per se, are not indicators of a division between public and private.

Notes

1 Stefano Bianca, *Urban Form in the Arab World, Past and Present* (New York: Thames & Hudson, 2000), 142.
2 Susan Parnell, 'The Urban', in *The Routledge Handbook on Cities of the Global South*, ed. Susan Parnell and Sophie Oldfield (London, New York: Routledge, 2014), 73–4; Ash Amin and Stephen Graham, 'Cities of Connection and Disconnection', in *Unsettling Cities*, ed. John Allen, Doreen Massey, and Michael Pryke (London, New York: Routledge, 1999), 7–48.
3 Ash Amin and Nigel Thrift, *Cities, Reimaging the Urban* (Cambridge: Polity Press, 2002), 22.
4 See Doreen Massey, 'Travelling Thoughts', in *Without Guarantees: In Honour of Stuart Hall*, ed. Paul Gilroy, Larry Grossberg, and Angela McRobbie (London: Verso, 2000), 225–32; 'On Space and the City', in *City Worlds*, ed. Doreen Massey, John Allen, and Steve Pile (London, New York: Routledge, 1999), 157–77; Michael Pryke, 'On the Openness of Cities', in *Unsettling Cities*, ed. John Allen, Doreen Massey, and Michael Pryke (London, New York: Routledge, 1999), 321–38; Derek Gregory, 'Interventions in the Historical Geography of Modernity', in *Place, Culture, Representation*, ed. James S. Duncan and David Ley (London: Routledge, 1993), 272–313.
5 Nezar Alsayyad, *The 'Real', the Hyper, and the Virtual Traditions in the Built Environment* (Abingdon: Routledge, 2014); Doreen Massey, 'Cities in the World', in *City Worlds*, ed. Doreen Massey, John Allen, and Steve Pile (London, New York: Routledge, 1999), 99–156.

6 See, for example, David Gartman, 'Culture and the Built Environment', in *Handbook of Cultural Sociology*, ed. John R. Hall, Laura Grindstaff, and Ming-cheng Lo (London, New York: Routledge, 2010), 347–56.; Ananya Roy, '"The Reverse Side of the World": Identity, Space, and Power', in *Hybrid Urbanism: On the Identity Discourse and the Built Environment*, ed. Nezar Alsayyad (London: Praeger, 2001), 229–45; David Harvey, *Spaces of Hope* (Edinburgh: Edinburgh University, 2000); Pierre Bourdieu, *The Logic of Practice* (Cambridge: Polity Press, 1990); Robert E. Park, 'The City', in *The City: Suggestions for Investigation of Human Behaviour in the Urban Environment*, ed. Robert E. Park, Ernest W. Burgess, and Morris Janowitz (Chicago: Chicago University Press, 1925), 1–46.
7 See Rob Shields, *Places on Margin* (Abingdon, UK: Routledge, 1991).
8 The reason why the selected paths could be proper representatives will be explained distinctively at the beginning of the chapter dedicated to each city.
9 I retain the description of sensual perceptions at a level of an experience that can be shared by many.
10 Amin and Thrift, *Cities, Reimaging the Urban*, 10–11. Michael Sheringham, 'City Space, Mental Space, Poetic Space: Paris in Breton, Benjamin and Réda', in *Parisian Fields*, ed. Michael Sheringham (London: Reaktion, 1996), 104 quoted in; Amin and Thrift, *Cities, Reimaging the Urban*, 10.
11 Deborah Stevenson, *Cities and Urban Cultures* (Maidenhead: Open University Press, 2003).
12 Amin and Thrift, *Cities, Reimaging the Urban*, 11.
13 Walter Benjamin, *Charles Baudelaire* (London, New York: Verso, 1997), 171, 169; quoted in Amin and Thrift, *Cities, Reimaging the Urban*, 10.
14 Amin and Thrift, *Cities, Reimaging the Urban*.
15 Michel de Certeau, *The Practice of Everyday Life* (Oakland, CA: University of California Press, 1988), 93, original emphasis.
16 Richard Dennis, *Cities in Modernity, Representations and Productions of Metropolitan Space, 1840–1930* (Cambridge: Cambridge University Press, 2008).
17 de Certeau, *The Practice of Everyday Life*, 117; Dennis, *Cities in Modernity, Representations and Productions of Metropolitan Space, 1840–1930*, 105.
18 de Certeau, *The Practice of Everyday Life*, 99, original emphasis.
19 Stevenson, *Cities and Urban Cultures*, 55; See, also, Fran Tonkiss, *Space, the City and Social Theory, Social Relations and Urban Forms* (Cambridge: Polity Press, 2005).
20 Michel de Certeau, *The Practice of Everyday Life* (Oakland, CA: University of California Press, 1984).
21 de Certeau, *The Practice of Everyday Life*, 119; Charlotte Linde and William Labov, 'Spatial Networks as a Site for the Study of Language and Thought', *Language*, no. 51 (1975).
22 de Certeau, *The Practice of Everyday Life*, 119, original emphasis.
23 Ibid., original emphasis.
24 Ibid.
25 Ibid.
26 Ibid.
27 Ibid., 97, original emphasis.
28 Ibid., 93.
29 Ibid., original emphasis.
30 The order is the law and rule in a place according to which the elements are positioned beside one another, 'each situated in its own "proper" and distinct location, a location it defines. . . . It [a place] implies an indication of stability.' Ibid., 117, original emphasis.
31 Ibid., original emphasis.

32 Roland Barthes, 'Semiology and the Urban', in *The City and the Sign: An Introduction to Urban Semiotics*, ed. Mark Gottdiener and Alexandros Lagopoulos (New York: Columbia University Press, 1986), 87–98; cited in Stevenson, *Cities and Urban Cultures*.
33 Amin and Thrift, *Cities, Reimaging the Urban*.
34 Ibid., 14.
35 See Anthony Edwin James Morris, *History of Urban Form, before the Industrial Revolutions*, third ed. (London, New York: Routledge, 1994).
36 See Spiro Kostof, *The City Shaped, Urban Patterns and Meanings through History* (Boston: Little, Brown, 1991); Brian Morris, *Anthropology of the Self: The Individual in Cultural Perspective* (London: Pluto Press, 1994). The locations of the historic cities in the Arab world were also related to important trade routes, geopolitical relationships, the availability of natural resources such as abundant water supply and an agricultural hinterland, and, sometimes, to the religious significance of certain places. The emergence and growth of most of the cities were affected by a combination of several of these factors. Bianca, *Urban Form in the Arab World, Past and Present*, 136.
37 Bianca, *Urban Form in the Arab World, Past and Present*, 9.
38 See, for example, Besim S. Hakim, 'Law and the City', in *The City in the Islamic World*, ed. Salma K. Jayyusi et al., vol. 1 (Leiden, Boston: Brill, 2008), 71–92; Besim Hakim, *Arabic-Islamic Cities: Building and Planning Principles* (New York: Routledge and Kegan Paul, 1986); Muddathir Abdel-Rahim, 'Legal Institutions', in *The Islamic City*, ed. Robert Bertram Serjeant (Paris: UNESCO, 1980), 41–51.
39 See, for example, Margaret Smith, *Al-Ghazzālī the Mystic* (London: Hijra International Publishers, 1944); Henri Corbin, *Creative Imagination in the Sufism of Ibn Arabi*, trans. Ralph Manheim (Princeton: Princeton University Press, 2016).
40 Zahrā Aharī, *Maktab Iṣfahān Dar Shahrsāzī (Isfahan School of Urban Design, the Syntax of Structure Design)* (Tehran: Farhangistān Hunar Press, 2006).
41 Seyyed Hossein Nasr, 'The Contemporary Muslim and the Architectural Transformation of the Islamic Urban Environment', ed. Renata Holod (Philadelphia: Aga Khan Award for Architecture, 1978), 2.
42 Bianca, *Urban Form in the Arab World, Past and Present*, 66.
43 See Siyid Muhsin Habībī, *Az Shar Tā Shahr (de La Cite a La Ville)* (Tehran: University of Tehran Press, 2006); Husiyn Sultānzādih, *Bazaar-Hāyi Īrānī* (Tehran: Daftar-i Pajūhish-i Farhangī, 2001); Heinz Gaube, *Iranian Cities* (New York: New York University Press, 1979); John Gulick, 'Private Life and Public Face: Cultural Continuites in the Domestic Architecture of Isfahan', *Iranian Studies* 7 (1974): 629–38.
44 The root of the word is Arabic. *Nīẓām* in both Arabic and Persian means (1) whatever makes a rope of diamonds; a chain, thread or rope of diamonds; a thread on which diamond beads are strung; (2) a medium of order and arrangement; (3) anything that is the basis and foundation of order; (4) the arrangement of everything; (5) method. See the *Dihkhudā* and *al-Maʿānī* dictionaries.
45 For further details, see Somaiyeh Falahat, 'Nizams: The Hidden Syntax under the Surafce, Urban Morphology in Traditional Islamic Cities', *Archnet-IJAR, International Journal of Architectural Research* 6, no. 1 (2012): 90–9.
46 See, for example, Habībī, *Az Shar Tā Shahr (de La Cite a La Ville)*; Husiyn Sultānzādih, *Muqadami-Ī Bar Tārīkhi Shahr va Shahrsāzī Dar Īrān (An Introduction to the History of City and Urbanism in Iran)* (Tehran: Amīr Kabīr, 1988); Gaube, *Iranian Cities*.
47 Aharī, *Maktab Iṣfahān Dar Shahrsāzī (Isfahan School of Urban Design, the Syntax of Structure Design)*.

48 Wilfrid Blunt, *Isfahan, Pearl of Persia* (New York: Stein and Day, 1966).
49 Zahrā Aharī, *Maktab Shahrsazi Iṣfahan* (Tehran: Hunar University Press, 2000).
50 Rizā Mukhtārī Isfahanī and Alīrizā Ismāīlī, *The Art of Isfahan through the Eyes of Travelers, from Safavids to Qajar* (Tehran: Farhangistān Hunar Press, 2006).
51 Brian Spooner, 'City and River in Iran: Urbanization and Irrigation of the Iranian Plateau', *Iranian Studies* 7 (1974): 681–713.
52 Vladimir Minorsky, ed., *Tadhkirat Al-Mulūk: A Manual of Safavid Administration (circa 1137/1725)*, trans. Vladimir Minorsky (London: Gibb Memorial Trust, 1943).
53 Bianca, *Urban Form in the Arab World, Past and Present.*
54 Roger Le Tourneau, *Fez in the Age of Marinides* (Norman: University of Oklahoma Press, 1961).
55 Halima Ferhat, 'Marinid Fez: Zenith and Signs of Decline', in *The City in the Islamic World*, ed. Salma Khadra Jayyusi, Renata Holod, Attilio Petruccioli, and André Raymond (Leiden, Boston: Brill, 2008), 247–67.
56 Habībī, *Az Shar Tā Shahr (de La Cite a La Ville).*
57 Bianca, *Urban Form in the Arab World, Past and Present*, 66.
58 See Spiro Kostof, *The City Assembled: The Elements of Urban Form through History* (Boston: Little, Brown, 1992).
59 Bianca, *Urban Form in the Arab World, Past and Present.*
60 Somaiyeh Falahat, 'Nizams: The Hidden Syntax under the Surface, Urban Morphology in Traditional Islamic Cities', *Archnet-IJAR, International Journal of Architectural Research* 6, no. 1 (2012): 90–9.
61 Hassan Radoine, 'French Territoriality and Urbanism: General Lyautey and Architect Prost in Morocco (1912–1925)', in *Colonial Architecture and Urbanism in Africa*, ed. Fassil Demissie (Farnham: Ashgate, 2012), 11.
62 Ibid., 26.
63 See, for example, Jonathan G. Katz, *Architecture as Symbol and Self-Identity* (Philadelphia: Aga Khan Award for Architecture, 1980). As a typical expression of scholarly understanding of the urban space of Fez medina, we can refer to Wirth and Escher, who write: 'erscheint in Fes alles ungeplant, behelfsmäßig, irgendwie improvisiert zusammengewürfelt. Es fehlen fast alle 'Landmarken', und damit findet sich ein Unkundiger nur schwer zurecht.' (In Fez, everything seems to be unplanned, provisional, somehow improvised. Almost all 'landmarks' are missing, and an uninformed person finds it difficult to handle.) Eugen Wirth and Anton Escher, *Die Medina von Fes, Geographische Beiträge Zu Persistenz Und Dynamik, Verfall Und Erneuerung Einer Traditionellen Islamischen Stadt in Handlungstheoretischer Sicht* (Germany: Fränkische Geographische Gesellschaft, 1992), 28.
64 Katz, *Architecture as Symbol and Self-Identity*; Stefano Bianca, 'Conservation and Rehabilitation Projects for the Old City of Fez', in *Adaptive Reuse: Integrating Traditional Areas into the Modern Urban Fabric*, ed. Bentley Sevcenko (Cambridge, MA: MIT Laboratory of Architecture and Planning, 1983). On preservation and rehabilitation projects or development plans in the medina of Fez, see, for example, World Bank, *Morocco – Fez Medina Rehabilitation Project* (Washington, DC: World Bank, 2006). http://documents.worldbank.org/curated/en/2006/06/6843147/morocco-fes-medina-rehabilitation-project. Genevieve Darles and Nicolas Lagrange, 'The Medina of Fez – Crafting a Future for the Past', *The UNESCO Courier* (October 1996), 36–39; Jean François Troin, 'Urbanization and Development: The Role of the Medina in the Maghreb', in *Urban Development in the Muslim World*, ed. Hooshang Amirahmadi and Salah S. El-Shakhs (New Brunswick: Center for Urban Policy Research, 1993), 94–108.

65 *Zāwīya* literally means 'corner' and is a spiritual place for Sufi orders. Burckhardt explains that *zāwīyas* were the result of people who had chosen a particular path of (religious) spirituality beginning to group together into individual brotherhoods. Word of the Sufi orders spread amongst the people, leading to the emergence of circles that aspired to take part in the spiritual life. Each Sufi order or brotherhood had a founder. When the founder was alive, the centre of the order was the founder's place of refuge or dwelling. After his death, it was his tomb. Both of these have been named *zāwīyas*. Later, individuals who had become prominent within an order took over its spiritual instruction and guidance as its spiritual masters, whereas formal authority, along with the administration of the sepulchral mosque, was retained by the family of the founder. Titus Burckhardt, *Fez: City of Islam* (Cambridge: Islamic Texts Society, 1992).
66 See Ferhat, 'Marinid Fez: Zenith and Signs of Decline'.
67 The following paragraphs on the history of the evolution of Fez are a summary mainly based on descriptions found in the following sources – which accord with common accounts of Fez's evolution: Clifford Edmund Bosworth, ed., *Historic Cities of the Islamic World* (Leiden, Boston: Brill, 2007); Bianca, *Urban Form in the Arab World, Past and Present*; Wirth and Escher, *Die Medina von Fes, Geographische Beiträge Zu Persistenz Und Dynamik, Verfall Und Erneuerung Einer Traditionellen Islamischen Stadt in Handlungstheoretischer Sicht*; Bianca, 'Conservation and Rehabilitation Projects for the Old City of Fez'; Le Tourneau, *Fez in the Age of Marinides*; Évariste Lévi-Provençal, 'La Fondation de Fès', *Annales de l'Institut d'Etudes Orientales* 4 (1938): 23–53; Ferhat, 'Marinid Fez: Zenith and Signs of Decline'.
68 Bianca, *Urban Form in the Arab World, Past and Present.*
69 Le Tourneau, *Fez in the Age of Marinides.*
70 Wirth and Escher, *Die Medina von Fes, Geographische Beiträge Zu Persistenz Und Dynamik, Verfall Und Erneuerung Einer Traditionellen Islamischen Stadt in Handlungstheoretischer Sicht.*
71 Bosworth, *Historic Cities of the Islamic World.*
72 Ibid.
73 Bianca, *Urban Form in the Arab World, Past and Present*; Le Tourneau, *Fez in the Age of Marinides.*
74 Bosworth, *Historic Cities of the Islamic World.*
75 Wirth and Escher, *Die Medina von Fes, Geographische Beiträge Zu Persistenz Und Dynamik, Verfall Und Erneuerung Einer Traditionellen Islamischen Stadt in Handlungstheoretischer Sicht.*
76 Bosworth, *Historic Cities of the Islamic World.*
77 Le Tourneau, *Fez in the Age of Marinides*, 10.
78 Wirth and Escher, *Die Medina von Fes, Geographische Beiträge Zu Persistenz Und Dynamik, Verfall Und Erneuerung Einer Traditionellen Islamischen Stadt in Handlungstheoretischer Sicht*; Bosworth, *Historic Cities of the Islamic World.*
79 Bianca, *Urban Form in the Arab World, Past and Present.*
80 Wirth and Escher, *Die Medina von Fes, Geographische Beiträge Zu Persistenz Und Dynamik, Verfall Und Erneuerung Einer Traditionellen Islamischen Stadt in Handlungstheoretischer Sicht.*
81 Ibid.
82 Le Tourneau, *Fez in the Age of Marinides.*
83 Bianca, *Urban Form in the Arab World, Past and Present.*
84 Ibid.
85 Bosworth, *Historic Cities of the Islamic World.*
86 Le Tourneau, *Fez in the Age of Marinides*, 40, 41.
87 Bosworth, *Historic Cities of the Islamic World*, 143.

88 Le Tourneau, *Fez in the Age of Marinides*, 17.
89 Bosworth, *Historic Cities of the Islamic World*, 140.
90 Wirth and Escher, *Die Medina von Fes, Geographische Beiträge Zu Persistenz Und Dynamik, Verfall Und Erneuerung Einer Traditionellen Islamischen Stadt in Handlungstheoretischer Sicht.*
91 Bosworth, *Historic Cities of the Islamic World.*
92 Wirth and Escher, *Die Medina von Fes, Geographische Beiträge Zu Persistenz Und Dynamik, Verfall Und Erneuerung Einer Traditionellen Islamischen Stadt in Handlungstheoretischer Sicht.*
93 Bosworth, *Historic Cities of the Islamic World*, 140.
94 Lévi-Provençal, 'La Fondation de Fès'.
95 Anton Escher, 'Die "Medina von Fès" Auf Dem Weg in Das 21. Jahrhundert?', *Trialog* 40 (1994): 46–51.
96 Ibid.
97 For example: 'Schèma Directeur d'Urbanisme de la Ville de Fès' (1978) by Moroccan planers, French urbanists and international experts.
98 Escher, 'Die "Medina von Fès" Auf Dem Weg in Das 21. Jahrhundert?'
99 Wirth and Escher, *Die Medina von Fes, Geographische Beiträge Zu Persistenz Und Dynamik, Verfall Und Erneuerung Einer Traditionellen Islamischen Stadt in Handlungstheoretischer Sicht*, 22.
100 Bianca, *Urban Form in the Arab World, Past and Present*, 306.
101 Lévi-Provençal, 'La Fondation de Fès'. In the 1950s, the nucleus of ᶜAyn Qadūs was planned as a residential site for low or middle-income families. It was located on a hillside north of Fez. Rural immigrants also established a number of informal settlements close to ᶜAyn Qadūs. Similar settlements developed spontaneously around the eastern periphery of the old city. Bianca, *Urban Form in the Arab World, Past and Present*, 304.
102 The *dirb* is a complex notion that has twofold significance although in spatial terms it usually refers to the community of the *dirb* which, I will describe in more detail later in this section. *Ḥuma* is another term that is associated to the notion of a *dirb*. According to Raftani, if a *dirb* refers to the alley or physical aspect, the term *ḥuma* is more appropriate to express the idea of the neighbourhood. For one woman, a resident of Sabaᶜ Lūyāt alley in the medina, a *ḥuma* is a zone which is larger than a *dirb*. For her, for example, her *ḥuma* also includes Ṣaffārīn Ṣaḥn – an urban space serving the whole city and located outside her immediate *dirb*. For another girl, her *ḥuma* is everything: 'her whole world', including all the people (even from other *dirb*s) whom she meets on the roof terrace, the suq, the hammam, the mosque, and so on.
103 In Fez, in the oral common knowledge of residents, different terminologies are used for naming the paths. They include the following: (a) *Ṭālaᶜ* is used only of the two main thoroughfares of the city which connect the central part – the al-Qarāwīyīn mosque complex and specialty market (*qiysarīyya*) – to the Bāb Būjlūd. The Ṭālaᶜ Ṣaghīra has less slope than the Ṭālaᶜ Kabīra. (b) *ᶜUqba* indicates the open-end passages which have a high degree of slope and might have steps. (c) *Zanqa* refers to an open-ended, connecting pathway without a great deal of slope or marked topographical features. (d) *Zuqāq* is similar to *zanqa*. (e) *Dirb* usually represents the closed-ended pathways leading to one or a number of houses, or the smallest scale of neighbourhood.
104 The prefix *sīdī*, literally meaning 'master', is added to names to indicate the importance of and respect to the person.
105 The typical house in the medina of Fez is called *dār* in Moroccan Arabic, a term used for both house and station or, in the astrological vocabulary, to refer

to a position of the stars. Stefania Pandolfo, *Impasse of the Angels* (Chicago: University of Chicago Press, 1997), 319. A *dār* is a house with a courtyard, often with two large rooms (*biyt*) on the ground floor facing each other. There is usually a fountain ornamented with mosaics (*zilīj*) on one of the walls around the courtyard – which is sometimes replaced by a marble fountain positioned in the centre. In the medina of Fez there are also other types of residential space: *duwiyrā*, which is a house smaller than a *dār*, often with only one large room (*biyt*) downstairs and one upstairs, a small courtyard and usually no pillars; *miṣrīyya*, which is a guest house located on the top floor of a larger house, used by male guests or sometimes the eldest son and his friends, and later his family; and *rīād*, which is a house with a garden either in the centre, or on the fourth side when the house is U-shaped. For details see Jacques Revault, Lucien Golvin, and Ali Amahan, 'Palais et Demeures de Fès', Demeures de Fès (XIVe-XVIIe Siècles) (Marseille: Institut de Recherches et d'études sur le monde arabe et musulman, 1985). David Amster, 'Introduction to Domestic Architecture in the Fez Medina', *Dar Bennis*, 2010, www.houseinfez.com/A%20Typical%20House%20in%20the%20Fez%20Medina.htm; Grillo Alessandra, 'Traditional Building Techniques in Fes', ed. Attilio Petruccioli, *Environmental Design: Journal of the Islamic Environmental Design Research Centre* 1, 2 (1988): 38–47.

106 However, even the courtyard is not the final innermost cell in a discovery journey of the city. In each house there are one or more rooms which are positioned at the end of the journey within the house. Their interiors can only be accessed after stages are traversed within the spatial arrangement of the house.

107 There used to exist numerous gates marking the entrances to *dirb*s all over the medina, cutting off the *dirb*s from the main (more public) routes. According to Raftani, they were used for the urban management of affairs but lost that function shortly after the beginning of the French Protectorate in 1912. They no longer have any function and most of them have been removed to facilitate free movement within the city.

108 As will be explained, these characteristics are typical of residential *dirb*s in Fez, particularly visible in the Sabaᶜ Lūyāt *dirb*.

109 The Bū ᶜAlī is a small mosque which hosts the prayers only two (out of five) daily prayer times.

110 The implicit precept that doors must not face each other in these four public buildings helps amplify the common claim in the existing literature that the phenomenon of staggering adjacent doors so that a direct line of view is not provided through multiple sets is solely connected with the preservation of privacy in residential buildings.

111 In Bū ᶜAlī, al-Dabāghīn, Zūwītan around two or three steps; al-Darᶜī is very deep and numerous steps lead to its two courtyards.

112 For example, in the *dirb* Bin Zīān I spotted a woman in casual (home) clothes, although with a scarf, came to the boundary of the *dirb*, waiting for a passer-by to take her bread to the oven (*farrān*). She would not enter the main alley (Sīdī Muḥammad al-Ḥāj) thus clad.

113 Relatively similar conditions are found around the Īdrīs *zāwīya* at the centre of the city. There are wooden borders in the surrounding alleys of the *zāwīya* which are set at a certain height to prevent the entry of animals.

114 Royaume du Maroc, *Schéma Directeur D'urbanisme de La Ville de Fès* (Paris: Ministère de l'habitat et de l'aménagement du territoire, 1980).

115 See, for example, Aharī, *Maktab Iṣfahān Dar Shahrsāzī (Isfahan School of Urban Design, the Syntax of Structure Design)*; Habībī, *Az Shār Tā Shahr (de La Cite a La Ville)*; Gaube, *Iranian Cities*; Blunt, *Isfahan, Pearl of Persia*.

116 Blunt, *Isfahan, Pearl of Persia*, 14.
117 Masashi Haneda, 'An Interpretation of the Concept of the "Islamic City"', in *Islamic Urban Studies, Historical Review and Perspectives*, ed. Masashi Haneda and Toru Miura (London, New York: Routledge and Kegan Paul, 1994), 236.
118 Habībī, *Az Shār Tā Shahr (de La Cite a La Ville)*, 93.
119 Aharī, *Maktab Iṣfahān Dar Shahrsāzī (Isfahan School of Urban Design, the Syntax of Structure Design)*.
120 See, for example, Gaube, *Iranian Cities*.
121 Lutfulāh Hunarfar, *Ganjīnih-yi Ā̱sār-i Tārīkhī-yi Iṣfahān (A Treasure of the Historical Monuments of Isfahan)* (Tehran: S̱aqafī, 1971); Blunt, *Isfahan, Pearl of Persia*. Jiy today is identified as the village known as Shahristān, which lies to the east of the modern city, on the north bank of the river. Yahūdīyyih, literally the Jewish quarter, has been identified as the Jūbārih neighbourhood to the northeast of the Friday Mosque (Masjid Jāmiᶜ).
122 Abulghāsim Rafīyī Mihrābādī, *Ā̱s̱āri Millīy-I Isfahān (The National Monuments of Isfahan)* (Tehran: Anjuman-i Ā̱s̱ār Millī, 1973).
123 Sulṭānzādih, *Muqadami-Ī Bar Tārīkh-i Shahr va Shahrsāzī Dar Īrān (An Introduction to the History of City and Urbanism in Iran)*.
124 Blunt, *Isfahan, Pearl of Persia*.
125 Lisa Golombek, 'Urban Patterns in Pre-Safavid Isfahan', *Iranian Studies* 7 (1974): 22.
126 Golombek, 'Urban Patterns in Pre-Safavid Isfahan'.
127 Rafīᶜyī Mihrābādī, *Ā̱s̱āri Millīy-I Isfāhān (The National Monuments of Isfahan)*.
128 Habībī, *Az Shār Tā Shahr (de La Cite a La Ville)*.
129 Golombek, 'Urban Patterns in Pre-Safavid Isfahan'.
130 Gaube, *Iranian Cities*; Stephen P. Blake, *Half the World: The Social Architecture of Safavid Isfahan, 1590–1722* (Costa Mesa: Mazda Publications, 1999).
131 Golombek, 'Urban Patterns in Pre-Safavid Isfahan'.
132 Mahmūd Falāmakī, 'Shahrnishīnī Dar Īrān (Urbanism in Iran)', in *Shahrhāy-I Īrān (Iranian Cities)*, ed. Mustafā Kīyānī (Tehran: Sāzmān-i Chāp va Intishārāt-i Vizarat-i Farhang va Irshād-i Islāmī, 1987).
133 Ministry of Culture and Arts of Iran, *Isfahan, the City of Light* (British Museum: Ministry of Culture and Arts of Iran, 1976); Peter Beaumont, Gerald H. Blake, and J. Malcom Wagstaff, *The Middle East: A Geographical Study* (London: John Wiley & Sons, 1976); Falāmakī, 'Shahrnishīnī Dar Īrān (Urbanism in Iran)'.
134 Ministry of Culture and Arts of Iran, *Isfahan, the City of Light*.
135 Golombek, 'Urban Patterns in Pre-Safavid Isfahan'; Gaube, *Iranian Cities*.
136 Gaube, *Iranian Cities*.
137 Roger Savory, *Iran under the Safavids* (Cambridge: Cambridge University Press, 1980).
138 Eckart Ehlers, 'Capitals and Spatial Organization in Iran: Esfahan, Shiraz, Tehran', in *Téhéran: Capitale Bicentenaire*, ed. Chahryar Adle and Bernard Hourcade, Bibliothèque Iranienne, 37 (Institut Français de Recherche en Iran, 1992), 160.
139 The central point of the city had been a square (*miydān-i Kuhnih*) when ᶜAbbās I adopted it as his capital.
140 Laurence Lockhart, 'Shah Abbas's Isfahan', in *Cities of Destiny*, ed. Arnold J. Toynbee (London: Thames & Hudson, 1976), 219.
141 Ibid.
142 Blake, *Half the World: The Social Architecture of Safavid Isfahan, 1590–1722*.
143 Golombek, 'Urban Patterns in Pre-Safavid Isfahan'; Gaube, *Iranian Cities*.
144 Klaus Herdeg, *Formal Structure in Islamic Architecture of Iran and Turkistan* (New York: Rizzoli, 1990).

145 Blake, *Half the World: The Social Architecture of Safavid Isfahan, 1590–1722*; Blunt, *Isfahan, Pearl of Persia*; Lockhart, 'Shah Abbas's Isfahan'.
146 Blake, *Half the World: The Social Architecture of Safavid Isfahan, 1590–1722.*
147 Savory, *Iran under the Safavids.*
148 Herdeg, *Formal Structure in Islamic Architecture of Iran and Turkistan.*
149 Wilhelm Barthold, *An Historical Geography of Iran* (Princeton: Princeton University Press, 1984).
150 George Nathaniel Curzon, *Persia and the Persian Question*, vol. 1 (Cambridge: Cambridge University Press, 1892).
151 John Chardin, *Travels in Persia 1673–1677* (New York: Dover, 1971).
152 Curzon, *Persia and the Persian Question.*
153 Alīriẓā Ismāʿīlī , 'Chāhārbāgh Dar Safarnāmihā (Chāhārbāgh in Travel Stories)', *Gulistān-I Hunar* 5 (2006): 39–47; Savory, *Iran under the Safavids*; For further discussions on urban developments in the Safavid era see also Somaiyeh Falahat and M. Reza Shirazi, 'Spatial Fragmentation and Bottom-Up Appropriations: The Case of Safavid Isfahan', *Urban History* 42, no. 1 (2015): 3–21; Somaiyeh Falahat and M. Reza Shirazi, 'New Urban Developments in Safavid Isfahan Continuity or Disjuncture?', *Planning Perspectives* 27, no. 4 (2013): 165–75.
154 Ministry of Culture and Arts of Iran, *Isfahan, the City of Light.*
155 Ann K.S. Lambton and Janine Sourdel-Thomine, 'Isfahan', in *Historic Cities of the Islamic World*, ed. C. Edmund Bosworth (Leiden, Boston: Brill, 2007), 178.
156 Based on on-site investigations, which also include interviews with local experts, such as Aḥmad Muntaẓir and Maryam Qāsimī.
157 *Kūchih*, like *dirb*, has a twofold significance. It means simultaneously an alley and a neighbourhood in terms of a sociospatial constellation. In the Lughatnāmih-yi Dihkhudā dictionary we can read two meanings for *kūchih*: (1) neighbourhood (*maḥallih*, *barzan*); (2) small, narrow way. *Kūchih* is the diminutive form of *kūy*. *Kūy*, similarly, indicates both: (1) a wide path which is a main road, passage; and (2) neighbourhood (*maḥallih*). Alī Akbar Dihkhudā, *Lughatnāmih* (Tehran: Tehran University Press, 1980).
158 *Muqarnas* is a decorative system of honeycombed or vaulted corners made up of intersecting niches which follow clear geometric principles. It is widely used in, for example, entrances or to line vaults and has been one of the most distinctive means of ornament in Islamic architecture since the twelfth century. Jennifer Scarce, 'Muqarnas', in *Encyclopedia of Islamic Civilisation and Religion*, ed. Ian Richard Netton (London, New York: Routledge, 2008).
159 Oleg Grabar, 'What Makes Islamic Art Islamic', *Aarp – Art and Archaeology Research Papers* 9 (1976): 3, original emphasis.
160 This play of perception differs from person to person, because of different worldviews, presuppositions and information. To each person, these views and layers of perception could be defined as different in quantity and quality, but what remains intact is the fact that this portal cannot be perceived in one or two stages, but it includes multiple different layers of seeing, discovering, understanding and reading. Similar to the bazaar, with its sub-spaces that the individual has to trace one after the other in order to experience and penetrate it, this portal has sub-layers of perception which should be conceptually traced in order to be understood. Each layer carries other layers inside it; the 'withins' which open inside each other. See Somaiyeh Falahat, 'Context-Based Conceptions in Urban Morphology: Hezar-Too, an Original Urban Logic?', *Cities* no. 36 (2014): 50–7.
161 One is the continuance of the south wing of the Naqsh-i Jahān bazaar, and the second the path of main city bazaar which terminates in one of the old city gates. The two of them with the shops on both sides and their roofed ceilings

are parts of the main bazaar and commercial space. But the third way is no longer roofed and its windowless mud walls confirm the beginning of a new space.

162 A *hashtī* was an intermediary space between the inside and outside of a house; an introductory space before the border of the gate. It has different forms and sizes ranging from a small recess or triangular space to an octagonal area with places to sit. Sometimes the doors of neighbouring houses opened into a single *hashtī*. Some *hashtī*s are decorated with ornamentation while others remain very simple. Muḥsin Nīkbakht and Siyid Abulqāsim Siyid Ṣadr, *Dāyiratulmaᶜārif-I Mimārī va Sharsāzī (Encyclopedia of Architecture and Urban Planning)* (Tehran: Āzādih, 2002).

163 Justin McGuinness, 'Neighbourhood Notes: Texture and Streetscape in the Médina of Tunis', *The Journal of North African Studies* 5, no. 4 (2000): 97–120.

164 Justin McGuinness, 'Political Context and Professional Ideologies: French Urban Conservation Planning Transferred to the Médina of Tunis', *The Journal of North African Studies* 2, no. 2 (1997): 34–56.

165 Ellen C. Micaud, 'Urbanization, Urbanism, and the Medina of Tunis', *International Journal of Middle East Studies* 9, no. 4 (1978): 432.

166 McGuinness, 'Neighbourhood Notes: Texture and Streetscape in the Médina of Tunis'.

167 Jellal Abdelkafi, *La Médina de Tunis* (Paris: Centre National de la Recherche Scientifique, 1989).

168 Anton Escher and Marianne Schepers, 'Revitalizing the Medina of Tunis as a National Symbol', *Erdkunde* 62, no. 2 (2008): 129.

169 Escher and Schepers, 'Revitalizing the Medina of Tunis as a National Symbol'.

170 Paul Sebag, *Tunis: Histoire D'une Ville* (Paris: L'Harmattan, 1998). For a detailed history of its evolution see Paul Sebag, 'Tunis', in *Historic Cities of the Islamic World*, ed. Clifford Edmund Bosworth (Boston: Brill, 2007), 535–49; Justin McGuinness, 'The Development of Conservation Management for a Pre-Industrial North African City: The Case of the Medina of Tunis' (Durham theses, Durham University, 1992), http://etheses.dur.ac.uk/6065/

171 André Laronde and Jean-Claude Golvin, *L'Afrique Antique: Histoire et Monuments (Lybie, Tunisie, Algérie, Maroc)* (Paris: Tallandier, 2001); Habib Boulares, *Histoire Générale de La Tunisie* (Tunis: Cérès, 2011).

172 Abou-Obeid El-Bekri, *Description de l'Afrique Septentrionale*, ed. Mac Guckin de Slane (Paris: Imprimerie Impériale, 1857).

173 D'Abd El-Wah'id Merrakechi, *Histoire Des Almohades*, trans. Edmond Fagnan (Alger: Adolphe Jourdan, 1893).

174 Ibn Naji, *Ma'alim Al-Imam Fi Ma'rifati Ahl Al-Qayrawan* (Tunis: n.p., 1902).

175 El-Bekri, *Description de l'Afrique Septentrionale.*

176 Ibid.

177 Ibid.

178 Sebag, *Tunis: Histoire D'une Ville.*

179 Muḥammad ibn Abi al-Qāsim Ibn Abi Dinār, *Al-Mu'nis Fī Akhbār Ifrīqīyah Wa-Tūnis* (n.p.: 1869).

180 Al-Zarkachi, *Chroniques Des Almohades et Des Hafsides*, trans. E. Fagnan (Constantine, 1895).

181 Ibn Khaldun, *Histoire Des Berbères et Des Dynasties Musulmanes de l'Afrique Septentrionale*, trans. Mac Guckin de Slane (Alger: Imprimerie du Gouvernement, 1852).

182 Al-Zarkachi, *Chroniques Des Almohades et Des Hafsides.*

183 Sebag, *Tunis: Histoire D'une Ville.*

184 Azzedine Guellouz et al., *Histoire Générale de La Tunisie: Les Temps Modernes, Tome III* (Tunis: Sud Editions, 2007).
185 Ibn Abi Dinār, *Al-Mu'nis Fī Akhbār Ifrīqīyah Wa-Tūnis.*
186 Dey, in the Ottoman government system, was an honouree title. In Tunis, in the late sixteenth century, a dey commanded the army and was in control of the state. The usage of the title ceased in the official structure by early eighteenth century. Bey, similarly, was a Turkish title traditionally given to rulers of tribal groups, to some members of noble families, and to important officials. In the Ottoman government system a bey was the governor of a province. In Tunis after 1705 the title became hereditary for the country's sovereign. The Editors of Encyclopædia Britannica, 'Bey', in *Encyclopædia Britanica* (Encyclopædia Britannica, Inc., 2016). www.britannica.com/topic/bey
187 Ibn Abi Dinār, *Al-Mu'nis Fī Akhbār Ifrīqīyah Wa-Tūnis.*
188 Djerbians are the habitants of the island of Djerba in Tunisia.
189 Ahmed Saadaoui, *Tunis, Ville Ottomane: Trois Siècles D'urbanisme et D'architecture* (Tunis: Centre de publication universitaire, 2010).
190 Sebag, *Tunis: Histoire D'une Ville.*
191 Saadaoui, *Tunis, Ville Ottomane: Trois Siècles D'urbanisme et D'architecture.*
192 Escher and Schepers, 'Revitalizing the Medina of Tunis as a National Symbol'.
193 McGuinness, 'Political Context and Professional Ideologies: French Urban Conservation Planning Transferred to the Médina of Tunis'.
194 McGuinness, 'Neighbourhood Notes: Texture and Streetscape in the Médina of Tunis', 99.
195 The Ḥamūda Pāshā mosque was built in 1655 by Ḥamūda Pāshā; the second mosque built by Ḥanafis in Tunis. For details about the building see Saadaoui, *Tunis, Ville Ottomane: Trois Siècles D'urbanisme et D'architecture.*
196 We can think of a rather similar case in Fez. The walls of the Īdrīs *zāwīya* are fully decorated in the outside passages surrounding the building, symbolising the sacredness of the inside space without revealing it. The difference between the two is that the walls of the Īdrīs *zāwīya* do not have any openings accessing the inside except for the two gates, and they do not provide any communication between the interior and exterior of the building.
197 A Dīwān, in the Ottoman governing system, was an imperial chancery headed by the grand vizier, with a consultative assembly of senior officials. In Islamic societies, the Dīwān was originally a register book and later a finance section in the administration structure, a government bureau, or an administration body. The first *dīwān* appeared in the seventh century as a pensions list. Later the term started to refer to a financial institution, and, in late seventh century, it meant a government bureau. The Editors of Encyclopaedia Britannica, 'Divan, Islamic Government Unit', n.d.
198 Ellen C. Micaud, 'Urbanization, Urbanism, and the Medina of Tunis', *International Journal of Middle East Studies* 9, no. 4 (1978): 431–47.
199 There is hammam on this passage in need of renovation which has long been out of use.
200 Two other houses that belonged to well-known persons, Bil Kādī and the al-Madanī, located at the corner of the Dīwān passage and the street of the Āghā, might have had a same affect.
201 Revault, *Palais et Demeures de Tunis (XVIIIe et XIXe).*
202 İlhami Yurdakul, 'Şeyhülislam (Shaykhulislam)', in *Encyclopedia of the Ottoman Empire*, ed. Gábor Ágoston and Bruce Alan Masters (New York: Facts on File, 2009).
203 Revault, *Palais et Demeures de Tunis (XVIIIe et XIXe).*
204 See, for example, ibid.

205 Interviewing local residents at the culs-de-sac at the Dīwān passage, do not show any social bound at the scale of the whole passage, at the current time period, which differs the role of passage here in comparison to the *dirb*s we investigated in Fez.

206 In contrast to the typical walls of an Islamic city which has windows that are too high or too small to provide visual access to what lies beyond, in this *zāwīya* windows are used in a new way. No longer merely auxiliary elements, they are, rather, important architectural elements that accord the walls a specific character that is visible even from the outside space of the pathway.

207 This feature can be expanded to many other cities in the Middle Eastern and North African region.

208 The courtyard is an exterior on which the interiors centre: the open space that gathers and orders the interiors around it. On the larger urban scale, however, the courtyard is an interior within the urban fabric, since it is socially and spatially closed off from the rest of the city and cannot be seen from outside the house.

209 I do not aim to claim that the paths were planned as boundaries by the original city makers. Such a claim would need detailed historical surveys to substantiate it. I am merely reading what exists of the city fabric of that era.

210 Thomas Nagel, 'Concealment and Exposure', *Philosophy and Public Affairs* 27, no. 1 (1998): 3; quoted in Ali Madanipour, *Public and Private Spaces of the City* (London, New York: Routledge, 2003), 59.

211 Madanipour, *Public and Private Spaces of the City.*

212 The path here refers to the regulation of movement and experiences while walking and moving around the city. These experiences are phenomenological, practical, social, and symbolic.

213 Moncef M'halla, 'La medina, un art de bâtir,' Africa: Fouilles, monuments et collections archéologiques en Tunisie (Tunis) 12, special issue: Arts et Traditions Populaires (1998): 44, 66 (kole safahat: 33–98), quoted in O'Meara, *Space and Muslim Urban Life: At the Limits of the Labyrinth of Fez*, 15.

214 Ludovico Micara, 'Lofty Chambers: The Interior Space in the Architecture of Islamic Countries', in *Understanding Islamic Architecture*, ed. Attilio Petruccioli and Khalil K. Pirani (London: Routledge, 2002), 52.

215 M'halla, 'La Médina, Un Art de Bâtir'.

216 Simon O'Meara, *Space and Muslim Urban Life: At the Limits of the Labyrinth of Fez* (London: Routledge, 2007), 15.

217 This is in contrast to, for example, gated communities, where one group of buildings is detached from its surroundings by a wall and the gate is set in the wall.

218 Sometimes the physical characters of the path provide the name of the neighbourhood – for example, Saba[c] Lūyāt means 'seven turns' and the cul-de-sac of the neighbourhood has indeed that number of turns.

219 For comparison, Wirth and Escher interpret the concept of neighbourhood (in the context of Fez) as a concretisation of the withdrawal from the public that aims at intimacy and the protection of the family. They note in Fez the bare, forbidding walled frontages along most of the thoroughfares and a few small square-like extensions in the medina of Fez that prove that the arterial roads are regarded only as an economic necessity, but not as public space which somehow or other needs to be designed. Roads and squares are negative space – the outcome of the spatial exclusion of urban open spaces which are for public and common use. The walls protect a private inner area, but are not a framework, frontage, back-drop or background for communal, public, urban life. Wirth and Escher, *Die Medina von Fes, Geographische Beiträge Zu Persistenz Und*

Dynamik, Verfall Und Erneuerung Einer Traditionellen Islamischen Stadt in Handlungstheoretischer Sicht, 29.

220 Maidans also have the typology of a courtyard. The Naqsh-i Jahān maidan in Isfahan, for instance, with its central void surrounded by rows of two-storey shops (arches), has the character of an enclosed space: a void space that is enclosed by the facades.

221 In Pandolof's anthropological research, the courtyard appeared as the most significant point in the visionary drawing of residents of a village in Morocco of their village. The courtyard was imaged as a specific location, a shorthand symbol for the interior of the village and a place of gatherings. (Pandolfo, *Impasse of the Angels*). This phenomenon is also apparent in other cities. Çelik, explaining the role of courtyard in Algiers, notes: 'Regardless of the family's income level or the size of the building, the houses of the casaba were organized around a court surrounded by arcades. This was the centre . . . Entrance to the court was indirect and achieved through several labyrinthine lobbies' (interiorised court). Zeynep Çelik, *Urban Forms and Colonial Confrontations, Algiers under French Rule* (Oakland, CA: University of California Press, 1997), 15.

222 Kamal Raftani, 'Fez', 2017.

223 Ibid.

224 See, for example, André Raymond, 'The Spatial Organization of the City', in *The City in the Islamic World*, ed. Renata Holod, Attilio Petruccioli, and André Raymond, vol. 1 (Leiden, Boston: Brill, 2008), 59, original emphasis; see also André Raymond, 'Espaces Publics et Espaces Privés Dans Les Villes Arabes Traditionnelles', *Maghreb-Machrek* 123 (1989): 194–201.

225 People have individual perceptions and imaginaries of their *dirb* which can expand beyond the alley or be delimited to only a certain part of it. For example, a girl in the Saba^c Lūyāt *dirb* in Fez included the hammam and square outside her alley as part of her neighbourhood. For one male respondent a *dirb* is where you feel you are almost home. In contrast, other residents in the Saba^c Lūyāt *dirb* consider only the parts of the pathway that surround their houses as their *dirb*, rather than seeing the whole alley in that light. Pandolfo presents another account: 'In the old qsar when a person died, the neighbors of the alley were charged with taking care of the funeral, cooking food for the guests, etc. at a funeral in the New Village, if one tried to understand what the logic was behind a certain woman's preparing the bread or another's cooking the meat, one had to go back to the layout of the old qsar. The two women lived far apart, and were not actual neighbors of the woman who died. Yet, without hesitation, they were referred to as *ahl d-dirb*, the "alley neighbors."' Pandolfo, *Impasse of the Angels*, 329.

Epilogue

Relying on reasoning and rationalising, as discussed, has reduced the descriptive, vivid features of Islamic city space into a common scientific framework. One reason for the omission of phenomenological characteristics in theory-making has been the lack of conceptual vocabulary in our global body of scholarly literature. Each spatial metaphor or concept can reveal specific structures of comprehension and shape representations. In the literature that actually acknowledges the phenomenological characteristics of Islamic cities – although mostly without incorporating such perceptions into theory-making – urban space is observed as enfolded, mysterious, inscrutable, *entr'ouvert*, simultaneously open and closed, ambiguous, maze-like and labyrinthine. Among the conceptualizations used to describe these features of the city, that of 'labyrinth' is the closest and most complex expression of the sensual experiences of the urban space. Despite its controversial applications in this context, the choice of this metaphor denotes a perception that goes beyond mere cognition. Yet, once again, this metaphor gives prominence to geometry, the element of the path and purposeful movement (i.e. movement as merely a linking activity in contrast to wandering).

In the course of exploring the urban space of the Islamic city on foot, focusing on its phenomenological features, I concluded that in the premodern structures, there is a tendency to embody the nodes of relationships or meanings in the form of interiors or centres separated from an imagined, practiced or material outside by numerous intermediary thresholds. This model has spatial characteristics that generate a constant 'revealing yet hiding' (connoting but not revealing directly): an in-between condition which is the result of a mode of boundary-making in which borders are opaque yet blurred, as they are constructed by a series of sociospatial, virtual and/or visual thresholds. In this setting, the material walls are not the key – and not the only – boundary-makers; more important and more salient are the architectural, virtual, symbolic and social containment zones whereby spatial relations are ordered through in-between spaces. Here, the multiple thresholds form boundaries – as mediators of relations in a dynamic manner – and edges between different cores throughout the city by deferring access to them.

We need to make this phenomenality of space legible, and integrate it into other aspects of space, to produce a new or more comprehensive reading of the Islamic city. A fresh perspective is needed that lays stress on the relations between spaces and in-between spaces: an approach that is based on continuity rather than segregation, where the continuity is constructed by endlessly establishing and transforming. We need to read the city by experiencing its space as a tour which – in contrast to a map – summarises and encapsulates it in terms of the in-between spaces experienced by a walker. To respond to this gap, as well as to explore and, more crucially, consolidate these features (in-betweenness, interiority and the experience of wandering) in our knowledge and scholarly understanding of cities, I have argued that we can use the conceptual vocabulary of Hezar-tu, borrowed from literature studies. I came at this concept while reworking the notion of labyrinth in the cultural-spatial context of Islamic city discourse, and believe, despite its specific geographical and cultural origins, Hezar-tu has the potential to serve as a universal concept for presenting a different vision of spatial ordering. Hezar-tu [hizār-tū], which consists of the two words of *tū* (inside) and *hizār* (thousand), literally means 'a thousand insides'. It denotes an abstraction, or an ever-elusive core, which is hidden or resides inside insides, requiring the negotiation of multiple thresholds to reach understanding of it. A *tū* is associated with concepts of insideness, enfoldedness, in-betweenness and sequential discovery, as well as acts of separating and concealing. Furthermore, the spatial structure that Hezar-tu connotes can be expanded by virtue of its two synonyms: *tū-bar-tū* (fold on fold) and *tū-dar-tū* (inside an inside). The former refers to a formation of two-dimensional folds and curves, and the latter to a composition of three-dimensional enclosed spaces. So Hezar-tu, as a spatial concept, expresses the characteristics of diverse types of structures and constellations. A reading of the city based on the conceptualization of Hezar-tu introduces urban space as a composition of *tū*s. Multiple nodes of relationships produce social, spatial, conceptual and symbolic *tū*s. The experience of walking through the city is like experiencing a Hezar-tu: *tū*s opening onto each other, one after the other, creating a fluid and continual condition of in-betweenness. We encounter this phenomenon at different scales and types in urban space, and not just the space of the Islamic city.

It is my hope that this work makes a theoretical contribution to both global urban theory and the discourse of urban studies of Islamic cities. In rethinking the contours of global urbanism, the approach introduced here presents an alternative reading of urban space: examining a new framework for conceptualising the city, promoting the logic of ambiguity and focusing on the phenomenology of space. New concepts derived from local terminology also help us tailor our global methods and theoretical structures to local contexts, allowing us to observe the peculiarities of each city while retaining global urban commonalities. They take us beyond urban theories and scholarship drawn principally from Western contexts, and offer knowledge that is diverse and democratic. In the context of Islamic cities studies, the perspective explored in this book helps transcend the idea of a city as merely a place of functions, patterns and rationales by illuminating the phenomenological characteristics of urban space. It takes us beyond rationalisation, revealing sensory features and drawing out neglected details.

Methodologically, this work encourages and follows a program of reading the city by approaching urban space and street-level indicators on foot, presenting narratives based on wandering in the city. Seen this way, the city becomes a place of nodes and thresholds. To reduce the limitations imposed on explorations of sensual, spatial features by singular personal interpretations, the number of walkers may be multiplied. The next step, in future research, should be to explore each *tū*, its characteristics and the relationships that create it as a node of sociospatial networks at different dimensions and scales. Then one could elaborate on each *tū*, the relationships that constitute it, the intersection of the relationships and their characteristics. Thus, in terms of further research (and to introduce Hezar-tu as a theory of urban space for Islamic cities), it will be necessary to expand case studies geographically by involving other cities, to change from a single perspective to an intersubjective one – making it possible to arrive at more comprehensive conclusions – and to integrate more detailed information about the historical, social and anthropological characters of specific urban spaces.

Glossary

ᶜĀlam-i-mis̱āl the Imaginal Realm
Baladīyih an urban institution that aimed at regulating urban space and urban life in Iranian cities
Bāṭīn inner side
Bunbast culs-de-sac (Persian)
ᶜIrfān Sufi ideas
ᶜUqba passages which have a high degree of slope and might have steps (Moroccan)
ᶜUrf social norm
Dirb, kūchih terms for a cul-de-sac or alley or the community associated with such a pathway. For details on *dirb* see page 158, on *kūchih* see page 161
Farrān oven
Ḥaml-maḥmūl literally means 'carrying and carried' or 'supporting and supported' and refers to the situation where an upper room is built on top of part of a dwelling below it, which belongs to a different person
Ḥānūt small local grocery
Hashtī an intermediary space between the inside and outside of a house
Iyvān loggia
Jāmīᶜ main mosque
Khīābān routes that were long and to a certain extent straight (Persian)
Kūchihbāgh alleys flanked by gardens (Persian)
Milk-mushtarak literally means 'shared property' and refers to situations in which part of a building is property shared among different owners
Muqarnas a decorative system of honeycomb or vaulted corners
Nahj passage (Tunisian)
Naẓm regularity and order and is manifested in regular, geometric patterns (Arabic and Persian)
Naẓmīyih the embryo institution that later became the police in Iran
Niẓām a kind of logic, a character, attitude or linking element (Arabic and Persian)
Qiysarīyya specialty market (Fez), royal bazaar (Isfahan)
Sābāṭ arched roof
Sāḥa open area in a passage

Saqā wall fountain

Ṣīnf craft union

Ṭāla[c] thoroughfare (Moroccan)

***Ṭarīqa* or the Way** the esoteric dimension which contrasts with the exoteric dimension of Islam that concerns the sharia or the Divine Law.

Ẓāhīr outer side

Zanqa, zuqāq passage (Moroccan)

Zāwīya literally means 'corner' and is a spiritual place for Sufi orders. For details see page 157.

Bibliography

Abdelkafi, Jellal. *La Médina de Tunis*. Paris: Centre National de la Recherche Scientifique, 1989.

Abdel-Rahim, Muddathir. 'Legal Institutions'. In *The Islamic City*, edited by Robert Bertram Serjeant, 41–51. Paris: UNESCO, 1980.

Abu-Lughod, Janet L. 'The Islamic City – Historic Myth, Islamic Essence, and Contemporary Relevance'. *International Journal of Middle Eastern Studies* 19, no. 2 (1987): 155–76.

———. 'Preserving the Living Heritage of Islamic Cities'. In *Toward an Architecture in the Spirit of Islam*, edited by Renata Holod, 61–75. Philadelphia: Aga Khan Award for Architecture, 1978.

Aharī, Zahrā. *Maktab Iṣfahān Dar Shahrsāzī (Isfahan School of Urban Design, the Syntax of Structure Design)*. Tehran: Farhangistān Hunar Press, 2006.

———. *Maktab Shahrsazi Iṣfahan*. Tehran: Hunar University Press, 2000.

Aḥmadī, Bābak. *Chāhār Guzārish Az Taẕkiratululīa (Four Reports of Attar's Taẕkiratululīa)*. Tehran: Markaz, 1997.

Akbar, Jamel A. *Crisis in the Built Environment: The Case of the Muslim City*. Singapore: Concept Media, 1988.

Alessandra, Grillo. 'Traditional Building Techniques in Fes'. Edited by Attilio Petruccioli. *Environmental Design: Journal of the Islamic Environmental Design Research Centre* 1, no. 2 (1988): 38–47.

Allen, John. 'Worlds within Cities'. In *City Worlds*, edited by Doreen Massey, John Allen, and Steve Pile. London: Routledge, 1999.

Alsayyad, Nezar. *Cities and Caliphs, on the Genesis of Arab Muslim Urbanism*. New York: Greenwood Press, 1991.

———. 'Medina-the "Islamic," "Arab," "Middle Eastern" City: Reflections on an Urban Concept'. In *Urban Design in the Arab World, Reconceptualising Boundaries*, edited by Robert Saliba. Farnham: Ashgate, 2015.

———. *The "Real", the Hyper, and the Virtual Traditions in the Built Environment*. Abingdon: Routledge, 2014.

Al-Zarkachi. *Chroniques Des Almohades et Des Hafsides*. Translated by E. Fagnan. Constantine, 1895.

Amin, Ash, and Stephen Graham. 'Cities of Connection and Disconnection'. In *Unsettling Cities*, edited by John Allen, Doreen Massey, and Michael Pryke, 7–48. London, New York: Routledge, 1999.

Amin, Ash, and Nigel Thrift. *Cities, Reimaging the Urban*. Cambridge: Polity Press, 2002.

Amster, David. 'Introduction to Domestic Architecture in the Fez Medina'. *Dar Bennis*, 2010. www.houseinfez.com/A%20Typical%20House%20in%20the%20Fez%20Medina.htm.

Antoniou, Jim. *Islamic Cities and Conservation*. Paris: UNESCO, 1981.

Arberry, Arthur J., ed. 'Introduction'. In *Fifty Poems of Hafiz [Hāfiz]*, 30–1. Cambridge: Cambridge University Press, 1970.

Ardalan, Nader. 'Color in Safavid Architecture: The Poetic Diffusion of Light'. *Iranian Studies* 7, no. 1–2 (1974): 164–78.

Ardalan, Nader, and Laleh Bakhtiar. *The Sense of Unity*. Chicago, London: University of Chicago Press, 1973.

Arnold, Arthur. *Through Persia by Caravan*. Vol. 2. New York: Harper & Brothers, 1877.

ᶜĀshūrī , Dāryūsh. *Hastīshināsī-Yi Ḥāfiẓ (Ontology of Hafiz)*. Tehran: Markaz, 1998.

Bakhtiar, Laleh. *Sufi: Expressions of the Mystic Quest*. London: Thames & Hudson, 1976.

Bancroft-Hunt, Norman. 'Labyrinth and Maze'. In *The Dictionary of Art*, edited by Jane Turner, 18:584–6. New York: Grove, 1996.

Barnes, Trevor J., and James S. Duncan. 'Introduction, Writing Worlds'. In *Writing Worlds: Discourse, Text and Metaphor in the Representation of Landscape*, edited by Trevor J. Barnes and James S. Duncan, 1–17. London, New York: Routledge, 1992.

Barthes, Roland. 'Semiology and the Urban'. In *The City and the Sign: An Introduction to Urban Semiotics*, edited by Mark Gottdiener and Alexandros Lagopoulos, 87–98. New York: Columbia University Press, 1986.

Barthold, Wilhelm. *An Historical Geography of Iran*. Princeton: Princeton University Press, 1984.

Beaumont, Peter, Gerald H. Blake, and J. Malcom Wagstaff. *The Middle East: A Geographical Study*. London: John Wiley & Sons, 1976.

Bell, David, and Mark Jayne. 'Small Cities? Towards a Research Agenda'. *International Journal of Urban and Regional Research* 33, no. 3 (2009): 683–99.

Benevolo, Leonardo. *The History of the City*. London: Scholar Press, 1980.

Benjamin, Walter. *The Arcades Project*. Cambridge, MA: Harvard University Press, 1999.

———. *The Arcades Project*. Edited by Howard Eiland and Kevin McLaughlin. Cambridge, MA: Harvard University Press, 2002.

———. *Charles Baudelaire*. London, New York: Verso, 1997.

———. *One-Way Street*. London: Verso, 1997.

Bianca, Stefano. *Architektur Und Lebensform*. Zürich, München: Architektur Artemis, 1979.

———. 'Conservation and Rehabilitation Projects for the Old City of Fez'. In *Adaptive Reuse: Integrating Traditional Areas into the Modern Urban Fabric*, edited by Bentley Sevcenko. Cambridge, MA: MIT Laboratory of Architecture and Planning, 1983.

———. *Urban Form in the Arab World, Past and Present*. New York: Thames & Hudson, 2000.

Bianquis, Thierry. 'Urbanism'. In *Medieval Islamic Civilization: An Encyclopaedia*, edited by Josef W. Meri. New York: Routledge, 2006.

Bin Khalaf Tabrīzī, Muḥammad Huṣiyn. *Burhān-I Qāṭic*. Edited by Muḥammad Mucīn. Tehran: Ibn Sīnā, 1951.

Blake, Stephen P. *Half the World: The Social Architecture of Safavid Isfahan, 1590–1722*. Costa Mesa: Mazda Publications, 1999.
Blunt, Wilfrid. *Isfahan, Pearl of Persia*. New York: Stein and Day, 1966.
Bode, Baron C.A. de. *Travels in Luristan and Arabistan*. London: J. Madden and Company, 1845.
Bord, Janet. *Mazes and Labyrinths*. London: Latimer New Dimensions, 1976.
Borges, Jorge Luis. 'The Garden of Forking Paths'. In *Collected Fictions*, translated by Andrew Hurley, 104–26. New York: Penguin Books, 1999.
Bosworth, C. Edmund, ed. *Historic Cities of the Islamic World*. Leiden, Boston: Brill, 2007.
Boulares, Habib. *Histoire Générale de La Tunisie*. Tunis: Cérès, 2011.
Bourdieu, Pierre. *The Logic of Practice*. Cambridge: Polity Press, 1990.
Brown, L. Carl. 'Introduction'. In *From Medina to Metropolis*, edited by L. Carl Brown, 15–49. Princeton: Darwin Press, 1973.
Brunschvig, Robert. 'Urbanisme Médiéval et Driot Musulman'. In *Revue Des Etudes Islamiques*, 127–55. Paris: Librairie orientaliste Paul Geuthner, 1947.
Burckhardt, Titus. *Fez: City of Islam*. Cambridge: Islamic Texts Society, 1992.
Buttimer, Anne. 'Musing on Helicon: Root Metaphors and Geography'. *Geografiska Annaler* 64B (1982): 89–96.
Calvino, Italo. 'La Sfida Al Labirinto [The Challenge to the Labyrinth]'. In *Una Pietra Sopra*, edited by Italo Calvino, 99–117. Milan: Mondadori, 1995.
Campbell, Ian. 'Tactile Labyrinths and Sacred Interiors: Spatial Practices and Political Choices in Abdelmajid Ben Jalloun's Fí Al-Tufúla and Ahmed Sefrioui's La Boîte À Merveilles'. In *World Languages and Cultures Faculty Publications*, Vol. Paper 24, 2014. http://scholarworks.gsu.edu/mcl_facpub.
Cassirer, Ernst. *An Essay on Man*. New Haven: Yale University Press, 1944.
Cavallaro, Dani. *The Mind of Italo Calvino*. North Carolina: McFarland, 2010.
Çelik, Zeynep. *Urban Forms and Colonial Confrontations, Algiers under French Rule*. Oakland, CA: University of California Press, 1997.
Certeau, Michel de. *The Practice of Everyday Life*. Oakland, CA: University of California Press, 1984.
Certeau, Michel de. *The Practice of Everyday Life*. Oakland, CA: University of California Press, 1988.
Chakrabarty, Dipesh. *Provincialising Europe: Postcolonial Thought and Historical Difference*. Princeton: Princeton University Press, 2000.
Chambers, Iain. *Migrancy, Culture, Identity*. London: Routledge, 1994.
Chardin, John. *Travels in Persia, 1673–1677*. New York: Dover, 1971.
Chittick, William C. *Ibn Al-Arabi's Metaphysics of Imagination: The Sufi Path of Knowledge*. Albany: State Univeristy of New York Press, 1989.
Clarke, John Innes. *The Iranian City of Shiraz*. Durham: University of Durham, 1963.
Clarke, John Innes, and Brian Drummond Clark. *Kermanshah, an Iranian Provincial City*. Durham: University of Durham, 1969.
Clifford, James. 'Introduction: Partial Truths'. In *Writing Culture: The Poetics and Politics of Ethnography*, edited by James Clifford and George E. Marcus, 1–26. Oakland, CA: University of California Press, 1986.
Colomina, Beatriz. *Privacy and Publicity*. Cambridge, London: MIT Press, 1996.
Connell, Raewyn. *Southern Theory*. Cambridge: Polity Press, 2007.
Conrads, Ulrich. 'Zeit Des Labyrinths'. *Bauwelt* 20 (1980): 830–6.

Conty, Patrick. *The Genesis and Geometry of the Labyrinth: Architecture, Hidden Language, Myths and Rituals*. Rochester: Inner Traditions International, 2002.

Corbin, Henri. *Creative Imagination in the Sufism of Ibn Arabi*. Translated by Ralph Manheim. Princeton: Princeton University Press, 2016.

———. *History of Islamic Philosophy*. London: Routledge, 1993.

Cresswell, Tim. *On the Move, Mobility in the Modern Western World*. New York, London: Routledge, 2006.

Curl, James Stevens. *Encyclopedia of Architectural Terms*. London: Donhead, 1992.

Curzon, George Nathaniel. *Persia and the Persian Question*. Vol. 1. Cambridge: Cambridge University Press, 1892.

Darles, Genevieve, and Nicolas Lagrange. 'The Medina of Fez – Crafting a Future for the Past'. *The UNESCO Courier* (October 1996), 36–39.

Deleuze, Gilles. 'The Fold'. Translated by Jonathan Strauss. *Yale French Studies* 80 (1991): 227–47.

———. *The Fold, Leibniz and the Baroque*. Translated by Tom Conley. London: The Athlone Press, 1993.

Deleuze, Gilles, and Felix Guattari. *A Thousand Plateaus, Capitalism and Schizophrenia*. Translated by Brian Massumi. Minneapolis, London: University of Minnesota Press, 2000.

Dennis, Richard. *Cities in Modernity, Representations and Productions of Metropolitan Space, 1840–1930*. Cambridge: Cambridge University Press, 2008.

De Planhol, Xavier. *The World of Islam*. Ithaca, NY: Cornell University Press, 1959.

Descartes, René. *Discourse on Method and the Meditations*. London: Penguin, 1968.

Dihkhudā, ʿAlī Akbar. *Lughatnāmih*. Tehran: Tehran University Press, 1980.

Djerbi, Ali. 'Sémiologie de La Médina'. In *The Living Medina: The Walled Arab City in Literature, Architecture, and History*. Tangiers, Morocco: unpublished, 1996.

Donald, James. 'Metropolis: The City as Text'. In *Social and Cultural Forms of Modernity*, edited by Robert Bocock and Kenneth Thompson, 418–70. Cambridge: The Open University, 1992.

Doob, Penelope Reed. *The Idea of the Labyrinth from Classical Antiquity through the Middle Ages*. London: Cornel University Press, 1990.

Driven, René, and Marjolijn Verspoor. *Cognitive Exploration of Language and Linguistics*. Amesterdam: John Benjamins Publishing Company, 1998.

Eco, Umberto. *Semiotics and the Philosophy of Language*. Bloomington: Indiana University Press, 1986.

Edensor, Tim, and Mark Jayne. 'Introduction, Urban Theory beyond the West'. In *Urban Theory beyond the West*, edited by Tim Edensor and Mark Jayne. Abingdon: Routledge, 2012.

———, eds. *Urban Theory beyond the West*. Abingdon: Routledge, 2012.

The Editors of Encyclopædia Britannica. 'Bey'. *Encyclopædia Britanica*. Encyclopædia Britannica, Inc., 2016. www.britannica.com/topic/bey.

———. 'Divan, Islamic Government Unit'. *Encyclopaedia Britannica*, n.d.

Ehlers, Eckart. 'Capitals and Spatial Organization in Iran: Esfahan, Shiraz, Tehran'. In *Téhéran: Capitale Bicentenaire*, edited by Chahryar Adle and Bernard Hourcade, 155–72. Bibliothèque Iranienne, 37. Paris, Tehran: Institut Français de Recherche en Iran, 1992.

———. 'City Models in Theory and Practice: A Cross-Cultural Perspective'. *Urban Morphology* 15, no. 2 (2011): 97–119.

Eisenstein, Sergei M. 'Piranesi, or the Fluidity of Forms'. In *The Sphere and the Labyrinth: Avant-Gardes and Architecture from Piranesi to the 1970s*, 65–91. Cambridge, MA, London: MIT Press, 1990.

El-Bekri, Abou-Obeid. *Description de l'Afrique Septentrionale*. Edited by Mac Guckin de Slane. Paris: Imprimerie Impériale, 1857.

El Goulli, Sophie. *Les Mystères de Tunis*. Tunis: Dar Annawras, 1993.

English, Paul Ward. *City and Village in Iran: Settlement and Economy in the Kirman Basin*. Madison: University of Wisconsin Press, 1966.

Escher, Anton. 'Die "Medina von Fès" Auf Dem Weg in Das 21. Jahrhundert?' *Trialog* 40 (1994): 46–51.

Escher, Anton, and Marianne Schepers. 'Revitalizing the Medina of Tunis as a National Symbol'. *Erdkunde* 62, no. 2 (2008): 129–41.

Ettinghausen, Richard. 'Muslim Cities: Old and New'. In *From Medina to Metropolis*, edited by L. Carl Brown, 290–318. Princeton: Darwin Press, 1973.

Falahat, Somaiyeh. 'Context-Based Conceptions in Urban Morphology: Hezar-Too, an Original Urban Logic?' *Cities*, no. 36 (2014): 50–7.

———. 'Nizams: The Hidden Syntax under the Surafce, Urban Morphology in Traditional Islamic Cities'. *Archnet-IJAR, International Journal of Architectural Research* 6, no. 1 (2012): 90–9.

———. *Reimaging the City, a New Conceptualisation of the Urban Logic of the "Islamic City"*. Wiesbaden: Springer Vieweg, 2014.

Falahat, Somaiyeh, and M. Reza Shirazi. 'New Urban Developments in Safavid Isfahan Continuity or Disjuncture?' *Planning Perspectives* 27, no. 4 (2013): 165–75.

———. 'Spatial Fragmentation and Bottom-Up Appropriations: The Case of Safavid Isfahan'. *Urban History* 42, no. 1 (2015): 3–21.

Falāmakī, Mahmūd. 'Shahrnishīnī Dar Īrān (Urbanism in Iran)'. In *Shahrhāy-I Īrān (Iranian Cities)*, edited by Mustafā Kīyānī. Tehran: Sāzmān-i Chāp va Intishārāt-i Vizarat-i Farhang va Irshād-i Islāmī, 1987.

Ferhat, Halima. 'Marinid Fez: Zenith and Signs of Decline'. In *The City in the Islamic World*, edited by Salma K. Jayyusi, Renata Holod, Attilio Petruccioli, and André Raymond, 247–67. Leiden, Boston: Brill, 2008.

Ford, Larry R. *The Spaces between Buildings*. Baltimore: Johns Hopkins University Press, 2000.

Gartman, David. 'Culture and the Built Environment'. In *Handbook of Cultural Sociology*, edited by John R. Hall, Laura Grindstaff, and Ming-cheng Lo, 347–56. London, New York: Routledge, 2010.

Gaube, Heinz. *Iranian Cities*. New York: New York University Press, 1979.

Golombek, Lisa. 'Urban Patterns in Pre-Safavid Isfahan'. *Iranian Studies* 7 (1974): 18–44.

Grabar, Oleg. 'The Architecture of the Middle Eastern City from Past to Present: The Case of the Mosque'. In *Middle Eastern Cities*, edited by Ira Marvin Lapidus, 26–46. Oakland, CA: University of California Press, 1969.

———. 'What Makes Islamic Art Islamic'. *Aarp – Art and Archaeology Research Papers* 9 (1976): 1–3.

Green, Nile. *The Love of Strangers*. Princeton, Oxford: Princeton University Press, 2016.

Gregory, Derek. 'Interventions in the Historical Geography of Modernity'. In *Place, Culture, Representation*, edited by James S. Duncan and David Ley, 272–313. London: Routledge, 1993.

Gregory, Derek, and Rex Walford. 'Introduction: Making Geography'. In *Horizons in Human Geography*, edited by Derek Gregory and Rex Walford, 1–7. London: Macmillan, 1989.

Grunebaum, Gustav E. von. 'Die Islamische Stadt'. *Saeculum* 6 (1955): 138–53.

———. *Islam: Essays in the Nature and Growth of a Cultural Tradition*. London: Routledge and Kegan Paul, 1955.

Guellouz, Azzedine, Abdelkader Masmoudi, Mongi Smida, and Ahmed Saadaoui. *Histoire Générale de La Tunisie: Les Temps Modernes*. Tome 3. Tunis: Sud Editions, 2007.

Gulick, John. 'Private Life and Public Face: Cultural Continuites in the Domestic Architecture of Isfahan'. *Iranian Studies* 7 (1974): 629–38.

Habībī, Siyid Muhsin. *Az Shar Tā Shahr (de La Cite a La Ville)*. Tehran: University of Tehran Press, 2006.

Hakim, Besim. *Arabic-Islamic Cities: Building and Planning Principles*. New York: Routledge and Kegan Paul, 1986.

Hakim, Besim S. 'Law and the City'. In *The City in the Islamic World*, edited by Salma K. Jayyusi, Renata Holod, Attilio Petruccioli, and André Raymond, 1:71–92. Leiden, Boston: Brill, 2008.

Haneda, Masashi. 'An Interpretation of the Concept of the "Islamic City"'. In *Islamic Urban Studies, Historical Review and Perspectives*, edited by Masashi Haneda and Toru Miura, 1–10. London, New York: Routledge and Kegan Paul, 1994.

Harley, John Brian. 'Deconstructing the Map'. In *Writing Worlds: Discourse, Text and Metaphor in the Representation of Landscape*, edited by Trevor J. Barnes and James S. Duncan, 231–47. New York: Routledge, 1992.

———. 'Maps, Knowledge and Power'. In *The Iconography of Landscape, Essays on the Symbolic Representation, Design and Use of Past Environments*, edited by Denis Cosgrove and Stephen Daniels, 277–312. Cambridge: Cambridge University Press, 1988.

Harvey, David. 'Models of the Evolution of Spatial Patterns in Human Geography'. In *Integrated Models in Geography*, edited by Richard Chorley and Peter Haggett, 549–608. London: Methuen, 1967.

———. *Paris, Capital of Modernity*. New York, London: Routledge, 2003.

———. 'Space as a Key Word'. In *A Critical Reader, David Harvey*, edited by Noel Castree and Derek Gregory. Malden, Oxford: Blackwell Publishing Limited, 2006.

———. *Spaces of Hope*. Edinburgh: Edinburgh University, 2000.

Herdeg, Klaus. *Formal Structure in Islamic Architecture of Iran and Turkistan*. New York: Rizzoli, 1990.

Hetherington, Kevin. *Expressions of Identity: Space, Performance, Politices*. London: Sage, 1998.

———. 'In Place of Geometry: The Materiality of Place'. In *Ideas of Difference*, edited by Kevin Hetherington and Rolland Munro. Oxford: Blackwell Publishing Limited, 1997.

Hillier, Bill, and Julienne Hanson. *The Social Logic of Space*. Cambridge: Cambridge University Press, 1984.

Hoffmann, Gerhard. 'The Labyrinth'. In *From Modernism to Postmodernism: Concepts and Strategies of Postmodern American Fiction*, edited by Gerhard Hoffmann, 415–19. Amesterdam: Rodopi, 1994.

Hourani, Albert H. 'Introduction: The Islamic City in the Light of Recent Research'. In *The Islamic City*, edited by Albert H. Hourani and Samuel M. Stern, 9–24. Oxford: Bruno Cassier, University of Pennsylvania Press, 1970.

Hunarfar, Lutfulāh. *A Treasure of the Historical Monuments of Isfahan*. Tehran: Saghafī, 1971.

Huyssen, Andreas, ed. *Other Cities, Other Worlds: Urban Imaginaries in a Globalizing Age*. Durham: Duke University Press, 2008.

Ibn Abi Dinār, Muḥammad ibn Abi al-Qāsim. *Al-Mu'nis Fī Akhbār Ifrīqīyah Wa-Tūnis*. 1869.

Ibn Khaldun. *Histoire Des Berbères et Des Dynasties Musulmanes de l'Afrique Septentrionale*. Translated by Mac Guckin de Slane. Alger: Imprimerie du Gouvernement, 1852.

Ibn Naji. *Ma'alim Al-Imam Fi Ma'rifati Ahl Al-Qayrawan*. Tunis: n.p., 1902.

Ismā'īlī, Alīriżā. 'Chāhārbāgh Dar Safarnāmihā (Chāhārbāgh in Travel Stories)'. *Gulistān-I Hunar* 5 (2006): 39–47.

Jinnai, Hidenobu. 'Microcosm of the Family around the Courtyard'. In *The Proceedings of International Conference on Urbanism in Islam (ICUIT)*, edited by Yukawa Takeshi, 2. Tokyo: Middle Eastern Culture Centre, 1989.

Katz, Jonathan G. *Architecture as Symbol and Self-Identity*. Philadelphia: Aga Khan Award for Architecture, 1980.

Kern, Hermann. *Through the Labyrinth, Designs and Meanings over 5,000 Years*. Munich, New York: Prestel, 2000.

Kheirabadi, Masoud. *Iranian Cities : Formation and Development*. Austin: University of Texas Press, 1991.

Khuramshāhī, Bahāidīn. *Ẕihn va Zābān-I Ḥāfiẕ (Mind and Language of Hafiz)*. Tehran: Ṣidā-yi Muāṣir, 1999.

Kolter, Jody. 'Abductive Reasoning as an Aesthetic of Interpretation and a Logic of Creativity in Umberto Eco's the Name of the Rose'. *Res Cogitans* 2 (2011): 165–73.

Kostof, Spiro. *The City Assembled: The Elements of Urban Form through History*. Boston: Little, Brown, 1992.

———. *The City Shaped, Urban Patterns and Meanings through History*. Boston: Little, Brown, 1991.

Kusha, Hamid R. 'Impediments to Police Modernisation in Iran, 1878–1979'. *Policing and Society* 23, no. 2 (2013): 164–82.

Lambton, Ann K.S., and Janine Sourdel-Thomine. 'Isfahan'. In *Historic Cities of the Islamic World*, edited by C. Edmund Bosworth, 167–79. Leiden, Boston: Brill, 2007.

Lapidus, Ira Marvin. 'Muslim Cities and Islamic Societies'. In *Middle Eastern Cities*, edited by Ira Marvin Lapidus, 47–76. Oakland, CA: University of California Press, 1969.

———. *Muslim Cities in the Later Middle Ages*. Cambridge, MA: Harvard University Press, 1967.

———. 'Traditional Muslim Cities: Structure and Change'. In *From Medina to Metropolis*, edited by L. Carl Brown, 51–72. Princeton: Darwin Press, 1973.

Laronde, André, and Jean-Claude Golvin. *L'Afrique Antique: Histoire et Monuments (Lybie, Tunisie, Algérie, Maroc)*. Paris: Tallandier, 2001.

Lassner, Jacob. *The Topography of Baghdad in the Early Middle Ages*. Detroit: Wayne State University Press, 1970.

Latham, Alan, Derek McCormack, Kim McNamara, and Donald McNeill. *Key Concepts in Urban Geography*. Los Angeles: Sage, 2010.
Le Bon, Gustave. *The Crowd*. Harmondsworth: Penguin, 1981.
Le Corbusier, and Pierre Jeanneret. *Oeuvre Complète*. Edited by Willi Boesiger. Vol. 2. 8 vols. Zurich: Grisbeger, n.d.
Lefebvre, Henri. *The Production of Space*. Translated by Nicholson-Smith. Oxford: Basil Blackwell, 1991.
Le Tourneau, Roger. *Fez in the Age of Marinides*. Norman: University of Oklahoma Press, 1961.
———. *Les Villes Musulmanes de L'Afrique Du Nord*. Virginia: La Maison des Livres, 1957.
Lévi-Provençal, Évariste. 'La Fondation de Fès'. *Annales de l'Institut d'Etudes Orientales* 4 (1938): 23–53.
Linde, Charlotte, and William Labov. 'Spatial Networks as a Site for the Study of Language and Thought'. *Language*, no. 51 (1975).
Lindemann, Hans-Eckhard. *Stadt Im Quadrat, Geschichte Und Gegenwart Einer Einprägsamen Stadtgestalt*. Bauwelt Fundamente, 121. Basel: Birkhäuser, 1999.
Lockhart, Laurence. 'Shah Abbas's Isfahan'. In *Cities of Destiny*, edited by Arnold J. Toynbee. London: Thames & Hudson, 1976.
Lonegren, Sig. *Labyrinths: Ancient Myths and Modern Uses*. Glastonbury: Gothic Image Publications, 1996.
Madanipour, Ali. *Designing the City of Reason, Foundations and Frameworks*. Abingdon: Routledge, 2007.
———. *Public and Private Spaces of the City*. London, New York: Routledge, 2003.
———. 'Public Spaces of European Cities'. 18, no. 1 (2005): 7–16.
———. *Tehran: The Making of a Metropolis*. Chichester: John Wiley & Sons, 1998.
Marback, Richard, Patrick Bruch, and Jill Eicher. *Cities, Cultures, Conservations: Readings for Writers*. Boston: Allyn and Bacon, 1998.
Marçais, George. 'L'Urbanisme Musulman'. *Reprinted in: Mélanges D'histoire et D'archélogie de L'occident Musulman, Articles et Confrénces de George Marçais*, 1939 1957, 211–31.
Marçais, William. 'L'Islamisme et La Vie Urbaine'. *Comptes-Rendus de l'Académie Des Inscriptions et Belles-Lettres*, (1928): 86–100.
Massey, Doreen. 'Cities in the World'. In *City Worlds*, edited by Doreen Massey, John Allen, and Steve Pile, 99–156. London, New York: Routledge, 1999.
———. 'On Space and the City'. In *City Worlds*, edited by Doreen Massey, John Allen, and Steve Pile, 157–77. London, New York: Routledge, 1999.
———. 'Travelling Thoughts'. In *Without Guarantees: In Honour of Stuart Hall*, edited by Paul Gilroy, Larry Grossberg, and Angela McRobbie, 225–32. London: Verso, 2000.
Matthews, William Henry. *Mazes and Labyrinths, a General Account of Their History and Developments*. Detroit: Singing Tree Press, 1969.
Mazower, Mark. *Salonica, City of Ghosts, Christians, Muslims and Jews, 1430–1950*. London: Haper Collins, 2004.
McGuinness, Justin. 'The Development of Conservation Management for a Pre-Industrial North African City: The Case of the Medina of Tunis'. Durham theses, Durham University, 1992. http://etheses.dur.ac.uk/6065/.
———. 'Neighbourhood Notes: Texture and Streetscape in the Médina of Tunis'. *The Journal of North African Studies* 5, no. 4 (2000): 97–120.

———. 'Political Context and Professional Ideologies: French Urban Conservation Planning Transferred to the Médina of Tunis'. *The Journal of North African Studies* 2, no. 2 (1997): 34–56.
Merrakechi, D'Abd El-Wah'id. *Histoire Des Almohades*. Translated by E. Fagnan. Alger: Adolphe Jourdan, 1893.
M'halla, Moncef. 'La Médina, Un Art de Bâtir'. *Africa: Fouilles, Monuments et Collections Archéologiques En Tunisie*, Special issue: Arts et Traditions Populaires, 12 (1998): 33–98.
Micara, Ludovico. 'Lofty Chambers: The Interior Space in the Architecture of Islamic Countries'. In *Understanding Islamic Architecture*, edited by Attilio Petruccioli and Khalil K. Pirani, 49–56. London: Routledge, 2002.
Micaud, Ellen C. 'Urbanization, Urbanism, and the Medina of Tunis'. *International Journal of Middle East Studies* 9, no. 4 (1978): 431–47.
Ministry of Culture and Arts of Iran. *Isfahan, the City of Light*. British Museum: Ministry of Culture and Arts of Iran, 1976.
Minorsky, Vladimir, ed. *Tadhkirat Al-Mulūk: A Manual of Safavid Administration (circa 1137/1725)*. Translated by Vladimir Minorsky. London: Gibb Memorial Trust, 1943.
Mīrzā Abūṭālibkhān. *Safarnāmih-Yi Mīrzā Abūtālibkhān (1789–1803) (Travel Diaries of Mīrzā Abūṭālibkhān)*. Edited by Husiyn Khadīv Jam. Tehran: Sāzmān-i Intishārāt-i va Āmūzish-i Inghilāb-i Islāmī, 1984.
Morris, A.E.J. *History of Urban Form, before the Industrial Revolutions*. Third. London, New York: Routledge, 1994.
Morris, Brian. *Anthropology of the Self: The Individual in Cultural Perspective*. London: Pluto Press, 1994.
Mukhtārī Isfahanī, Rizā, and Alīrizā Ismāīlī. *The Art of Isfahan through the Eyes of Travelers, from Safavids to Qajar*. Tehran: Farhangistān Hunar Press, 2006.
Nagel, Thomas. 'Concealment and Exposure'. *Philosophy and Public Affairs* 27, no. 1 (1998): 3–30.
Nash, Catherine. 'Post-Colonial Geographies'. In *Envisioning Human Geographies*, edited by Paul Cloke, Mark Goodwin, and Phil Crang. London: Arnold, 2004.
Nasr, Seyyed Hossein. 'Contemporary Man, between the Rim and the Axis'. *Studies in Comparative Religion* 7, no. 2 (1973): 113–26.
———. 'The Contemporary Muslim and the Architectural Transformation of the Islamic Urban Environment'. In *Toward an Architecture in the Spirit of Islam*, edited by Renata Holod. Philadelphia: Aga Khan Award for Architecture, 1978.
———. 'Foreword'. In *The Sense of Unity*, edited by Nader Ardalan and Laleh Bakhtiar, xi–xv. Chicago: University of Chicago Press, 1973.
———. *Islamic Art and Spirituality*. Albany: State University of New York Press, 1987.
———. *Islamic Life and Thought*. London: Taylor and Francis, 2007.
Neglia, Giulia Annalinda. 'Some Historical Notes on the Islamic City with Particular Reference to the Visual Representation of the Built City'. In *The City in the Islamic World*, edited by Renata Holod, Attilio Petruccioli, and André Raymond, 1. Boston: Brill, 2008.
Nieuwenhuijze, Christoffel A.O. van. *Sociology for the Middle East: A Stocktaking and Interpretation*. Leiden: Brill, 1971.
Nīkbakht, Muḥsin, and Siyid Abulqāsim Siyid Ṣadr. *Dāyiratulmaᶜārif-I Miᶜmārī va Sharsāzī (Encyclopedia of Architecture and Urban Planning)*. Tehran: Āzādih, 2002.

Norberg-Schultz, Christian. *The Concept of Dwelling*. New York: Rizzoli, 1985.
Norberg-Schulz, Christian. 'The Architecture of Unity'. In *Architectural Education in the Islamic World*, edited by Ahmet Evin. Singapore: Concept Media/Aga Khan Award for Architecture, 1986.
Nujūmīān, Amīr ᶜAlī. 'Hizār Tū-Yi Shahr Dar Hizār Tū-Yi Matn, Yik Barasī-Yi Nishānihshinākhtī (City's Hizār Tū in Text's Hizār Tū, a Semiotic Investigation)'. In *Maghālāt Duvumīn Hamandīshī Nishānihshināsī Hunar (Second Symposium of Semiotics of Art)*, 213–30. Tihrān: Farhangistān Hunar Press, 2006.
O'Meara, Simon. *Space and Muslim Urban Life: At the Limits of the Labyrinth of Fez*. London: Routledge, 2007.
Pandolfo, Stefania. *Impasse of the Angels*. Chicago: The University of Chicago Press, 1997.
Panelli, Ruth. 'Social Geographies: Encounters with Indigenous and More-than-White/Angelo Geographies'. *Progress in Human Geography* 32, no. 6 (2008): 801–11.
Park, Robert E. 'The City'. In *The City: Suggestions for Investigation of Human Behaviour in the Urban Environment*, edited by Robert E. Park, Ernest W. Burgess, and Morris Janowitz, 1–46. Chicago: Chicago University Press, 1925.
Parnell, Susan. 'The Urban'. In *The Routledge Handbook on Cities of the Global South*, edited by Susan Parnell and Sophie Oldfield, 73–4. London, New York: Routledge, 2014.
Pennick, Nigel. *Mazes and Labyrinths*. London: Robert Hale, 1990.
Pryke, Michael. 'On the Openness of Cities'. In *Unsettling Cities*, edited by John Allen, Doreen Massey, and Michael Pryke, 321–38. London, New York: Routledge, 1999.
Psarra, Sophia. *Architecture and Narrative*. London, New York: Routledge, 2009.
———. '"The Book and the Labyrinth Were One and the Same" – Narrative and Architecture in Borges' Fictions'. *The Journal of Architecture* 8 (2003): 369–91.
Raban, Jonathan. *Soft City*. London: Hamish Hamilton, 1974.
Radoine, Hassan. 'French Territoriality and Urbanism: General Lyautey and Architect Prost in Morocco (1912–1925)'. In *Colonial Architecture and Urbanism in Africa*, edited by Fassil Demissie, 11–31. Farnham: Ashgate, 2012.
Rafīᶜyī Mihrābādī, Abulghāsim. *Āṣāri Millīy-I Iṣfāhān (The National Monuments of Isfahan)*. Tehran: Anjuman-i Āṣār Millī, 1973.
Raftani, Kamal. 'Fez', Email correspondence, 2017.
Random House Webster's Unabridged Dictionary. New York: Random House, 2000.
Raymond, André. *Arab Cities in the Ottoman Period: Cairo, Syria and the Maghreb*. Variorumncollected Studies Series. Aldershot: Ashgate, 2002.
———. 'Espaces Publics et Espaces Privés Dans Les Villes Arabes Traditionnelles'. *Maghreb-Machrek* 123 (1989): 194–201.
———. *Grandes Villes Arabes À L'époque Ottomane*. Paris: Sindbad, 1985.
———. 'The Spatial Organization of the City'. In *The City in the Islamic World*, edited by Renata Holod, Attilio Petruccioli, and André Raymond, 1:47–70. Leiden, Boston: Brill, 2008.
———. 'Urban Life and Middle Eastern Cities, the Traditional Arab City'. In *A Companion to the History of the Middle East*, edited by Youssef M. Choueiri, 207–26. Oxford: Blackwell Publishing Limited, 2005.
Rendell, Jane. 'Introduction: "Gender, Space"'. In *Gender, Space, Architecture, an Interdisciplinary Introduction*, edited by Jane Rendell, Barbara Penner, and Lain Borden, 101–11. London: Routledge, 2000.

Revault, Jacques. *Palais et Demeures de Tunis (XVIIIe et XIXe)*. Paris: Centre National de la Recherche Scientifique, 1971.

Revault, Jacques, Lucien Golvin, and Ali Amahan. 'Palais et Demeures de Fès'. Demeures de Fès (XIVe-XVIIe Siècles). Marseille: Institut de Recherches et d'études sur le monde arabe et musulman, 1985.

Robinson, Jennifer. *Ordinary Cities, between Modernity and Development*. Abingdon: Routledge, 2006.

———. 'Postcolonialising Geography: Tactics and Pitfalls'. *Singapore Journal of Tropical Geography* 24, no. 3 (2003): 273–89.

Roncato, Sergio. 'Piranesi and the Infinite Prisons'. *Spatial Vision* 21, no. 1–2 (2007): 3–18.

Rorty, Richard. *Contingency, Irony, and Solidarity*. Cambridge: Cambridge University Press, 1989.

Rosso, Stefano. 'A Correspondence with Umberto Eco'. Translated by Carolyn Springer. *Boundary 2* 12, no. 1 (1983): 1–13.

Roy, Ananya. 'The 21st-Century Metropolis: New Geographies of Theory'. *Regional Studies* 43, no. 6 (2009): 819–30.

———. '"The Reverse Side of the World": Identity, Space, and Power'. In *Hybrid Urbanism: On the Identity Discourse and the Built Environment*, edited by Nezar Alsayyad, 229–45. London: Praeger, 2001.

Royaume du Maroc. *Schéma Directeur D'urbanisme de La Ville de Fès*. Paris: Ministère de l'habitat et de l'aménagement du territoire, 1980.

Saadaoui, Ahmed. *Tunis, Ville Ottomane: Trois Siècles D'urbanisme et D'architecture*. Tunis: Centre de publication universitaire, 2010.

Said, Edward W. *Orientalism*. New York: Vintage Books, 1979.

Sauvaget, Jean. *Alèp: Essai Sur Le Développement D'une Grande Ville Syrienne, Des Origins Au Milieu Du XIXe Siècle*. Paris: P. Geuthner, 1941.

———. 'Le Plan de Laodicée-Sur-Mer'. *Bulletin D'études Orientales* 4 (1934): 81–114.

Savory, Roger. *Iran under the Safavids*. Cambridge: Cambridge University Press, 1980.

Scarce, Jennifer. 'Muqarnas'. In *Encyclopedia of Islamic Civilisation and Religion*, edited by Ian Richard Netton. London, New York: Routledge, 2008.

Schimmel, Annemarie. *Islam, and Introduction*. New York: State University of New York Press, 1992.

Sebag, Paul. 'Tunis'. In *Historic Cities of the Islamic World*, edited by C. Edmund Bosworth, 535–49. Boston: Brill, 2007.

———. *Tunis: Histoire D'une Ville*. Paris: L'Harmattan, 1998.

Seigworth, Gregory. 'Banality for Cultural Studies'. *Cultural Studies* 14, no. 2 (2000): 227–68.

Serjeant, Robert Bertram, ed. *The Islamic City: Selected Papers from the Colloquium Held at the Middle East Centre, Faculty of Oriental Studies, Cambridge, United Kingdom, from 19 to 23 July 1976*. Paris: UNESCO, 1980.

Sheringham, Michael. 'City Space, Mental Space, Poetic Space: Paris in Breton, Benjamin and Réda'. In *Parisian Fields*, edited by Michael Sheringham. London: Reaktion, 1996.

Shields, Rob. *Places on Margin*. London and New York: Routledge, 1991.

———. *Spatial Questions, Cultural Topologies and Social Spatialisations*. Los Angeles: Sage, 2013.

Smith, Margaret. *Al-Ghazzālī the Mystic*. London: Hijra International Publishers, 1944.
Smith, Neil, and Cindy Katz. 'Grounding Metaphor: Towards a Spatialized Politics'. In *Place and the Politics of Identity*, edited by Michael Keith and Steve Pile, 67–83. London: Routledge, 1993.
Spender, Stephen. *World within World*. London: Hamish Hamilton, 1951.
Spooner, Brian. 'City and River in Iran: Urbanization and Irrigation of the Iranian Plateau'. *Iranian Studies* 7 (1974): 681–713.
Stevenson, Deborah. *Cities and Urban Cultures*. Maidenhead: Open University Press, 2003.
Stoppani, Teresa. 'Voyaging in Piranesi's Space: A Contemporary Re-Reading of the Beginnings of Modernity'. *Haecceity Papers* 1, no. 2 (2006): 32–54.
Sulṭān Siyyid Rižā Khān. *Dārulsalṭanih-Yi Iṣfahan*. Isfahan: Saḥāb Cartography Centre, 1923.
Sulṭānzādih, Ḥusiyn. *Bazaar-Hāyi Īrānī*. Tehran: Daftar-i Pajūhish-i Farhangī, 2001.
———. *Muqadami-Ī Bar Tārīkhi Shahr va Shahrsāzī Dar Īrān (An Introduction to the History of City and Urbanism in Iran)*. Tehran: Amīr Kabīr, 1988.
Tchumi, Bernard. *Architecture and Distinction*. Cambridge, MA: MIT Press, 1996.
Tocqueville, Alexis de. *Democracy in America*. New York: Harper & Row, 1966.
Tonkiss, Fran. *Cities by Design, the Social Life of Urban Form*. Cambridge: Polity Press, 2013.
———. *Space, the City and Social Theory, Social Relations and Urban Forms*. Cambridge: Polity Press, 2005.
Troin, Jean François. 'Urbanization and Development: The Role of the Medina in the Maghreb'. In *Urban Development in the Muslim World*, edited by Hooshang Amirahmadi and Salah S. El-Shakhs, 94–108. New Brunswick: Center for Urban Policy Research, 1993.
Twagilimann, Aimable. 'Italo Calvino's If on a Winter's a Night, a Traveler and the Labyrinth'. In *The Labyrinth*, edited by Harold Bloom and Blake Hoppy. New York: Infobase Publishing, 2009.
Tyler, Stephen A. 'Ethnography, Intertextuality, and the End of Description'. In *The Unspeakable: Discourse, Dialogue and Rhetoric in the Postmodern World*, 89–106. Madison: University of Wisconsin Press, 1987.
Weiss, Beno. *Undesrtanding Italo Calvino*. South Carolina: University of South Carolina, 1993.
Wheatley, Paul. 'Levels of Space Awareness in the Traditional Islamic City'. *Ekistics*, no. 253 (1976): 354–66.
White, Hayden. *Tropics of Discourse: Essays in Cultural Criticism*. Baltimore: The Johns Hopkins University Press, 1978.
Wilson, Elizabeth. *The Sphinx in the City: Urban Life, the Control of Disorder, and Women*. Oakland, CA: University of California Press, 1991.
Wirth, Eugen. 'The Concept of the Oriental City: Privacy in the Islamic East versus Public Life in Western Culture'. *Environmental Design: Journal of the Islamic Environmental Design Research Centre* 18, no. 1–2 (2001/2000): 10–21.
———. 'Die Orientalische Stadt, Ein Überblick Aufgrund Jüngerer Forschungen Zur Materiellen Kultur'. *Saeculum* 26, no. 1 (1975): 45–94.
———. *Die Orientalische Stadt Im Islamischen Vorderasien Und Nordafrika: Städtische Bausubstanz Und Räumlische Ordnung, Wirtschaftsleben Und Soziale Organisation*. Vol. 1–2. Mainz: Philipp von Zabern, 2000.

———. 'Zur Konzeption Der Islamischen Stadt: Privatheit Im Islamischen Orient versus Öffentlichkeit in Antike Und Okzident'. *Die Welt Des Islams* 31, no. 1 (1991): 50–92.

Wirth, Eugen, and Anton Escher. *Die Medina von Fes, Geographische Beiträge Zu Persistenz Und Dynamik, Verfall Und Erneuerung Einer Traditionellen Islamischen Stadt in Handlungstheoretischer Sicht.* Germany: Fränkische Geographische Gesellschaft, 1992.

World Bank. *Morocco – Fez Medina Rehabilitation Project.* Washington, DC: World Bank, 2006. http://documents.worldbank.org/curated/en/2006/06/6843147/morocco-fes-medina-rehabilitation-project.

Yurdakul, İlhami. 'Şeyhülislam (Shaykhulislam)'. In *Encyclopedia of the Ottoman Empire*, edited by Gábor Ágoston and Bruce Alan Masters. New York: Facts on File, 2009.

Index

abstraction 2, 35, 43, 167
Abū ᶜAnan 105
Abu-Lughod, J. L. 24–26, 35, 36, 42, 81
actuality 8
administrative units 21, 26
Ahmad Alīkhān Zand 32
al-Āghā 134
al-bilād al-ᶜArabī 130
al-ᶜĀlīya 103
al-ᶜAmrānī 113
al-Ghazālī 85
al-Ḥafṣīyūn 6, 132, 133
al-Ḥalfāwīn 132
al-Ḥuluq 132
al-Marākishī 131
al-Mārīuns 105, 106
al-Murāvīds 104
al-Muvaḥidūns 104, 105, 132
al-Qumāsh 132
al-Rum 114
al-Shāwāshīn 133
al-Shurafā 107, 109, 110
al-Suwayqa 132
al-Tawfīq 132
al-ʾUmawīyya 131
Aleppo 41
Algerian *see* house
Algiers 39, 41, 42, 165
Ālibūyih 119
Alsayyad, N. 45, 48
ambiguity 47, 63, 64, 66, 67, 125, 167; as a characteristic of cities 4; in perception 65; in Hafiz 85; and negotiable boundaries 34; topological ambiguity 91, 92n27; *see also* atmosphere; *see also* logic; *see also* spatial
Amin, A. 43, 73, 75
Amīr Iqtidār Hukmrān 33
Ānandirāj 82
Arab 4, 6, 11, 37, 40, 41, 48, 81, 89, 93, 131, 149, 153; Arab cities 37, 41, 81
Association de Sauvegarde de la Médina de Tunis [ASM] 130
atmosphere 109, 124, 129, 139; of ambiguity, 125
ausgrenzen 89n4
Außerhalb-sein 89n4
authoritative knowledge 2

Bāb Abī Saᶜadūn 132
Bāb al-Baḥr 131
Bāb al-ᶜUluj 132
Bāb al-Falla 132
Bāb al-Jazīra 131, 132, 133
Bāb al-Khaḍrā 132
Bāb al-Saqqāīn 131
Bāb ᶜAlīwa 132
Bāb Khālid 132
Bāb Qarṭājina 131
Bāb ʾArṭā 131
baladīyih 33
barzakh 11, 86, 87, 92
barzan 162n157
bāshmāq 133
bāṭīn 84
bazaar 6, 18, 20–23, 27, 28, 37, 102, 118–128, 139, 145, 147, 148, 161, 162
being-in-between 86
bend 82, 83, 90n8, 124, 128, 147, 148
Benjamin, W. 74, 95
beys 132, 133
bildīya 130
Bin Zīān 107, 113, 153, 159n112
body: being analogous to the human body 27; bodily encounters 47

border 11, 34, 45, 102, 130, 135, 138, 139, 148, 152, 159n113, 166; ownership 34
Borges, J. L. 62, 63, 64, 66
boundary 7, 8, 12, 21, 24, 28, 31–33, 42, 44, 46, 86, 87, 92, 101, 102, 105, 107, 111, 113, 114, 123, 124, 128, 135, 141, 145, 147–149, 152, 159n112, 164; boundary-makers 153; dynamic boundary 81, 150; in maps 34; natural boundary 100; porous boundary 11, 89; *see also* ambiguity; sociospatial boundary 109; symbolic boundary 146; three types of boundary 25; walls as boundary-makers 4
brightness 123, 124, 129, 139, 140
Brunschvig, R.14, 18, 49
bunbast 32
Bureau Topographique du Maroc Occidental 29, 33
Burhān-i Ghāti[c] 82

[c]Abbās I 119, 120
Cairo 21, 38, 55
[c]Ālam-i-miṣāl 86, 99
[c]Alawīds 106
[c]Ayn Qadūs 158n101
calligraphy 113, 124, 126, 148
Calvino, I. 63, 64
[c]Aqba Sabā[c] 114
caravanserai 24, 27, 32, 35, 51, 119, 120, 147
Carceri d'invenzione 63
Carthage 131
casbah 39, 131, 132, 133
cell 17, 34, 122, 126, 127; cells of residence 26; *see also* privacy: *see also* spatial
de Certeau, M. 16, 67, 87, 96, 97
Chāhārbāgh *see* Isfahan
chīn 82, 90n8
Clifford, J. 69
code of space 10, 36
cognitive interpretations 16
collective identities 152
colonial cities 29
colonial 29, 130
colonialism 130
concept 48; concept-of-space 7; *see also* spatial
containment 11, 89, 114, 121, 124, 126, 139, 140, 145, 146, 148, 166; containment zone 126, 135, 166; zone of containment 146
Corbin, H. 86
courtyard 18, 22–24, 27–29, 34, 35, 37, 40, 42, 44, 67, 74, 88, 89, 95, 105–107, 109–111, 113, 114, 124, 130, 135, 138, 141, 145, 146–149, 151, 159n105, 159n106, 159n111, 164, 165; courtyard houses 22
craft union see *ṣīnf*
cultures of space 7
[c]urf 102
curved 64
curve 82, 83, 90n8, 97, 109, 124, 126, 128, 130, 139, 146, 148, 167

Daedalus 58, 67, 84, 90n11
Dār al-Baṭḥā 106
Dār al-Biyḍā 106
Dār-ul-Funūn 29
darkness 85, 123, 124, 128, 129, 139, 140
De Planhol X. 18, 35
deferring 2, 11, 85, 88, 145, 150, 166
Deleuze, G. 62, 64, 65
deys 132
dirb 107–117, 134, 137, 141, 144–147, 151–153, 159n107, 159n108, 159n112, 161, 164, 165; definition 158n102
disciplinary backgrounds 9, 14, 17
Divine Isfahan School 117
Divine Law 28, 29, 91n17
Dīwān 134, 135, 137, 140, 141, 142, 143, 144, 145, 146, 163, 164

Eco, U. 63, 64
edge 12, 81, 86, 87, 100, 120, 135, 149, 150, 166; *see also* spatial
eingrenzen 89n4
enfolded 41, 44, 45, 147, 148, 166
enfoldedness 146–147, 167; instrument of enfoldedness 145; tendency towards enfoldedness 145
entr'ouvert 37, 44, 166
entre-deux 11, 87
epistemological tool 82
exterior *see* urban exterior
exteriority 4, 29, 102, 109, 135, 138, 141

farrān 107, 159n112
feeling of being lost 61, 63

feeling of belonging 88, 145, 152
Fez 4, 11–12, 20, 22, 29, 33, 34, 37, 41, 42, 87, 89, 93–95, 100–112, 115–117, 135, 138, 140–142, 145, 146, 147, 149, 151–153; al-Dabāghīn 110, 111, 113, 159n111; al-Darᶜī 111–113, 159n111; al-Qarāwīyīn mosque 103–105, 107, 117; Bū ᶜAlī mosque 110, 111, 113, 114; Bū ᶜAnānyyia 105; Būjlūd 104, 106, 107, 158n103; ᶜAṭṭārīn 105; Fez al-Bālī 103, 105–112, 115, 116, 151; Fez al-Jdīd 103, 105–107; history 103–107; Madīnat Fās 103; Mellah 107; Miṣbāhīyya 105; Sabaᶜ Lūyāt 107, 108, 117, 135, 153, 158n102, 159n108, 164, 165; Ṣaffārīn 105; Sbāyīn 105; *see also* Fès; Shāwī *zāwīya* 114; Shāwī 107, 108, 114–116, 145, 146; Sīdī Muḥammad al-Ḥāj 107, 109, 110, 114, 153; Ṭālaᶜ Kabīra 104, 158; Ṭālaᶜ Ṣaghīra 104, 107, 158; Zūwītan 110, 111, 113, 159n111; Wād Ṣarrāfīn 114
flâneur 74, 95, 98
fluidity of view 126
foldedness 11
folds-on-folds 148
French Protectorate 133, 159n107
French 42, 84, 107, 130, 133
frontier 87, 88
fusion of times 94

Garden of Forking Paths 63
geometry 5, 19, 20, 30, 36, 44, 47, 58, 66, 71, 98, 126, 166
Global South 3, 153
Grabar, O. 20, 21
Grand Mufti 140
die Grenze 89n4

ḥaml-maḥmūl 152
Ḥammūda Pāshā Bey 133
ḥānūt 107
hashtī 128, 130, 162
Harvey, D. 53n94, 69, 74
Hassan Ibn Nuᶜmān 131
heritage 8, 103, 106, 132–134
Hezar-tu 2, 4, 5, 10, 11, 12n2, 48, 75, 81; city as Hezar-tu 93, 95, 145–147, 167, 168; as a space 87–89; as a text 84; as vocabulary 82–84;
Hezar-tu-ness 11
hezar 10, 82; *see also hizār*
hikmat 98
Hillier, B. 15n32
hizār-khānih 83
hizār-lā 83
hizār 2, 10, 82, 83, 90n11, 91n11, 167
Hourani, A. 21
house 38, 42
Ḥusaynid 133
ḥuma 159n102

Ibn al-Arabi 86
Ibn Ḥayūn 153
Ibn Khaldūn 131
Ibn Nājī 131
Īdrīs I, 103
Īdrīs II, 103
Īdrīsīd: age 104; dynasty 103
Ifriqiya 131, 132
Imaginal Realm 86, 99; *see also ᶜĀlam-i-miṡāl*
immigrants 106, 121, 130, 158n101
imtīyāz and *takhsīs* 100
in-between 2, 11, 12, 82, 83, 86–89, 90n8, 95, 111, 113, 145, 146, 148, 150, 166, 167
in-betweenness 2, 11, 82, 86–89, 145, 148, 167
indoor 29, 30, 35
infinity 62
infrastructure *see* modern infrastructure 32
inner *see bāṭīn*
Innerhalb-sein 23, 44, 89n4
inside 2, 12, 26, 44, 58, 62, 71, 72, 82, 83, 87–89, 100, 109–111, 113, 114, 119, 121, 124, 128, 130, 135, 138, 139, 141, 146, 148, 151, 152, 161, 162, 163, 167
insideness 2, 10, 23, 82, 89, 145, 167
insides-in-insides 148
Institute Nationale du Patrimoine [INP] 130
interior 4, 27–29, 36, 38, 72, 82, 102, 107, 109, 112, 113, 121, 124, 135, 138, 139, 141, 147–149, 152, 163–165
interiority 4, 29, 37, 88, 89, 109, 135, 138, 139, 141, 146, 167
intermediacy 87
intermediary 22, 86, 89, 114, 138, 162, 166

intermediary realm 22
intermediate zone 11, 87
interpretations of space 69, 70
Iran 6, 27, 33, 117, 118, 120
Iranian cities 27, 118, 121
ᶜ*irfān* 84, 92
Iraq 41
Irrweg 62
Isfahan Urbanism School 117
Isfahan 4, 11, 12, 28–33, 38, 40, 87, 93, 95, 100–102, 117–123, 125, 127, 129, 135, 138, 139, 141, 142, 149, 151; Allāh Virdī Khān Bridge 120; ᶜĀlī-Qāpū 120; Chāhārbāgh 38, 120, 121, 161; Dardasht 119; Imāmzādih Īsmāᶜīl shrine 31; Jiy 118, 160; Jūbārih 119, 160; Kārān 119; Khājū Bridge 28; Khūsīnān 118; Kūchih-yi Masjid 128; Masjid Jāmiᶜ 118; Masjid-i Shāh 28; Miydān-i Kuhnih 28; Najafī house 130; Naqsh-i Jahān 28, 120, 121, 122, 124, 148, 161, 165; Pusht-i Masjid neighbourhood 121, 127, 129, 151; *see also* map; Shah Abbas 38, 160, 161; Shāh mosque 120, 121, 128; Shiykh Luṭfullāh mosque 120, 125, 127; Yahūdīyyih 118, 119, 160; Zāyandihrūd 28, 100, 117
Islamic city 2, 75, 93, 98, 99, 102, 103, 117; as a concept 5, 9; countering a myth 148, 149; house 152; Islamic city studies 1, 4, 9, 10, 16; labyrinth and Islamic city 45–48, 72; maps and diagrams 29, 35; as a mode of spatialisation 8; navigator of urban space 20; perceptions 35, 36, 38; public-private pattern 22–23; publicness and privacy 150; rationalised phenomenology 39–45; schematic conceptions 19, 20; segregation 24; socio-administrational structure 21; space 166, 167; as a spatial-physical object 20; symbolic conception 27; as a shorthand 12n1; theories 17–26; urban space 12, 81, 88, 89n4, 91n25; wall 26, 149;
īvān 141

Jāmaᶜ al-Jdīd 133
Jāmiᶜ al-Andalus 103
Jāmiᶜ al-Qarāwīn 103
jāmiᶜ 135
jūy 100

Kairouanian 103, 105
kham 82, 90n8
khīābān 32
Khuramshāhī B. 86
knowledge-production 1, 9
Kriziz, A. 29
kūchih 32, 52, 124, 130, 147, 151, 152; definition 161n157
kūchihbāgh 32
kūy 162n157

L'Agence pour le Développement et la Réhabilitation de la ville de Fès [ADER-Fez] 108
lā-bar-lā, 83, 90n8 148
lā 82, 83, 90n8
lābīrint 83, 84
labyrinth 2, 4, 10, 75; and Islamic cities 16, 18– 20, 26, 37, 39, 40–48, 166, 167; Christian labyrinths 60; Cretan labyrinth 60, 68, 90n11; definition 58; etymology 61, 62; flower-bed labyrinths 61; history 59–61; infinity 62–65; labyrinthine city 67, 68; multi-path labyrinth 61, 65; Persian translation 83, 84; representation 68, 70–72; spatial model 65–67; labyrinthine 4, 10, 18, 19, 37, 39, 40, 44–47, 58, 60, 63, 64, 66–68, 70–72, 90n11, 165, 166
labyrinthinity 10, 47, 48, 66
Lapidus, I. M. 21
Le Corbusier 88, 92
Lefebvre, H. 6, 43, 70
Le Tourneau R. 20, 22, 42, 46, 105, 106
legal borders of ownership 152
Liebniz, G. W. 64
life-world 70, 99, 100, 106, 117
liminal 1, 37, 81, 87, 121
liminality 2
lingering 61, 66, 67
lintel 109, 110, 113, 117
lived space 34
local 4, 5, 19, 21, 29, 31, 32, 41, 60, 69, 93, 95, 98, 99, 100, 114, 153, 161, 164, 167
logic: of ambiguity 2, 11, 89, 167; of the subdivision 25

mādī 100
madrasa 105, 119, 132

maḥallih 162n157
maidan 119, 120, 124, 165
Maliki 6
map 29, 35, 47, 70, 72, 90n11, 95, 97, 167; cartographic 17, 79n105, 94; cities as maps 43, 45; Dārulsalṭanih map of Isfahan 29; Pier Colin's map of Tunis 29; mental map 96; view 96;
mapping 1, 29, 32, 34, 35, 46
marginality 3
Marrakesh 104
maze: and Islamic cities 4, 18, 38, 44, 46, 47; city 67, 68, 166; definition and history 58, 59, 61–65; maze-like 4, 46, 58, 64, 166; spatial concept 66
medina 37, 40, 93, 94, 95, 103; courtyard 147; of Fez 104, 106, 107, 109, 113, 117, 152; house 153; sociospatial network 153; structure 149; of Tunis 130–137, 140, 142–144; urban fabric 147; urban form 98; walls 26, 149, 152;
metaphor 2, 7, 8, 10, 17, 45, 58, 63, 64, 68, 71–74, 85, 89, 166; spatial 10, 44, 48, 65, 71, 75, 81, 166; urban 82;
metaphorical city 97
metaphorical space 46
methodological problems 21
Middle East 2, 5, 6, 8, 10, 16, 27, 29
Middle Eastern 2, 4, 6, 23, 82, 99
milk-mushtarak 152
mīrāb 100
modern 9, 12, 32, 39, 46, 94, 99, 103; analytical structure 40; city, 10, 37, 46, 67, 68, 72, 74, 133; functions 107; institutions 33, 53n87; labyrinth 62, 76n25; maps 17, 29; modern product 5; modern understanding 3, 29, 32; planning standards 107; representations 8, 29, 32; Tunis 130; urban life 53n94; urban planning 106; *see also* infrastructure
modernisation 6, 52n82, 95, 117
modernising 121; impacts 11
modernist 10, 17, 46, 72
modernity 3, 93
Morocco 6, 41, 92, 105, 106
morphology 19, 26, 27, 45, 133
morphological 5, 8, 22, 24
mosque 18, 19, 24, 27; accessibility 51n35; centrality of mosque 6; in maps 30, 33, 35; mosque as public realm 22, 23; mosques and aesthetics of city 38; mosques and water 101; mosques in Fez 103–107, 110, 113, 114, 117; mosques in Isfahan 118–121, 125, 128; mosques in Tunis 131–133, 135, 136, 139, 141, 142; as navigator of urban space 20, 21; orthogonal pattern of mosque 14n21; as an urban function 6, 20
movement 10, 24, 27, 28, 29, 30, 32, 34, 38, 43, 45, 46, 47, 59, 63, 65, 66, 67, 70, 71, 72, 73, 86, 90n11, 96, 114, 121, 127, 128, 149, 150, 159n107, 164, 166
moving 2, 3, 28, 36, 43, 60, 66, 68, 71, 88, 96, 113, 120, 146, 148, 164
muhtasib 101
Mūlāy al-Rashīd 106
Mulāy Īdrīs 103, 105, 146
multilayered-ness 127
muqaddima 86
muqarnas 125, 126
mysticism 117
myth 12, 39, 47, 58, 60, 70, 148

namings 39
narration of the path 11, 95
narrative maps 96
Nasr, S. H. 85, 99
National Institute of Patrimony 130
navigator 20
Nāẓimulaṭibā 82
naẓm 99
naẓmīyih 32, 33, 52n82
neighbourhood 6, 19, 22–27, 30, 31, 33, 37, 81, 95, 100, 101, 102, 105, 107, 119, 121, 134, 146, 148, 152; *see also barzan*; *see also kūy*; *see also maḥallih*; *see also* quarter; *see also* residential
nīẓām 98, 99, 100
niẓām 99, 102
node 2, 64, 87, 88, 89, 114, 123, 126, 139, 140, 145, 147, 152, 153, 166, 167, 168
vertical social nodes 152
North Africa 2, 5, 8, 10, 16, 19, 20, 27, 29, 104
North African 2, 6, 82, 99, 162, 164
nuclei 10, 72

occidental 23
order of differences 87

orient 7
oriental 6, 23
Orientalist 9, 19, 38, 41, 46
Ottoman 102, 132, 133, 140, 163
outdoor 29, 30, 34
outer *see ẓāhir*
outside 3, 11, 22, 26, 34, 41, 43, 46, 71, 82, 83, 88, 89, 93, 113, 114, 124, 130, 135, 138, 139, 140, 141, 146, 152, 158n102, 162, 163, 164, 165, 166
outsideness 2
outside spaces 34

paradise 99, 126
pardih 82, 83
path 2, 10, 20, 30, 38, 58, 59, 61, 62, 64–66, 71, 73, 96, 97, 107, 109, 114, 140, 149, 150, 166
perception 2, 3, 7, 9, 30, 61, 65, 69, 70, 73, 85, 154n9, 166; deformed perception 10; immediate perception 11; obscuring perceptions 124; patriarchal perception 19; perception and labyrinth 67; perception of urban diversity 2; perception of urban space 1, 2, 39, 44; perceptions of a walker 139, 150; perceptions of Islamic city 35, 36, 38, 39; phenomenological perceptions 44, 45, 72; play of perceptions 161n160; sensual perception 2, 3, 40, 46, 70, 96, 109, 148; verbalising perceptions 44
perceptual 37, 68, 95
phenomenology: phenomenality 4, 5, 10, 16, 39, 43, 44, 45, 46, 74, 75, 167; *see also tū*; phenomenological 1, 4, 5, 10, 11, 17, 30, 43, 44, 45, 47, 72, 73, 81, 102, 117, 146, 147, 148, 149, 150, 164, 166, 167, 168; phenomenology of *tū*ness 147
physical qualities 123
Piranesi, G. B. 62, 63, 66
place-images 4, 39, 44, 47
postcolonial 3, 4, 92, 130
postmodern 63, 64, 67–69, 90n11
postmodernism 68
premodern 4, 5, 14n27, 32, 37, 66, 94, 95, 166; Fez, 114; Isfahan 100, 117
privacy 12, 19, 22, 23, 25, 27, 35, 40, 42, 44, 102, 150, 153; cell of privacy 152
private 1, 4, 12, 17–19, 22–24, 29, 37, 39, 40–42, 51, 94, 98, 101, 106, 109, 120, 128, 130, 135, 140, 146, 148, 149, 152, 153; collective-private 22
Protectorate 141
public-private: division 22; sociospatial relations 22
public 1, 4, 12, 18, 19, 21, 22, 29, 36, 37, 38, 40, 41, 81, 94, 101, 103, 121, 128, 134, 135, 139, 141, 146, 147, 148, 149, 152, 153; space, 23, 24, 30, 34, 42, 164; *see also* urban; *see also* semi-public

Qarāwīnian 105
Qarāwīyīn *see* Fez
Qasba 134
qiysarīyya 103–105, 120, 158n103
quarter 20, 22, 23, 41, 105, 107, 119, 130, 160; *see also* neighbourhood; *see also* residential
Quran 6, 84, 85, 86, 91n25, 92, 99, 111, 140

rational relations 16
rationale 20, 29, 41
rationalisation 16, 48, 168
rationality 16, 34, 45, 46, 48
Raumkonzept 2, 24
räumliche Gliederung 22
räumliche Organization 22
Raymond, A. 18, 19, 41, 48
reasoning 1
representation 4, 6, 7, 8, 17, 19, 29, 30, 32, 34, 35, 38, 45, 47, 48, 61, 64, 66, 68, 69, 70, 71, 72, 86, 87, 94, 96, 166
residential: quarter 19, 22, 23, 24, 28, 35, 100, 121; zone 19
revealing yet hiding 88, 166
rhizome 64, 65
Robinson, J. 3, 13
Roman Empire 131
Roy, A. 3

sābāṭ 109, 114, 115, 117, 139, 140, 141, 145, 147
Saᶜdī 106
sacredness of centrality 127
Safavid 28, 33, 40, 91, 100, 102, 117, 119, 120, 121, 160, 161
Safeguarding of the Medina of Tunis 130
sāḥa 114
Saḥāb Geographic and Drafting Institute 31

Said, E. 7
Saljuqid era 100
saqā 113, 114, 115
Sassanid 118
Schéma Directeur D'urbanisme de La Ville de Fès 108
schematic 6, 19, 35; conceptions 19; urban understanding 19
scientific conception 5, 8, 45
segregation 1, 24, 25, 26, 42, 100, 102, 167; of the sexes 25
semi-public 134, 135
sensation 4
senselessness 68
sensory 1, 12, 43, 47, 74, 75, 95, 98, 123, 140, 168
sensual 1, 4, 5, 7, 11, 16, 17, 30, 35, 37, 39, 40, 43, 44, 46, 47, 64, 68, 70, 72, 86, 89, 91, 95, 96, 109, 140, 142, 148, 150, 154n9, 166, 168; *see also* perception
sequential discovery 11, 83, 145, 167
shared private ownership 23
sharia 28, 91n17, 98, 140
Shāri^c Biyn al-Qaṣrīn 21
Shaykh al-Islām 140
shikan 82, 90n8
Shīshīās Kabīr suq 138
Sīāj 107, 108, 114, 115, 146; Sīāj *tū* 146
Sīdī Ahmad bin Nāṣir al-Dar^cī 110
Sīdī bin Arūs 134
Sīdī ^cAlāl al-Baqalī 113
Sīdī Ṣāfī 107
ṣīnf 30
social: difference 146; edges 149: *see also* node; *see also tū*; units 24, 30
socio-administrational fabric 21
socio-administrational structure 21
sociospatial 4, 22, 24, 26, 32, 35, 42, 44, 73, 94, 102, 103, 109, 110, 113, 139, 140, 145, 146, 147, 148, 151, 153, 161, 166, 168; *see also tū*s
space between 88, 110, 130, 138, 162
space of absence-presence 88
space of opposites 88
space-ordering 2, 24, 42
spatial: *see tū*; ambiguity 2; arrangements 20, 22, 94, 104, 145; category 7; cells 34, 121, 126, 127, 128; concept 1, 2, 9, 17, 44, 45, 48, 114, 167; conditions of edges 2, 11; continuity 28, 36, 81; depth 88; experience 28, 73, 81; juxtaposition 12; logic 24, 36; milieu 5–7, 10, 48; model 63, 65, 71; obscurity 128; ordering 4, 66, 167; orders 21, 63; organisation 11, 18, 23–25, 40, 81; organiser 42; practice 10, 45, 47, 67, 71, 88, 96; principles 7, 26, 46; proximity 150; regulator 21; relations 2, 3, 5, 34, 58, 62, 66, 69, 70, 93, 150, 166; relationships 7–9, 17, 20, 34; stories 96; structures 2, 20, 47, 75, 83, 84, 90n11, 146; typology 20; unit of understanding 10, 71
spatial-physical object 20
spatialisation 7, 8, 9, 44, 71, 92
spatiality of the Islamic city 8
spiritual progress 127
structural-functional relationships 18
street 5, 6, 17, 18, 19, 20, 29, 32, 33, 37, 38, 40–42, 44, 45, 47, 58, 69, 94, 95, 96, 98, 117, 119, 132, 134, 138, 149, 168
sub-space 35, 110, 113, 123, 124, 126, 138, 139, 140, 147, 148, 161
subjective 11, 34, 68, 95
sufi 84, 85, 91n25, 92, 113, 141, 157n65; *see also* ^c*irfān*
Sūlṭān Siyyid Rižā Khān 30, 33
symbolic conception 27
symbolic space 69
Syria 19, 41, 55

tā 82, 83, 90n8
ṭabaghih 82, 90n8
Tabriz 121
Tārīkīhā alley 121, 128, 129
ṭarīqa 28, 84, 98
telegraph 32
temporalities 8, 12, 74, 93
terminologies 5, 9, 44, 81, 158
territoriality 150
the Way 28, 84, 91n17, 91n25, 98
theoretical: generalisations 21; vocabulary, 5
theory-making 1, 5, 166
thought-motifs 1, 8, 9
thousand 2, 83, 87, 121, 167
threshold 2, 22, 24, 36, 81, 85, 86, 89, 102, 111, 113, 117, 128, 130, 138, 145, 146, 148, 150, 166, 167, 168
Thrift, N. 43, 73, 75
Tonkiss, F. 2
tour 45, 96, 97, 107, 118, 121, 134, 167

tradition 7, 10, 27, 74, 84, 85, 95, 106
tū or *tu* 2, 4, 5, 10, 11, 48, 75, 82–84, 86, 87, 88, 89, 90n8, 91n11, 92, 93, 145–148, 150–152, 167, 168; phenomenological *tū* 147; social *tū* 147; sociospatial *tū* 147; spatial *tū* 146, 147, 150; spiritual *tū* 146; symbolic *tū* 147, 167; virtual *tū* 146, 148; visual *tū* 147, 148
tū-bar-tū 83, 148, 167
tū-dar-tū 83, 84, 90n8, 92, 148, 167
*tū*ness 147; visuality of *tū*ness 147
Tunis 4, 6, 11, 12, 14, 29, 87, 93, 95, 102, 130, 136, 137, 140–144, 146, 147, 149, 151; al-ᶜAṭṭārīn suq 132; Ḥamūda Pāshā mosque 135, 139; history 131–134; Shamāᶜiya madrasa 132; Silāmī house 140, 141; Siyyida ᶜAjūla passage 134; Zaytūna mosque 131, 132, 133
tūy 82, 90n8
Tschumi, B. 67

UNESCO 103, 107, 121, 131, 134
unexpectedness 47, 67, 138
unity, 21, 28, 36, 85, 127, 152; of being 85
universal 1, 85, 167
urban: concept 81, 82–89; diversity 4; exterior 1, 4, 34, 36, 38, 59, 82, 109, 113, 135, 138, 141, 149, 163, 164; fabric 12, 31, 36, 40, 93, 94, 102, 109, 121, 124, 134, 138, 139, 140, 147, 148, 164; form 3, 11, 12, 14, 17, 20, 24, 35, 40, 93, 98, 100; milieu 6, 96; order 17; *see also* negation of urban order 17; *see also* exterior; space 1, 2, 4, 5, 7, 9, 10–12, 18, 20, 27, 29, 30, 32–39, 42–48, 70–72, 75, 81, 82, 89, 93–96, 102, 104, 107, 109, 114, 135, 145, 146, 148, 150, 166–168; spatial pattern 22; stories 98; studies 2, 3, 4, 11, 67, 74, 75, 90n5, 95, 167; theory 2, 3, 43, 167; typologies of the urban fabric 19; vocabulary 1

Ville Européenne 133
Ville Nouvelle 103, 106, 107, 133
virtual reality 8, 9
virtuality 8, 74
visual 24, 25, 29, 30, 36, 37, 60, 61, 63, 66, 81, 88, 89, 97, 109, 113, 117, 124–126, 128, 138–141, 145, 147, 148, 150, 151, 164; thresholds 166; *see also tū*
vocabulary 1, 5, 7, 16, 35, 36, 73, 82, 101, 158, 166, 167
void 88, 109, 113, 114, 121, 124, 138, 141, 147, 148, 150–152, 165

walker 36, 58, 65, 66, 67, 81, 95, 96, 124, 125, 127, 128, 135, 138–140, 149, 150, 167
walking 4, 11, 37, 39, 45, 47, 88, 95, 96, 97, 108, 122, 125, 134, 135, 139, 146, 148, 164, 167
wall 4, 22, 23, 34, 35, 37, 38, 45, 47, 67, 72, 149–153, 166; blank walls 26, 27; as a boundary-maker 4, 12; city walls 100, 101; as a concept 26; Fez city walls 104, 105; Isfahan city walls 119, 120; labyrinth depicted on walls 59, 69; representative component of city 44; shared wall 153; spatial organiser 42; walled enclosure 37, 149; walls and *tū*s 147, 148: walls behind walls 82; walls in Fez 110, 113, 115, 163n196; walls in Isfahan 124–130; walls in Tunis 135, 138–141, 145
wandering 64, 97, 166, 167, 168
Wandermänner 96
water 27, 28, 98–102, 117, 118, 121, 155n36
West 3, 5, 12
Western academy 2
Western-centric 2
Western 2, 3, 32, 70, 131, 167
World Heritage Site 131
Wirth, E. 22, 23, 35, 37, 89n4, 104

Yemen 41
Yusuf Dey 133

ẓāhīr 84
zanqa 110, 115, 158n103
Zarbaṭānā 113, 114
zāwīya 33, 103, 107, 110, 111, 112, 113, 114, 115, 141, 142, 145, 146, 148, 159n196, 163, 164; definition 157n65
zone: of attachment 146; *see also* containment
Zoroastrianism 118
Zwischenraum 88